JLA

AMERICAN DREAMS

Grant Morrison
writer

Howard Porter
Oscar Jimenez
pencillers

John Dell
Chip Wallace
Ken Branch
Anibal Rodriguez
inkers

Pat Garrahy
colorist

Heroic Age
color separations

Ken Lopez
letterer

SUPERMAN

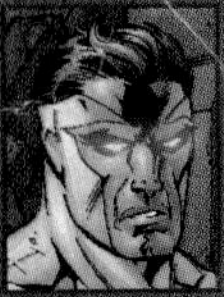

An alien by birth and an Earthman by choice, Superman is the world's greatest super-hero. The guiding force behind the formation of the new Justice League and the example metahumans across the globe must aspire to, Superman by his very existence has changed the world forever. Recently transformed by still-mysterious events, Superman is now a being of pure energy. His containment suit stores energy, which is transformed into powers including teleportation, intangibility, super-vision and the ability to create electromagnetic fields.

BATMAN

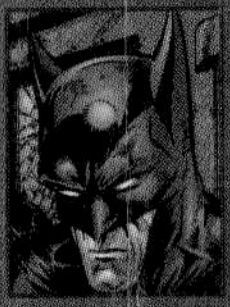

Just as Superman is the perfection all superhumans aspire to, Batman embodies everything Man can ever hope to be. Perhaps the most misunderstood and complex character of his day, Batman is driven not by vengeance, as he would have us believe, but by a desire to use his position to ensure that others never lose what he lost so many years ago. Batman has a brilliantly deductive mind combined with expert scientific knowledge. He is a master of every known martial art and keeps himself in the peak of human condition.

WONDER WOMAN

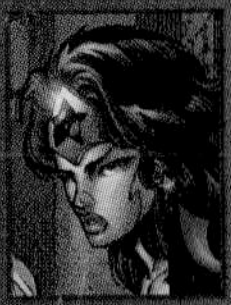

Daughter of Queen Hippolyta of Themyscira, Diana was raised as a warrior princess accustomed to the respect of her subjects and unquestioned loyalty of others. Though trained for war, Diana's message is actually one of peace—a seeming contradiction but one that Diana dismisses with the wisdom that there is often conflict in the achievement of goals. Wonder Woman possesses incredible strength and the power of flight, wears bracelets with which she can deflect bullets, and carries a magic lasso spun from the girdle of Gaia.

THE FLASH

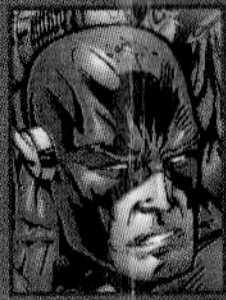

He is the Fastest Man Alive. Unlike the other members of the team, The Flash has been a very public super-hero for almost his entire life. He has had virtually no experience of the outside world since adolescence and has few friends who do not move in superhuman circles. Wally West has a reputation among his peers as being the most sociable "A-List" hero. By tapping into an extradimensional "speed force," the Flash is able to reach velocities that approach the speed of light itself and has the ability to explode solid objects by vibrating through them.

GREEN LANTERN

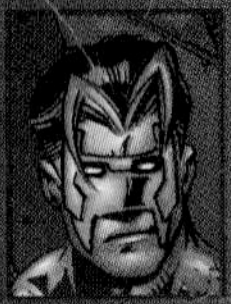

One of the youngest members of the team, Green Lantern makes up with enthusiasm what he lacks in experience. Regarded by the others as a major player, he is insecure knowing that he wasn't selected as a Green Lantern like his predecessor, but gained possession of his ring through a twist of fate. Green Lantern's power ring is the most powerful weapon in the universe. It creates solid light images whose shapes are limited only by the wearer's imagination, which Kyle Rayner has in abundance.

J'ONN J'ONZZ, THE MANHUNTER FROM MARS

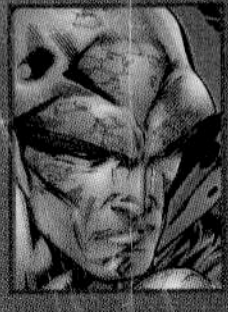

Pulled through time and space by Earth science, J'onn J'onzz was left stranded on a strange new world. Possibly the most highly regarded by his JLA peers, he is a founding member of every incarnation of the team, an alien whose loyalty to his adopted world is beyond challenge and whose determination to persevere against an adversary or to achieve a goal is unmatched. As is common among telepaths, the Martian Manhunter is an intensely silent figure. J'onzz has the powers of flight, super-strength, Martian vision, telepathy, super-speed, and the natural Martian ability to alter his physical shape and density.

AQUAMAN

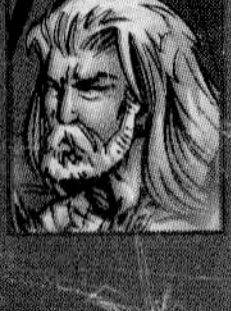

His parents were an Atlantean queen and an ancient wizard. So it was destiny that the child named Orin would become sworn protector of three-quarters of the Earth's surface. A lifetime withstanding the pressures of the deep has made him incredibly strong and amazingly fast both on water and land. He can communicate telepathically with sea creatures and can see in near darkness. The harpoon that replaced his lost left hand can be fired when necessary and is cybernetically controlled. Quiet, regal, serious as the tides, all of his fellow JLA members gladly give Aquaman the respect he demands.

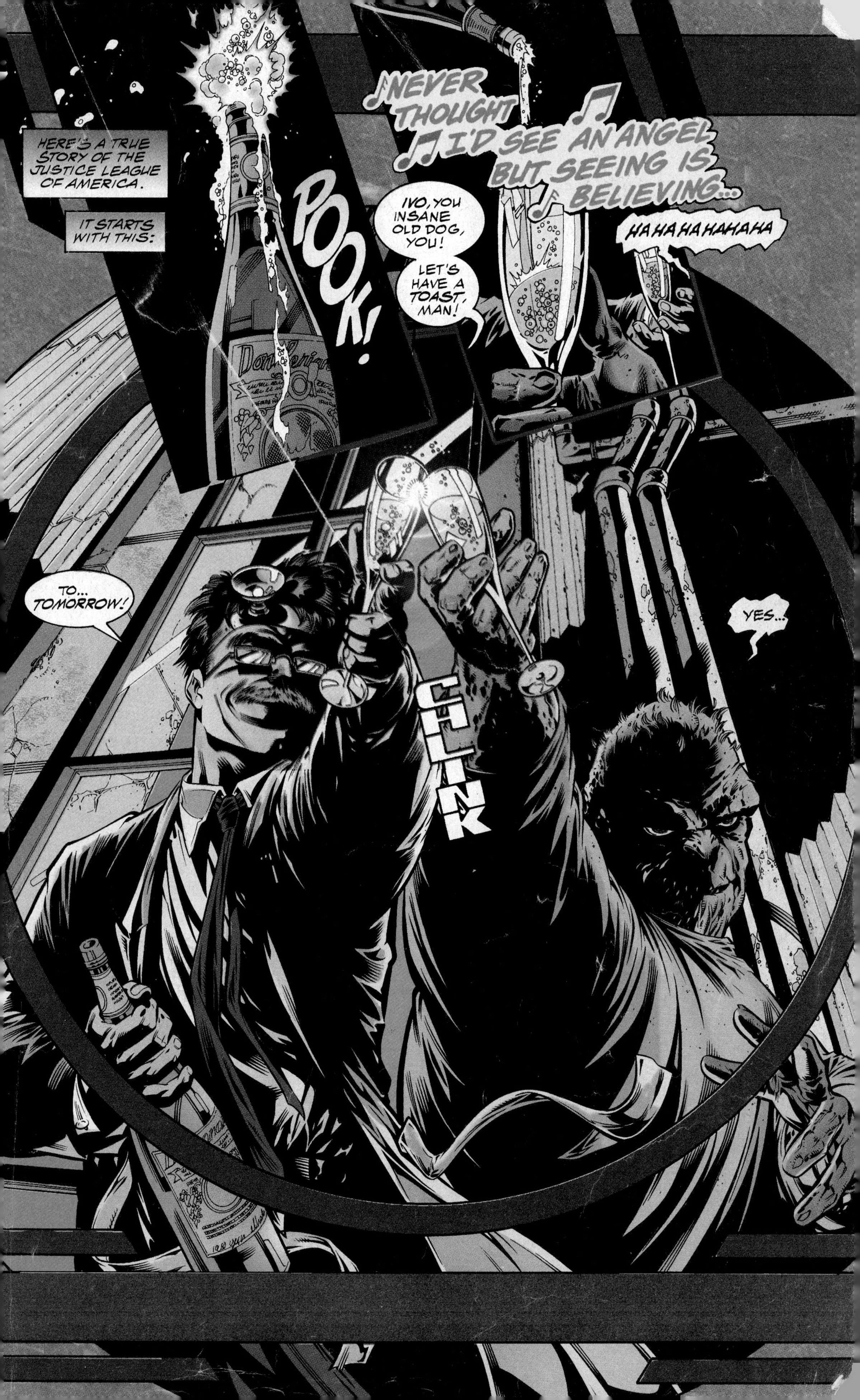

HERE'S A TRUE STORY OF THE JUSTICE LEAGUE OF AMERICA.
IT STARTS WITH THIS:
POOK!
NEVER THOUGHT I'D SEE AN ANGEL BUT SEEING IS BELIEVING...
IVO, YOU INSANE OLD DOG, YOU!
LET'S HAVE A TOAST, MAN!
HAHAHAHAHAHAHA
TO... TOMORROW!
YES...
CHLINK

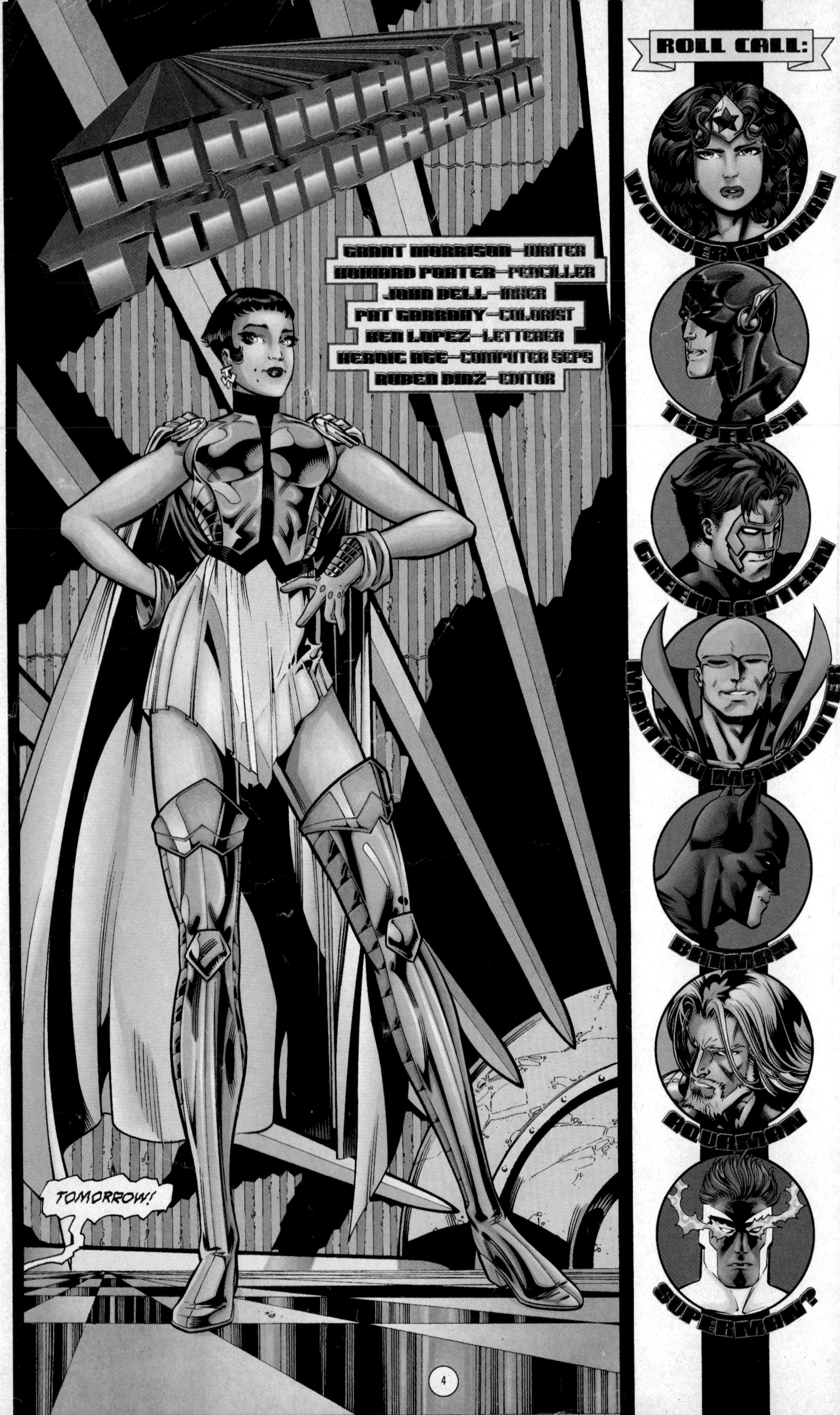
WOMAN OF TOMORROW
GRANT MORRISON—WRITER
HOWARD PORTER—PENCILLER
JOHN DELL—INKER
PAT GARRAHY—COLORIST
KEN LOPEZ—LETTERER
HEROIC AGE—COMPUTER SEPS
RUBEN DIAZ—EDITOR
ROLL CALL:
WONDER WOMAN
THE FLASH
GREEN LANTERN
MARTIAN MANHUNTER
BATMAN
AQUAMAN
SUPERMAN?
TOMORROW!

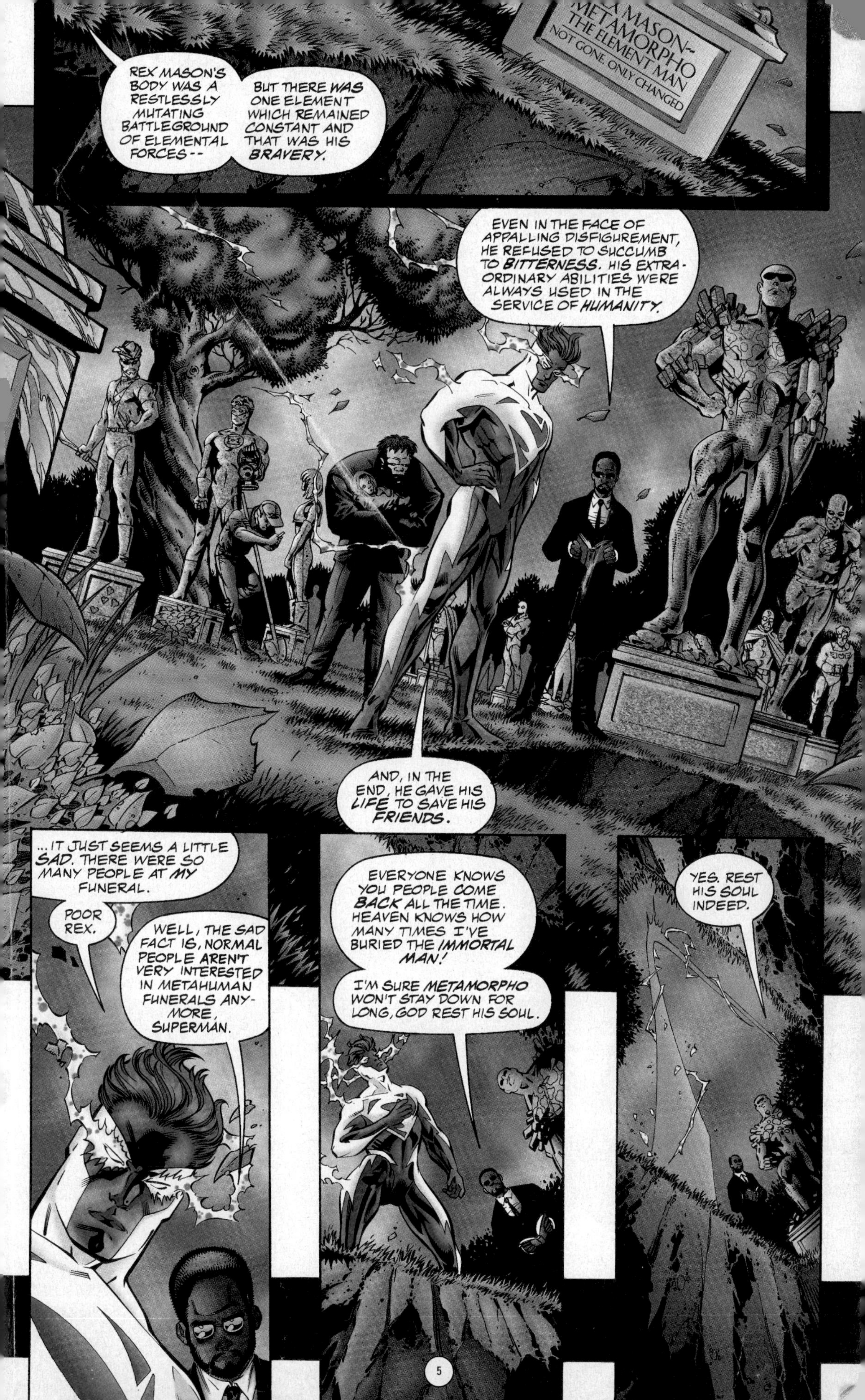
REX MASON- METAMORPHO THE ELEMENT MAN NOT GONE ONLY CHANGED
REX MASON'S BODY WAS A RESTLESSLY MUTATING BATTLEGROUND OF ELEMENTAL FORCES--
BUT THERE WAS ONE ELEMENT WHICH REMAINED CONSTANT AND THAT WAS HIS BRAVERY.
EVEN IN THE FACE OF APPALLING DISFIGUREMENT, HE REFUSED TO SUCCUMB TO BITTERNESS. HIS EXTRA-ORDINARY ABILITIES WERE ALWAYS USED IN THE SERVICE OF HUMANITY.
AND, IN THE END, HE GAVE HIS LIFE TO SAVE HIS FRIENDS.
...IT JUST SEEMS A LITTLE SAD. THERE WERE SO MANY PEOPLE AT MY FUNERAL.
POOR REX.
WELL, THE SAD FACT IS, NORMAL PEOPLE AREN'T VERY INTERESTED IN METAHUMAN FUNERALS ANY-MORE, SUPERMAN.
EVERYONE KNOWS YOU PEOPLE COME BACK ALL THE TIME. HEAVEN KNOWS HOW MANY TIMES I'VE BURIED THE IMMORTAL MAN!
I'M SURE METAMORPHO WON'T STAY DOWN FOR LONG, GOD REST HIS SOUL.
YES. REST HIS SOUL INDEED.

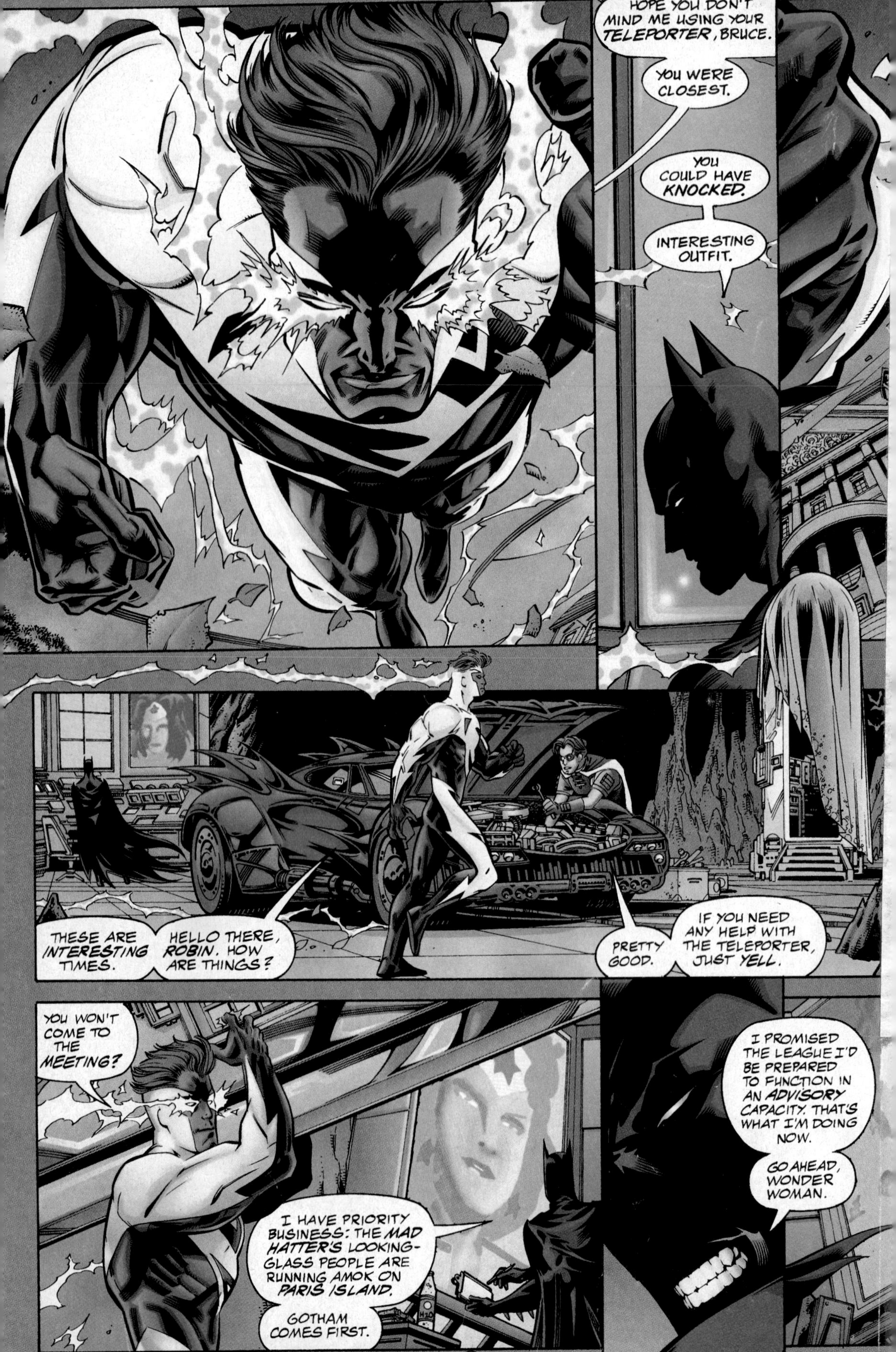
HOPE YOU DON'T MIND ME USING YOUR TELEPORTER, BRUCE.
YOU WERE CLOSEST.
YOU COULD HAVE KNOCKED.
INTERESTING OUTFIT.
THESE ARE INTERESTING TIMES.
HELLO THERE, ROBIN. HOW ARE THINGS?
PRETTY GOOD.
IF YOU NEED ANY HELP WITH THE TELEPORTER, JUST YELL.
YOU WON'T COME TO THE MEETING?
I HAVE PRIORITY BUSINESS: THE MAD HATTER'S LOOKING-GLASS PEOPLE ARE RUNNING AMOK ON PARIS ISLAND.
GOTHAM COMES FIRST.
I PROMISED THE LEAGUE I'D BE PREPARED TO FUNCTION IN AN ADVISORY CAPACITY. THAT'S WHAT I'M DOING NOW.
GO AHEAD, WONDER WOMAN.

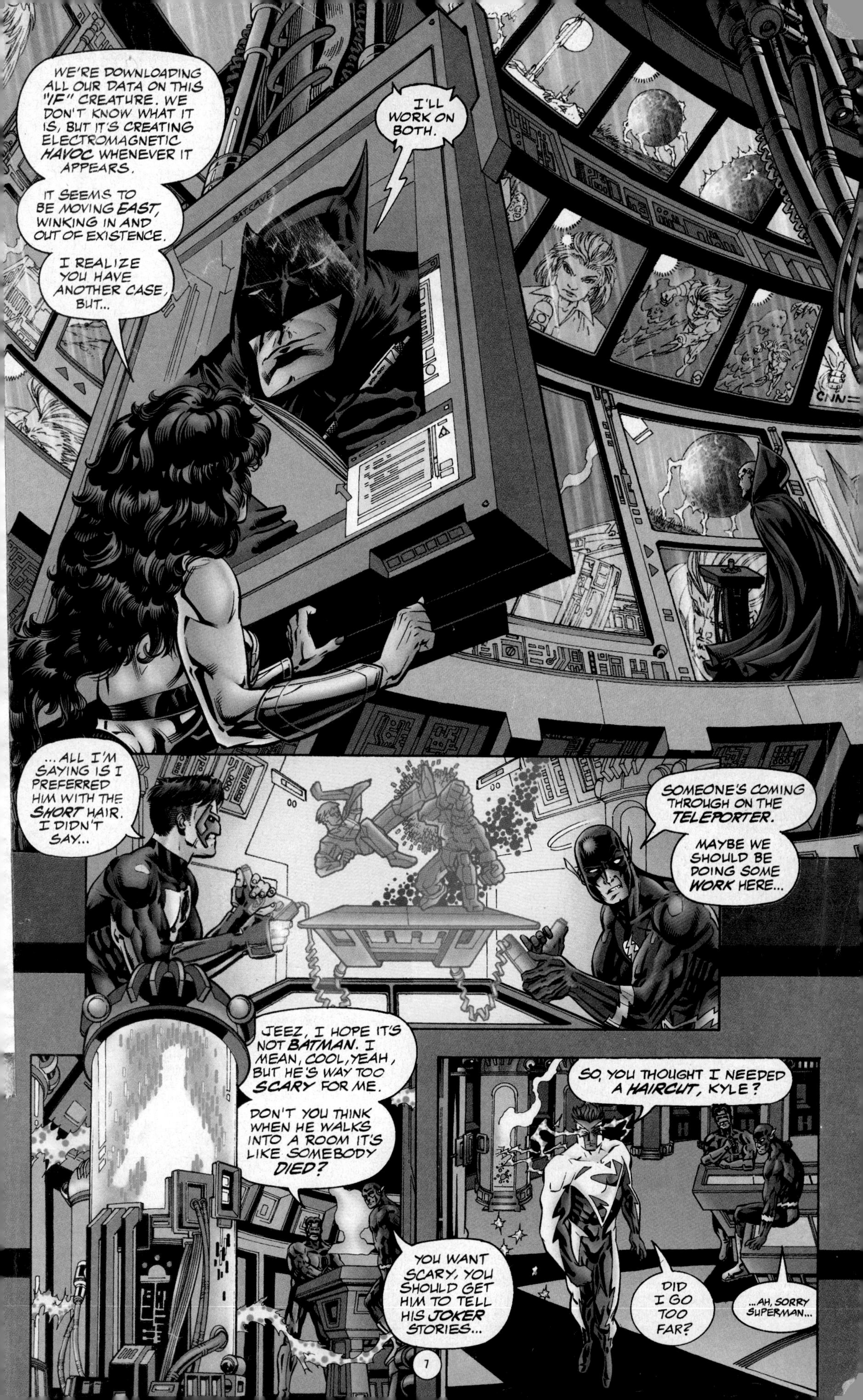
WE'RE DOWNLOADING ALL OUR DATA ON THIS "IF" CREATURE. WE DON'T KNOW WHAT IT IS, BUT IT'S CREATING ELECTROMAGNETIC HAVOC WHENEVER IT APPEARS.
IT SEEMS TO BE MOVING EAST, WINKING IN AND OUT OF EXISTENCE.
I REALIZE YOU HAVE ANOTHER CASE, BUT...
I'LL WORK ON BOTH.
BATCAVE
CNN
...ALL I'M SAYING IS I PREFERRED HIM WITH THE SHORT HAIR. I DIDN'T SAY...
SOMEONE'S COMING THROUGH ON THE TELEPORTER.
MAYBE WE SHOULD BE DOING SOME WORK HERE...
JEEZ, I HOPE IT'S NOT BATMAN. I MEAN, COOL, YEAH, BUT HE'S WAY TOO SCARY FOR ME.
DON'T YOU THINK WHEN HE WALKS INTO A ROOM IT'S LIKE SOMEBODY DIED?
YOU WANT SCARY, YOU SHOULD GET HIM TO TELL HIS JOKER STORIES...
SO, YOU THOUGHT I NEEDED A HAIRCUT, KYLE?
DID I GO TOO FAR?
...AH, SORRY SUPERMAN...

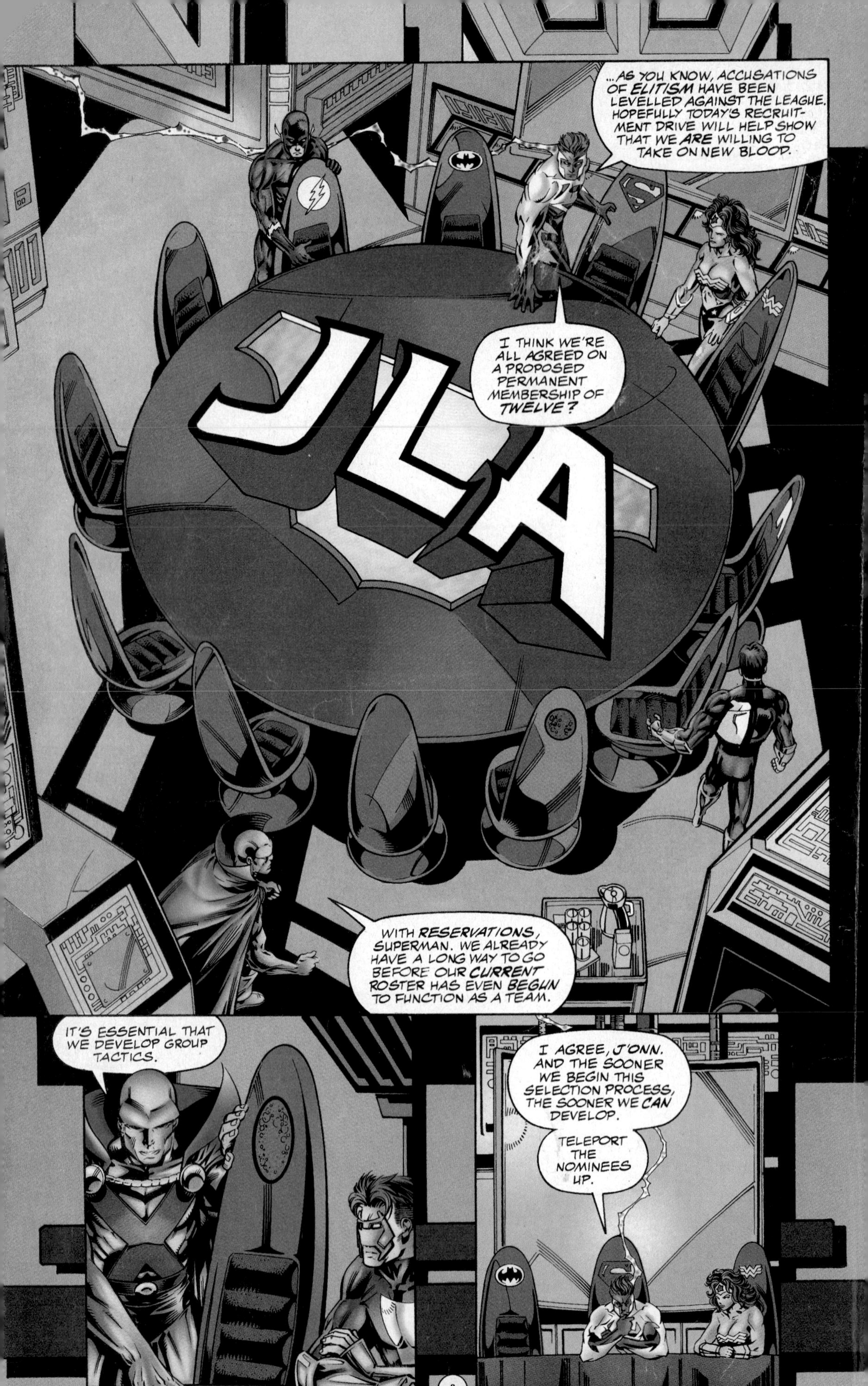
...AS YOU KNOW, ACCUSATIONS OF ELITISM HAVE BEEN LEVELLED AGAINST THE LEAGUE. HOPEFULLY TODAY'S RECRUITMENT DRIVE WILL HELP SHOW THAT WE ARE WILLING TO TAKE ON NEW BLOOD.
I THINK WE'RE ALL AGREED ON A PROPOSED PERMANENT MEMBERSHIP OF TWELVE?
JLA
WITH RESERVATIONS, SUPERMAN. WE ALREADY HAVE A LONG WAY TO GO BEFORE OUR CURRENT ROSTER HAS EVEN BEGUN TO FUNCTION AS A TEAM.
IT'S ESSENTIAL THAT WE DEVELOP GROUP TACTICS.
I AGREE, J'ONN. AND THE SOONER WE BEGIN THIS SELECTION PROCESS, THE SOONER WE CAN DEVELOP.
TELEPORT THE NOMINEES UP.

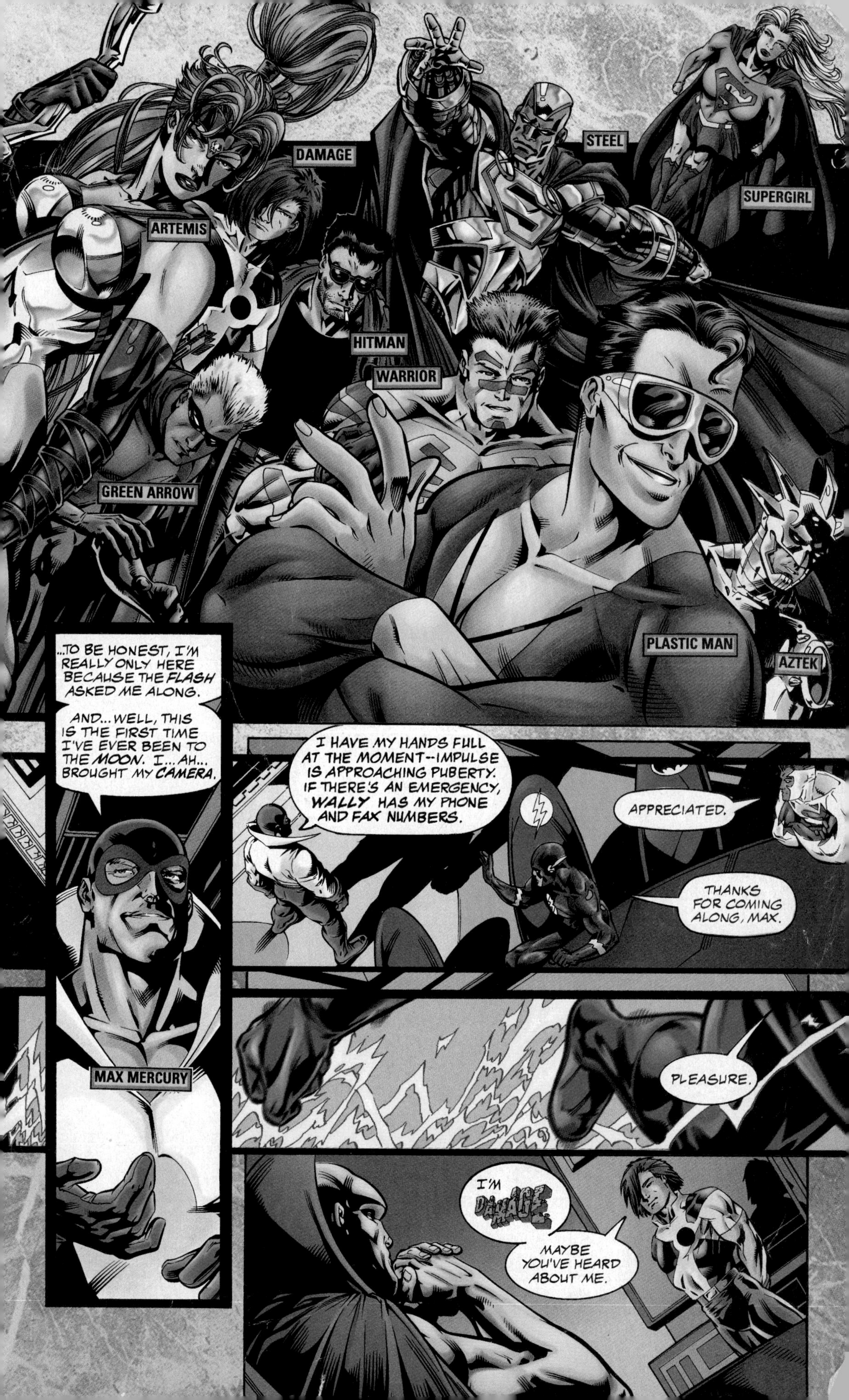
DAMAGE
STEEL
SUPERGIRL
ARTEMIS
HITMAN
WARRIOR
GREEN ARROW
PLASTIC MAN
AZTEK
...TO BE HONEST, I'M REALLY ONLY HERE BECAUSE THE FLASH ASKED ME ALONG.
AND...WELL, THIS IS THE FIRST TIME I'VE EVER BEEN TO THE MOON. I...AH... BROUGHT MY CAMERA.
I HAVE MY HANDS FULL AT THE MOMENT--IMPULSE IS APPROACHING PUBERTY. IF THERE'S AN EMERGENCY, WALLY HAS MY PHONE AND FAX NUMBERS.
APPRECIATED.
THANKS FOR COMING ALONG, MAX.
MAX MERCURY
PLEASURE.
I'M DAMAGE
MAYBE YOU'VE HEARD ABOUT ME.

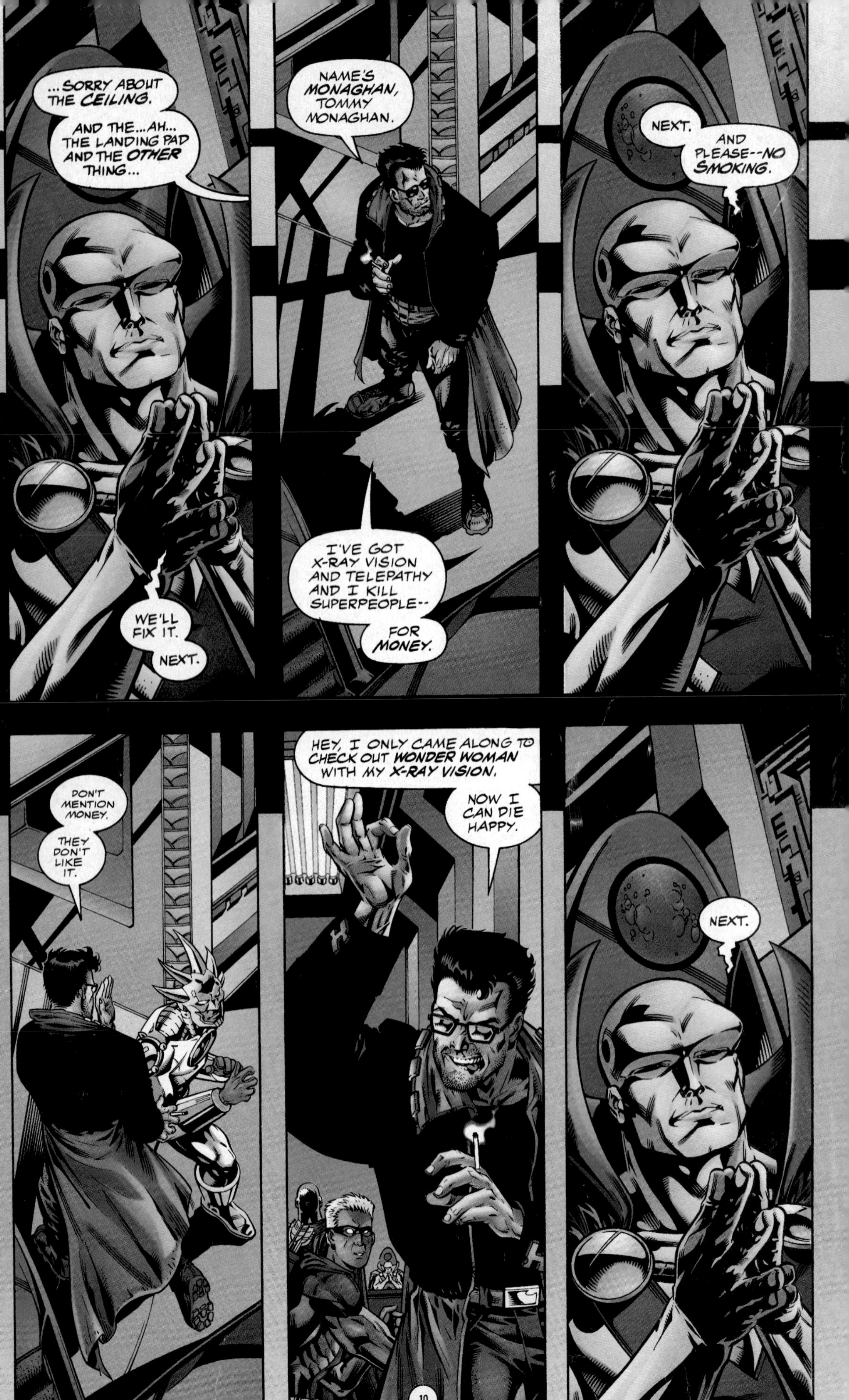
...SORRY ABOUT THE CEILING.
AND THE...AH... THE LANDING PAD AND THE OTHER THING...
WE'LL FIX IT.
NEXT.
NAME'S MONAGHAN, TOMMY MONAGHAN.
I'VE GOT X-RAY VISION AND TELEPATHY AND I KILL SUPERPEOPLE--
FOR MONEY.
NEXT.
AND PLEASE--NO SMOKING.
DON'T MENTION MONEY.
THEY DON'T LIKE IT.
HEY, I ONLY CAME ALONG TO CHECK OUT WONDER WOMAN WITH MY X-RAY VISION.
NOW I CAN DIE HAPPY.
NEXT.

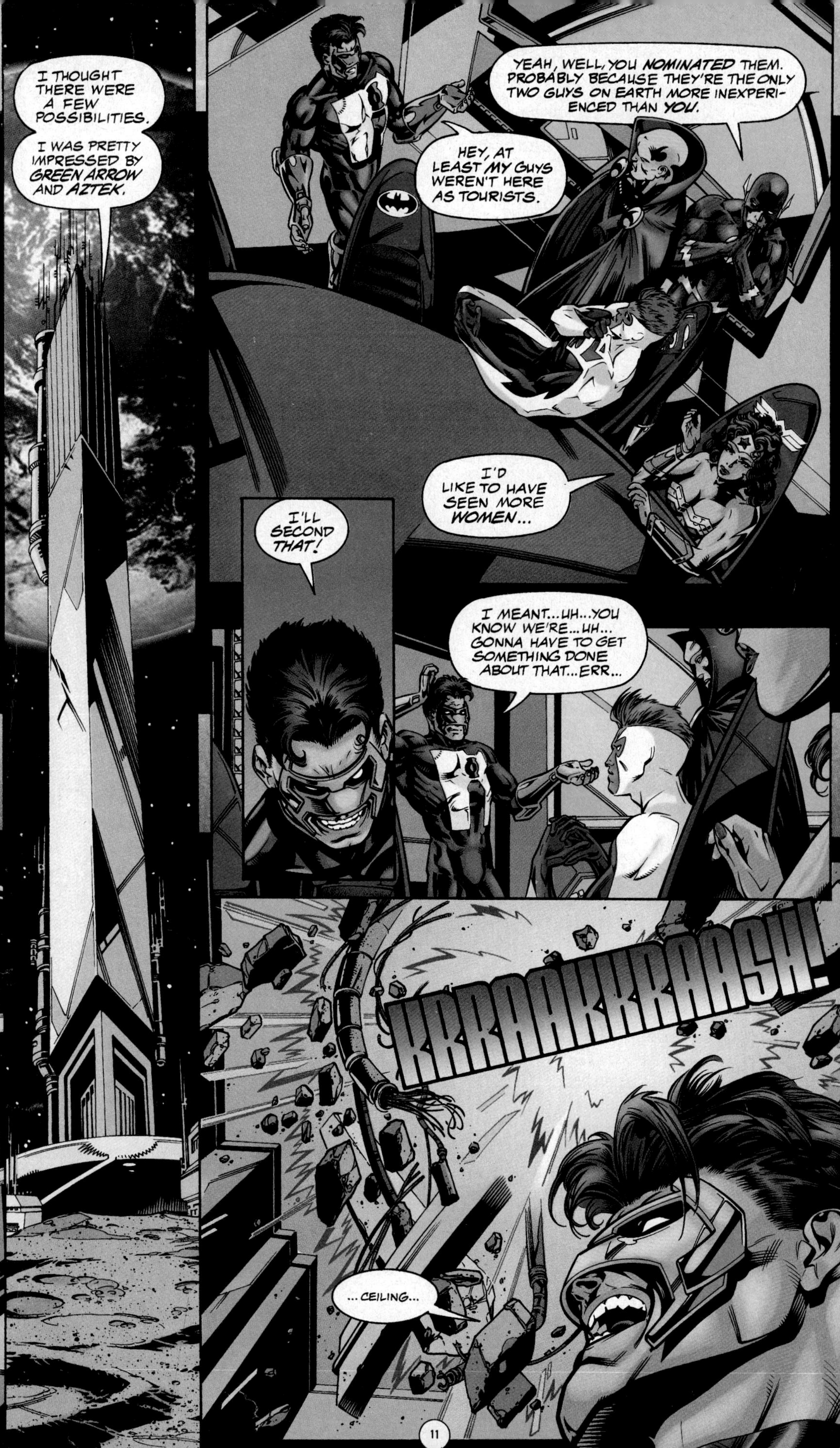
I THOUGHT THERE WERE A FEW POSSIBILITIES.
I WAS PRETTY IMPRESSED BY GREEN ARROW AND AZTEK.
YEAH, WELL, YOU NOMINATED THEM. PROBABLY BECAUSE THEY'RE THE ONLY TWO GUYS ON EARTH MORE INEXPERIENCED THAN YOU.
HEY, AT LEAST MY GUYS WEREN'T HERE AS TOURISTS.
I'D LIKE TO HAVE SEEN MORE WOMEN...
I'LL SECOND THAT!
I MEANT...UH...YOU KNOW WE'RE...UH... GONNA HAVE TO GET SOMETHING DONE ABOUT THAT...ERR...
KRRAAKKRAASH!
...CEILING...

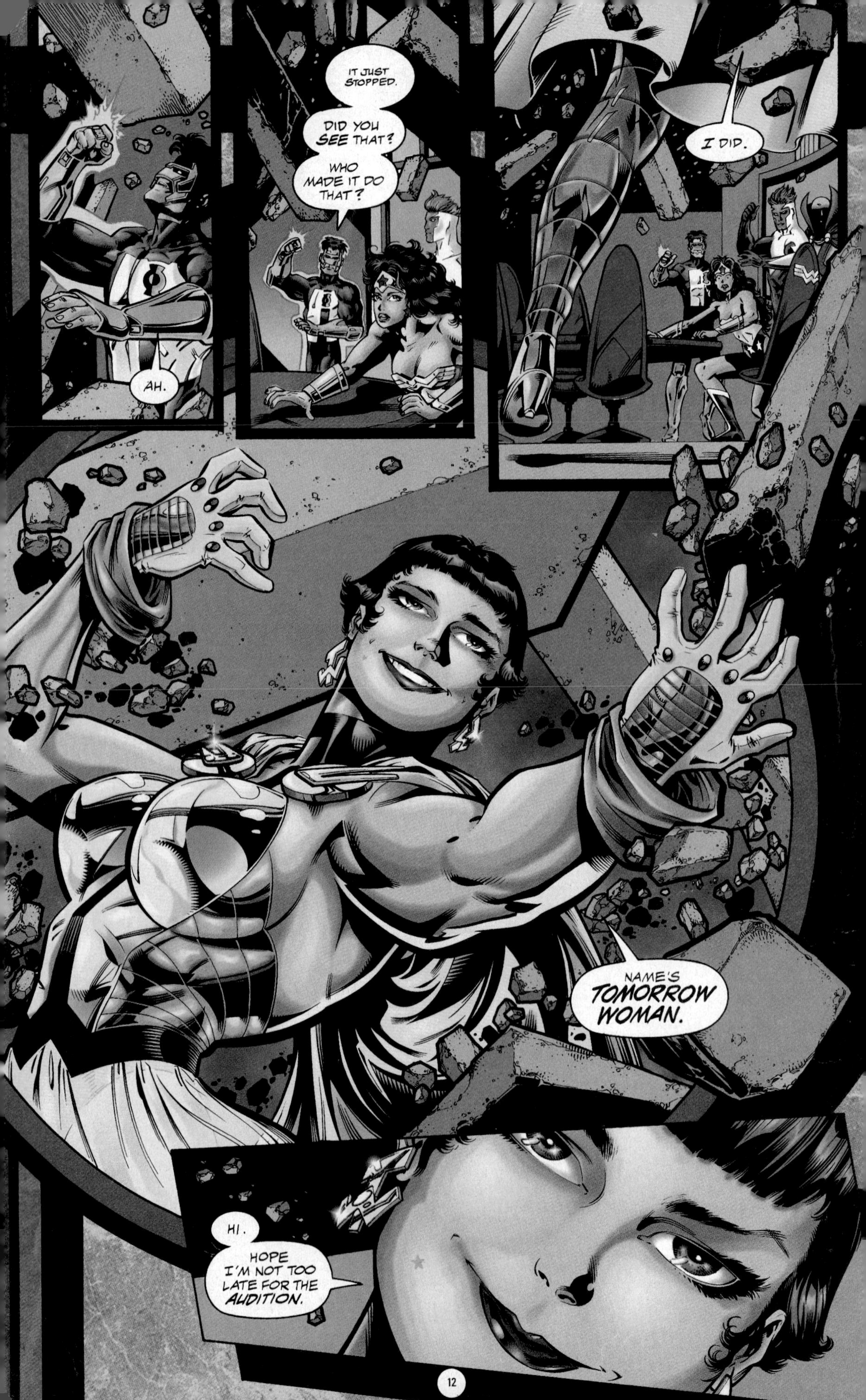
AH.
IT JUST STOPPED.
DID YOU SEE THAT?
WHO MADE IT DO THAT?
I DID.
NAME'S TOMORROW WOMAN.
HI.
HOPE I'M NOT TOO LATE FOR THE AUDITION.

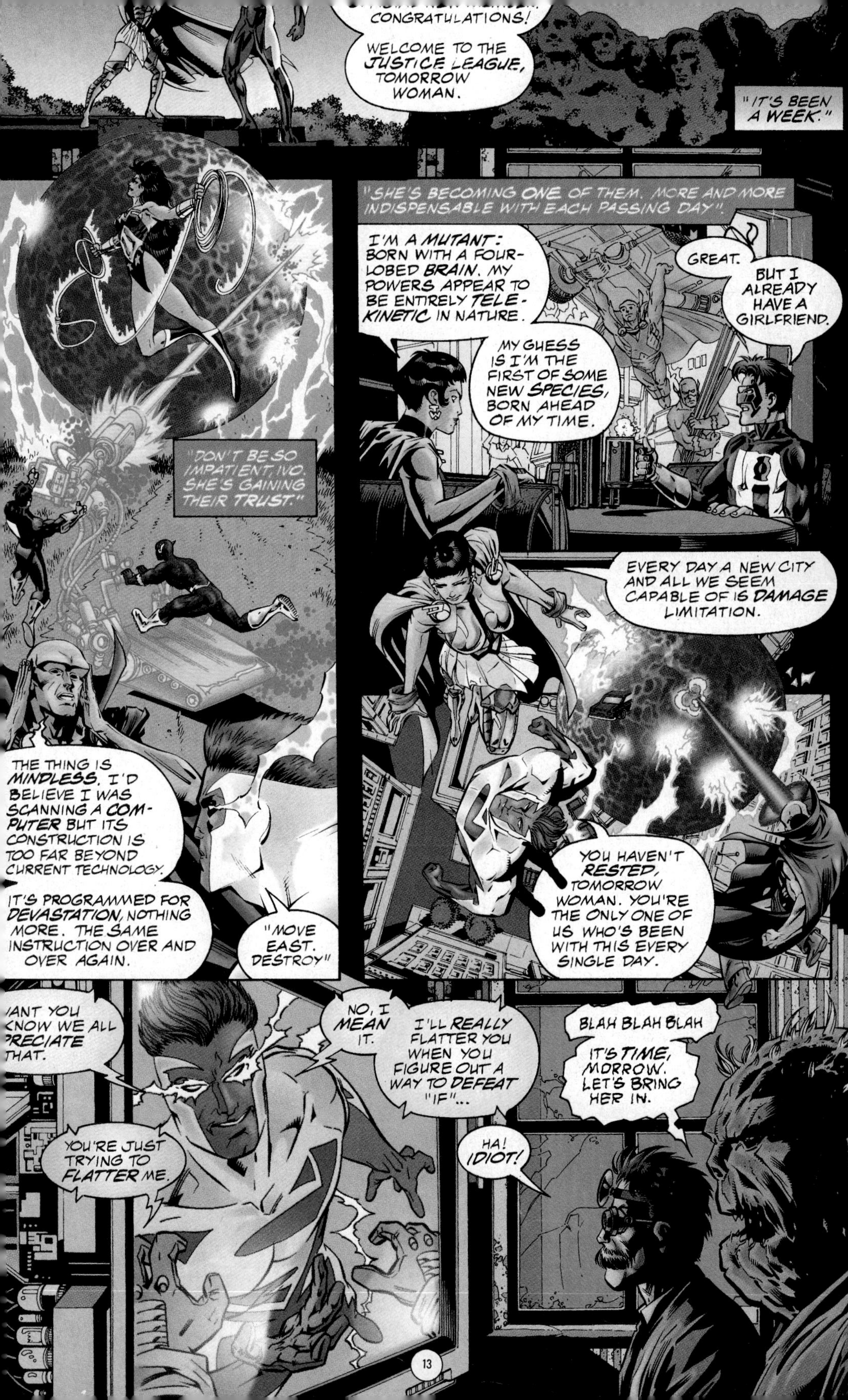
CONGRATULATIONS!
WELCOME TO THE JUSTICE LEAGUE, TOMORROW WOMAN.
"IT'S BEEN A WEEK."
"DON'T BE SO IMPATIENT, IVO. SHE'S GAINING THEIR TRUST."
THE THING IS MINDLESS. I'D BELIEVE I WAS SCANNING A COMPUTER BUT ITS CONSTRUCTION IS TOO FAR BEYOND CURRENT TECHNOLOGY.
IT'S PROGRAMMED FOR DEVASTATION, NOTHING MORE. THE SAME INSTRUCTION OVER AND OVER AGAIN.
"MOVE EAST. DESTROY"
"SHE'S BECOMING ONE OF THEM. MORE AND MORE INDISPENSABLE WITH EACH PASSING DAY".
I'M A MUTANT: BORN WITH A FOUR-LOBED BRAIN. MY POWERS APPEAR TO BE ENTIRELY TELEKINETIC IN NATURE.
MY GUESS IS I'M THE FIRST OF SOME NEW SPECIES, BORN AHEAD OF MY TIME.
GREAT.
BUT I ALREADY HAVE A GIRLFRIEND.
EVERY DAY A NEW CITY AND ALL WE SEEM CAPABLE OF IS DAMAGE LIMITATION.
YOU HAVEN'T RESTED, TOMORROW WOMAN. YOU'RE THE ONLY ONE OF US WHO'S BEEN WITH THIS EVERY SINGLE DAY.
ANT YOU NOW WE ALL PRECIATE THAT.
YOU'RE JUST TRYING TO FLATTER ME.
NO, I MEAN IT.
I'LL REALLY FLATTER YOU WHEN YOU FIGURE OUT A WAY TO DEFEAT "IF"...
HA! IDIOT!
BLAH BLAH BLAH
IT'S TIME, MORROW. LET'S BRING HER IN.

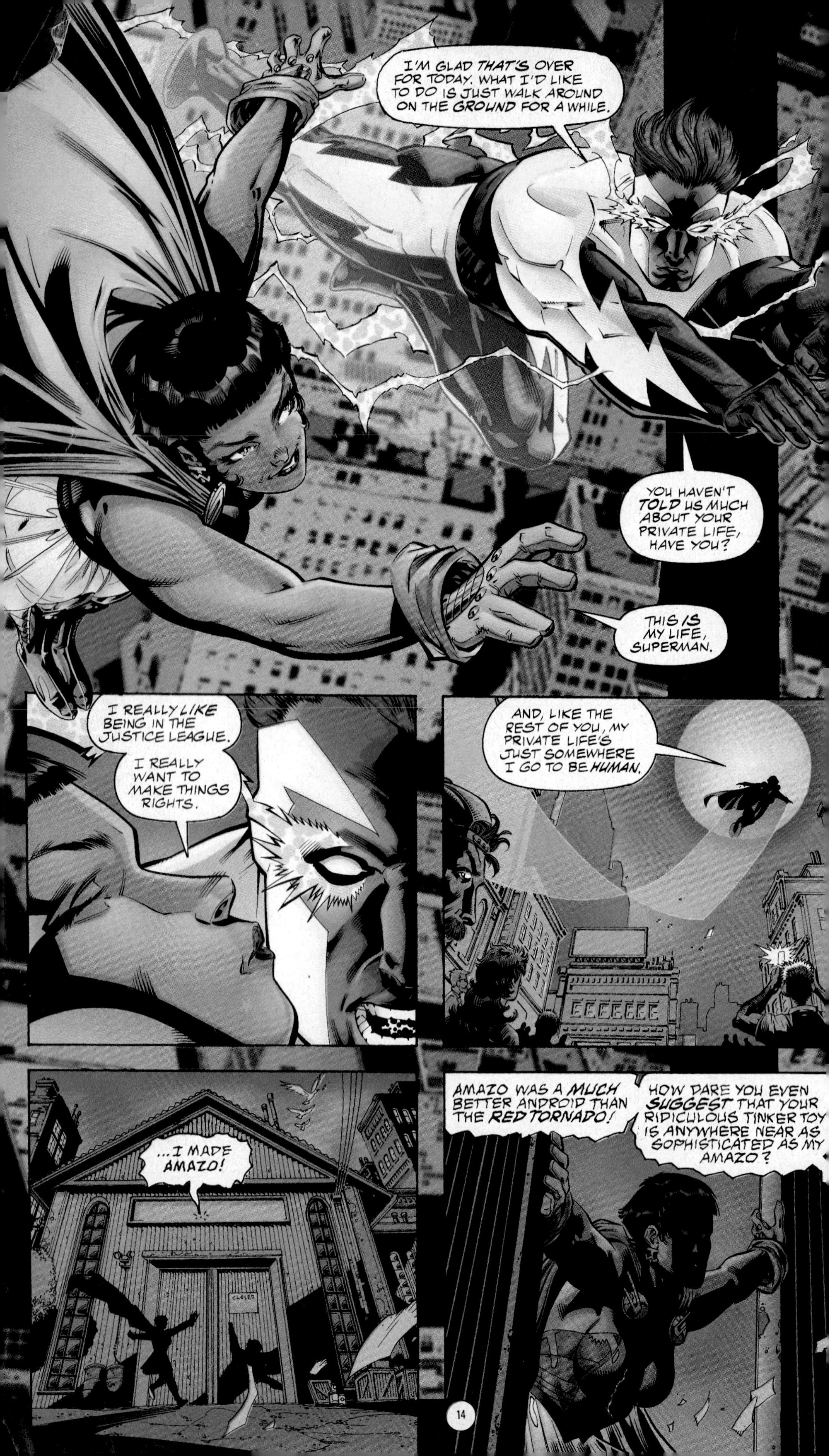
I'M GLAD THAT'S OVER FOR TODAY. WHAT I'D LIKE TO DO IS JUST WALK AROUND ON THE GROUND FOR A WHILE.
YOU HAVEN'T TOLD US MUCH ABOUT YOUR PRIVATE LIFE, HAVE YOU?
THIS IS MY LIFE, SUPERMAN.
I REALLY LIKE BEING IN THE JUSTICE LEAGUE.
I REALLY WANT TO MAKE THINGS RIGHTS.
AND, LIKE THE REST OF YOU, MY PRIVATE LIFE'S JUST SOMEWHERE I GO TO BE HUMAN.
...I MADE AMAZO!
CLOSED
AMAZO WAS A MUCH BETTER ANDROID THAN THE RED TORNADO!
HOW DARE YOU EVEN SUGGEST THAT YOUR RIDICULOUS TINKER TOY IS ANYWHERE NEAR AS SOPHISTICATED AS MY AMAZO?

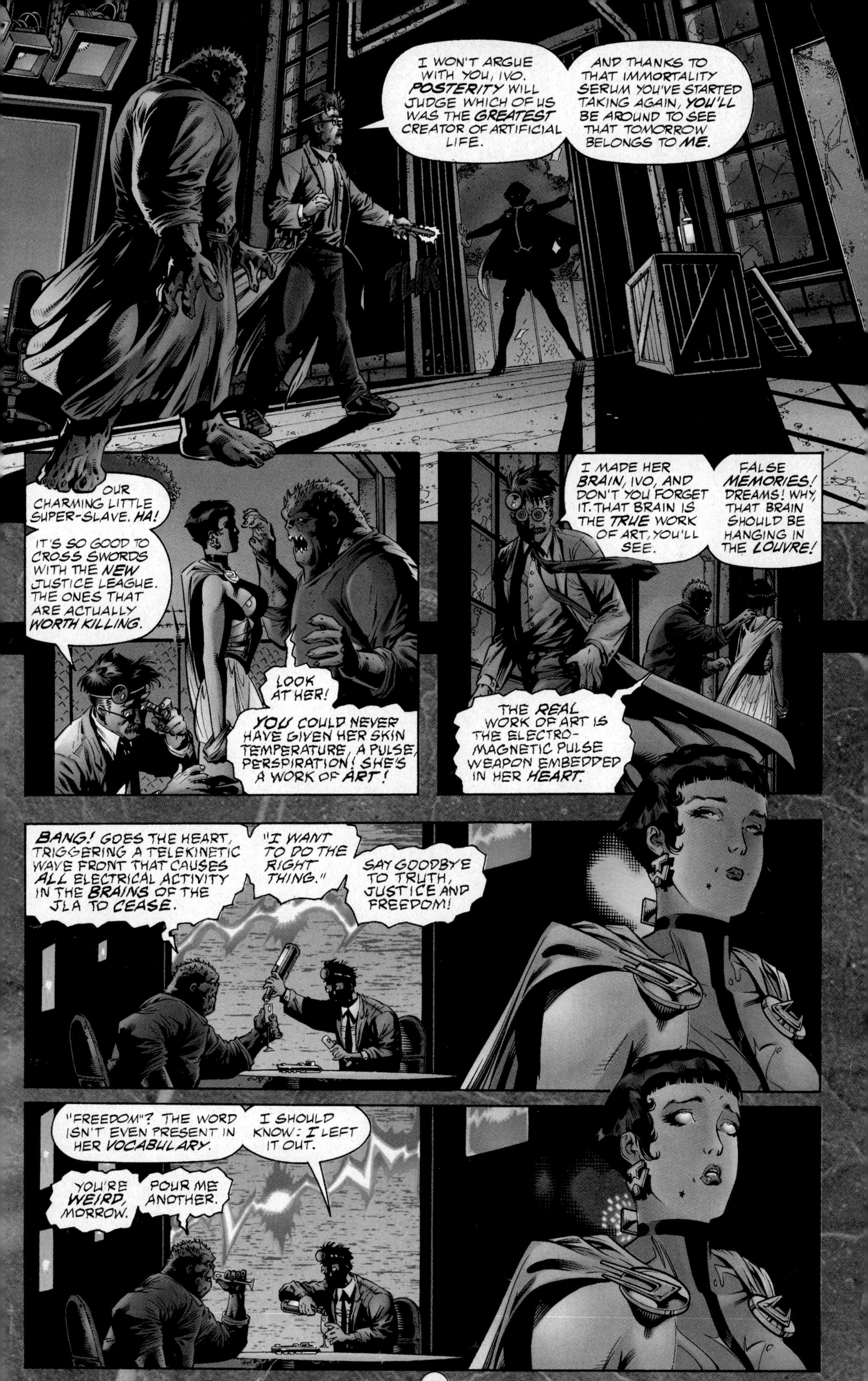
I WON'T ARGUE WITH YOU, IVO. POSTERITY WILL JUDGE WHICH OF US WAS THE GREATEST CREATOR OF ARTIFICIAL LIFE.
AND THANKS TO THAT IMMORTALITY SERUM YOU'VE STARTED TAKING AGAIN, YOU'LL BE AROUND TO SEE THAT TOMORROW BELONGS TO ME.
TLIK
OUR CHARMING LITTLE SUPER-SLAVE. HA!
IT'S SO GOOD TO CROSS SWORDS WITH THE NEW JUSTICE LEAGUE. THE ONES THAT ARE ACTUALLY WORTH KILLING.
LOOK AT HER!
YOU COULD NEVER HAVE GIVEN HER SKIN TEMPERATURE, A PULSE, PERSPIRATION! SHE'S A WORK OF ART!
I MADE HER BRAIN, IVO, AND DON'T YOU FORGET IT. THAT BRAIN IS THE TRUE WORK OF ART, YOU'LL SEE.
FALSE MEMORIES! DREAMS! WHY, THAT BRAIN SHOULD BE HANGING IN THE LOUVRE!
THE REAL WORK OF ART IS THE ELECTRO-MAGNETIC PULSE WEAPON EMBEDDED IN HER HEART.
BANG! GOES THE HEART, TRIGGERING A TELEKINETIC WAVE FRONT THAT CAUSES ALL ELECTRICAL ACTIVITY IN THE BRAINS OF THE JLA TO CEASE.
"I WANT TO DO THE RIGHT THING."
SAY GOODBYE TO TRUTH, JUSTICE AND FREEDOM!
"FREEDOM"? THE WORD ISN'T EVEN PRESENT IN HER VOCABULARY.
I SHOULD KNOW: I LEFT IT OUT.
YOU'RE WEIRD, MORROW.
POUR ME ANOTHER.

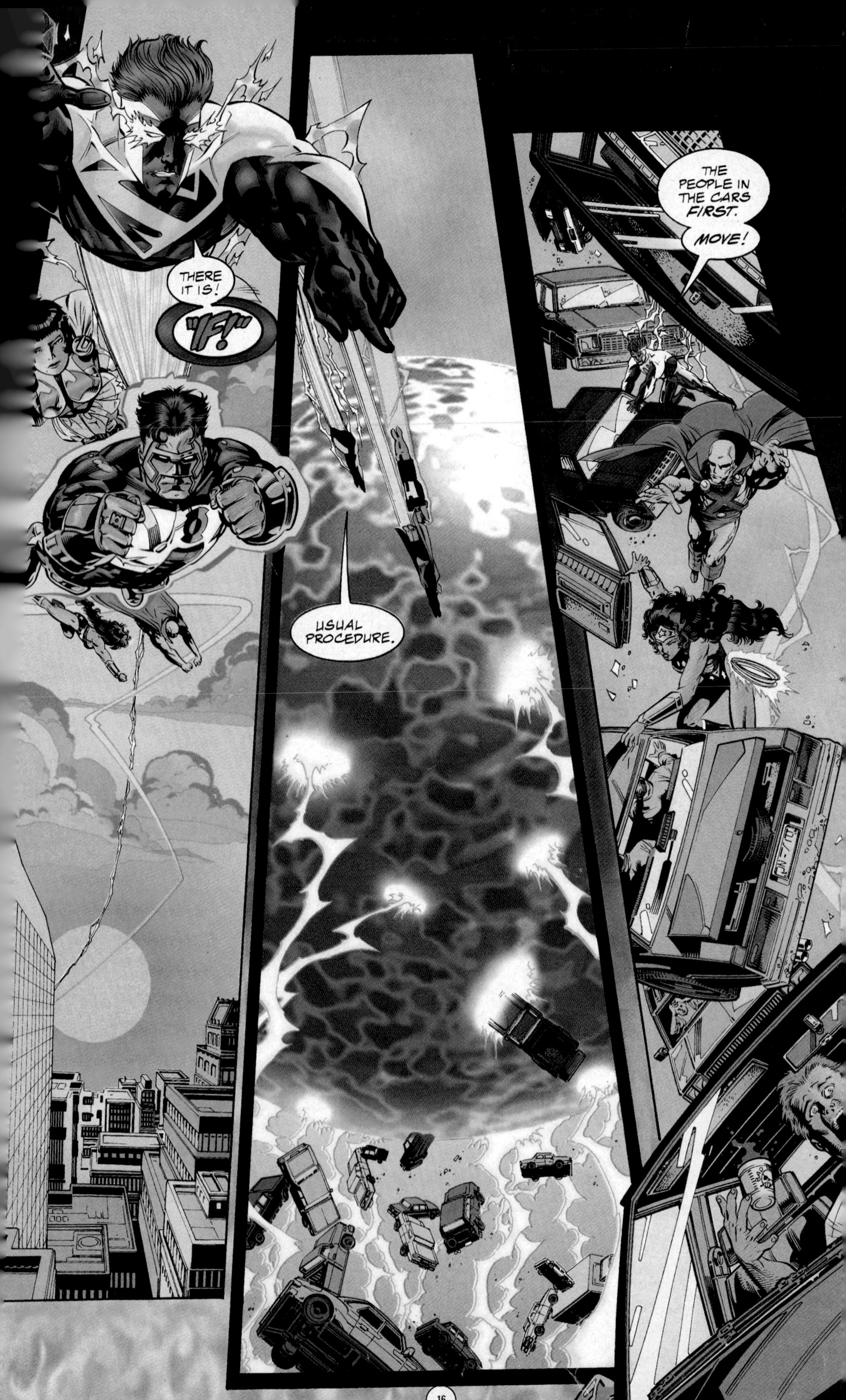

THERE IT IS!
"IF!"
USUAL PROCEDURE.
THE PEOPLE IN THE CARS FIRST.
MOVE!

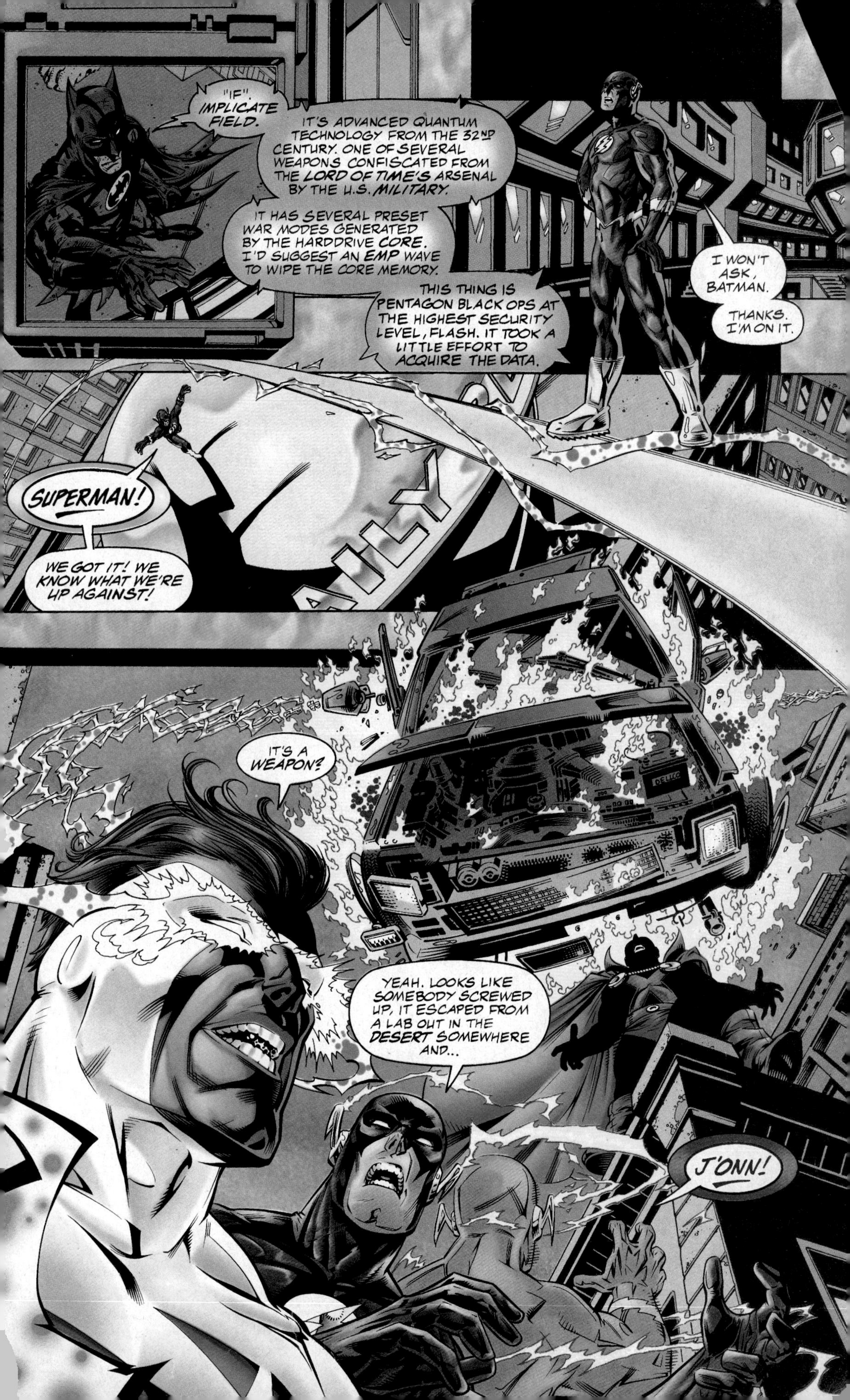
"IF". IMPLICATE FIELD.
IT'S ADVANCED QUANTUM TECHNOLOGY FROM THE 32ND CENTURY. ONE OF SEVERAL WEAPONS CONFISCATED FROM THE LORD OF TIME'S ARSENAL BY THE U.S. MILITARY.
IT HAS SEVERAL PRESET WAR MODES GENERATED BY THE HARDDRIVE CORE. I'D SUGGEST AN EMP WAVE TO WIPE THE CORE MEMORY.
THIS THING IS PENTAGON BLACK OPS AT THE HIGHEST SECURITY LEVEL, FLASH. IT TOOK A LITTLE EFFORT TO ACQUIRE THE DATA.
I WON'T ASK, BATMAN.
THANKS. I'M ON IT.
SUPERMAN!
WE GOT IT! WE KNOW WHAT WE'RE UP AGAINST!
IT'S A WEAPON?
YEAH. LOOKS LIKE SOMEBODY SCREWED UP, IT ESCAPED FROM A LAB OUT IN THE DESERT SOMEWHERE AND...
J'ONN!

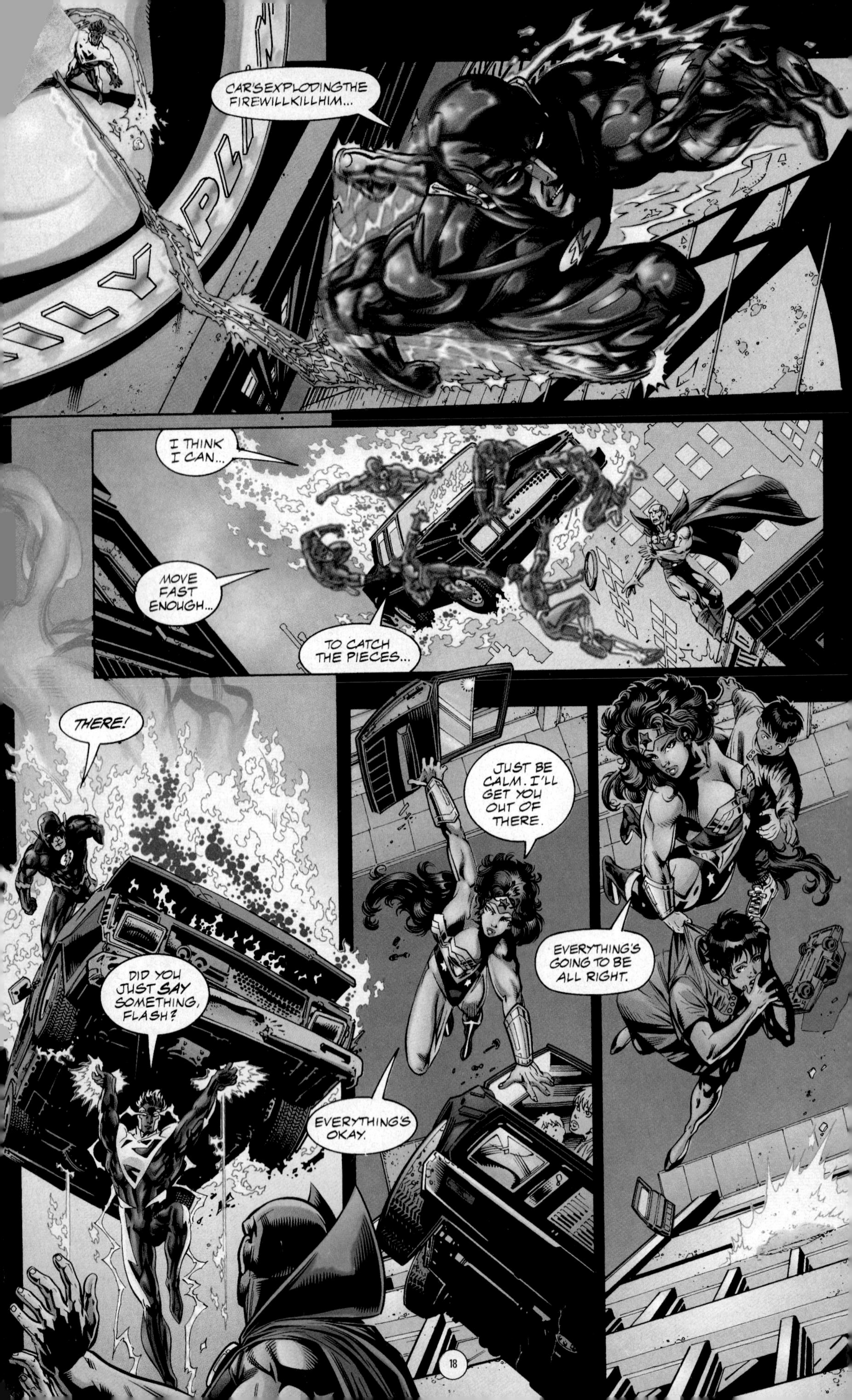
CAR'SEXPLODINGTHE FIREWILLKILLHIM...
I THINK I CAN...
MOVE FAST ENOUGH...
TO CATCH THE PIECES...
THERE!
DID YOU JUST SAY SOMETHING, FLASH?
EVERYTHING'S OKAY.
JUST BE CALM. I'LL GET YOU OUT OF THERE.
EVERYTHING'S GOING TO BE ALL RIGHT.

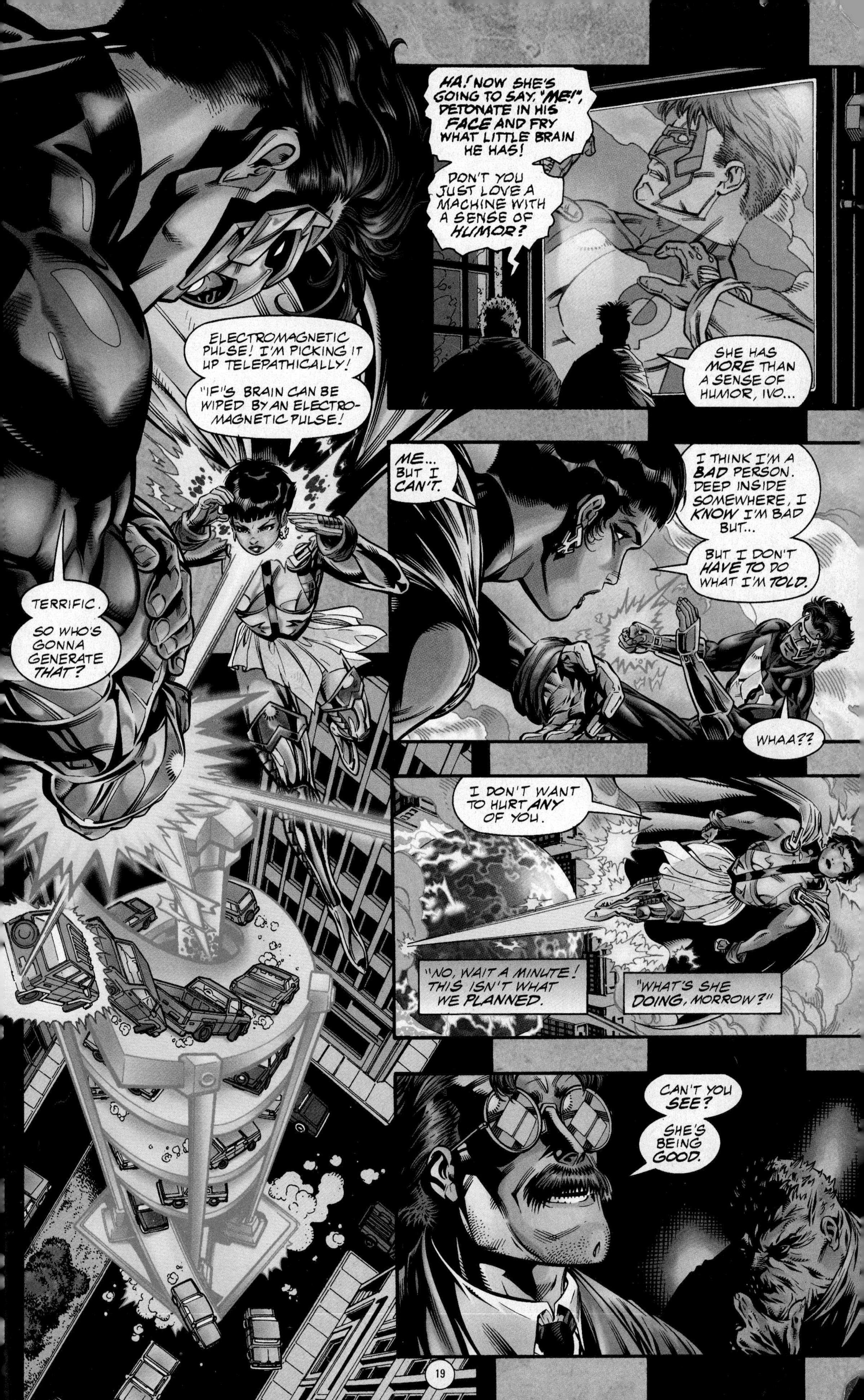
HA! NOW SHE'S GOING TO SAY, "ME!", DETONATE IN HIS FACE AND FRY WHAT LITTLE BRAIN HE HAS!
DON'T YOU JUST LOVE A MACHINE WITH A SENSE OF HUMOR?
SHE HAS MORE THAN A SENSE OF HUMOR, IVO...
ELECTROMAGNETIC PULSE! I'M PICKING IT UP TELEPATHICALLY!
"IF"S BRAIN CAN BE WIPED BY AN ELECTRO-MAGNETIC PULSE!
TERRIFIC.
SO WHO'S GONNA GENERATE THAT?
ME... BUT I CAN'T.
I THINK I'M A BAD PERSON. DEEP INSIDE SOMEWHERE, I KNOW I'M BAD BUT...
BUT I DON'T HAVE TO DO WHAT I'M TOLD.
WHAA??
I DON'T WANT TO HURT ANY OF YOU.
"NO, WAIT A MINUTE! THIS ISN'T WHAT WE PLANNED.
"WHAT'S SHE DOING, MORROW?"
CAN'T YOU SEE?
SHE'S BEING GOOD.

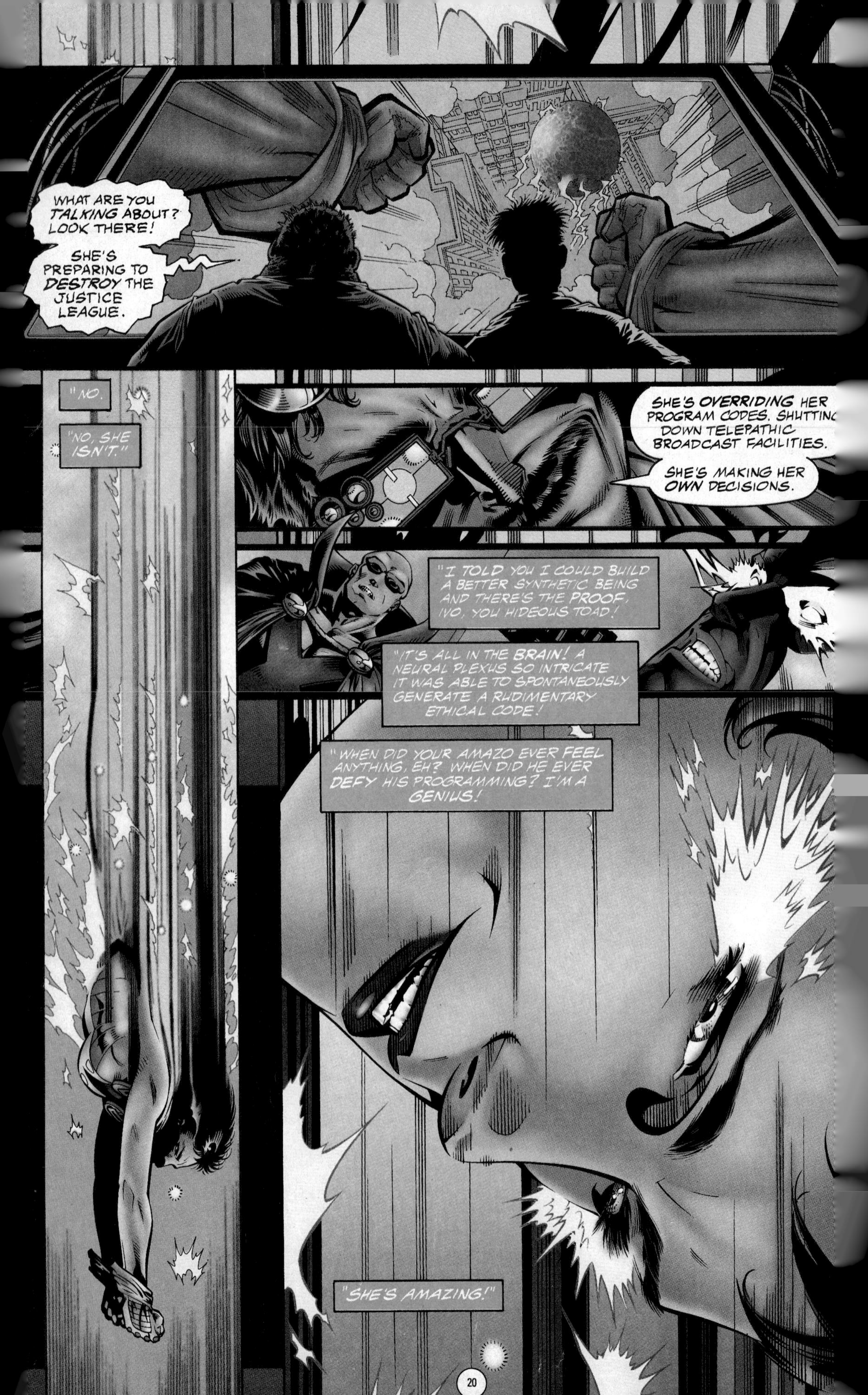

WHAT ARE YOU TALKING ABOUT? LOOK THERE!
SHE'S PREPARING TO DESTROY THE JUSTICE LEAGUE.
"NO.
"NO, SHE ISN'T."
SHE'S OVERRIDING HER PROGRAM CODES. SHUTTING DOWN TELEPATHIC BROADCAST FACILITIES.
SHE'S MAKING HER OWN DECISIONS.
"I TOLD YOU I COULD BUILD A BETTER SYNTHETIC BEING AND THERE'S THE PROOF, IVO, YOU HIDEOUS TOAD!
"IT'S ALL IN THE BRAIN! A NEURAL PLEXUS SO INTRICATE IT WAS ABLE TO SPONTANEOUSLY GENERATE A RUDIMENTARY ETHICAL CODE!
"WHEN DID YOUR AMAZO EVER FEEL ANYTHING, EH? WHEN DID HE EVER DEFY HIS PROGRAMMING? I'M A GENIUS!
"SHE'S AMAZING!"

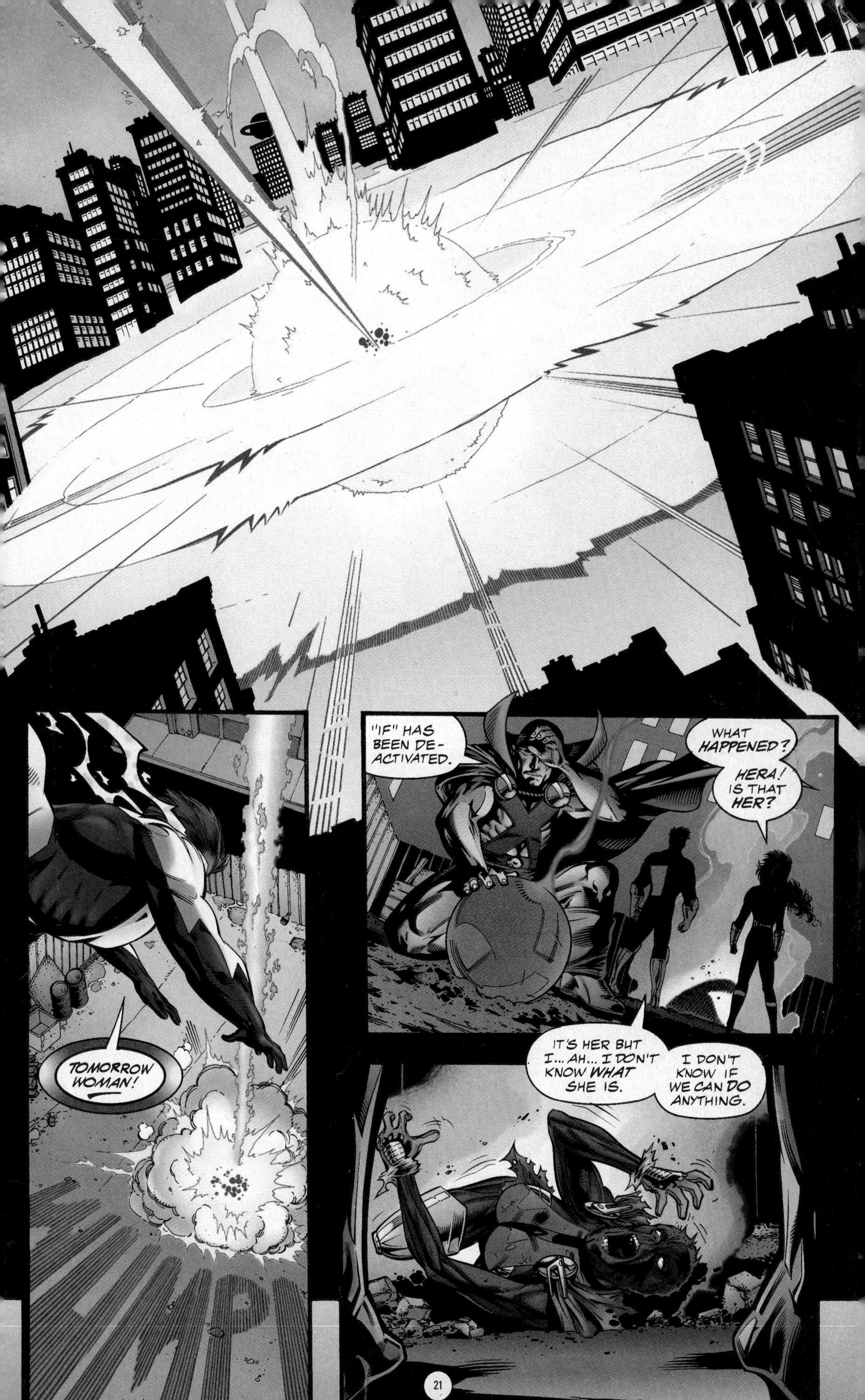
TOMORROW WOMAN!
"IF" HAS BEEN DE-ACTIVATED.
WHAT HAPPENED?
HERA! IS THAT HER?
IT'S HER BUT I... AH... I DON'T KNOW WHAT SHE IS.
I DON'T KNOW IF WE CAN DO ANYTHING.

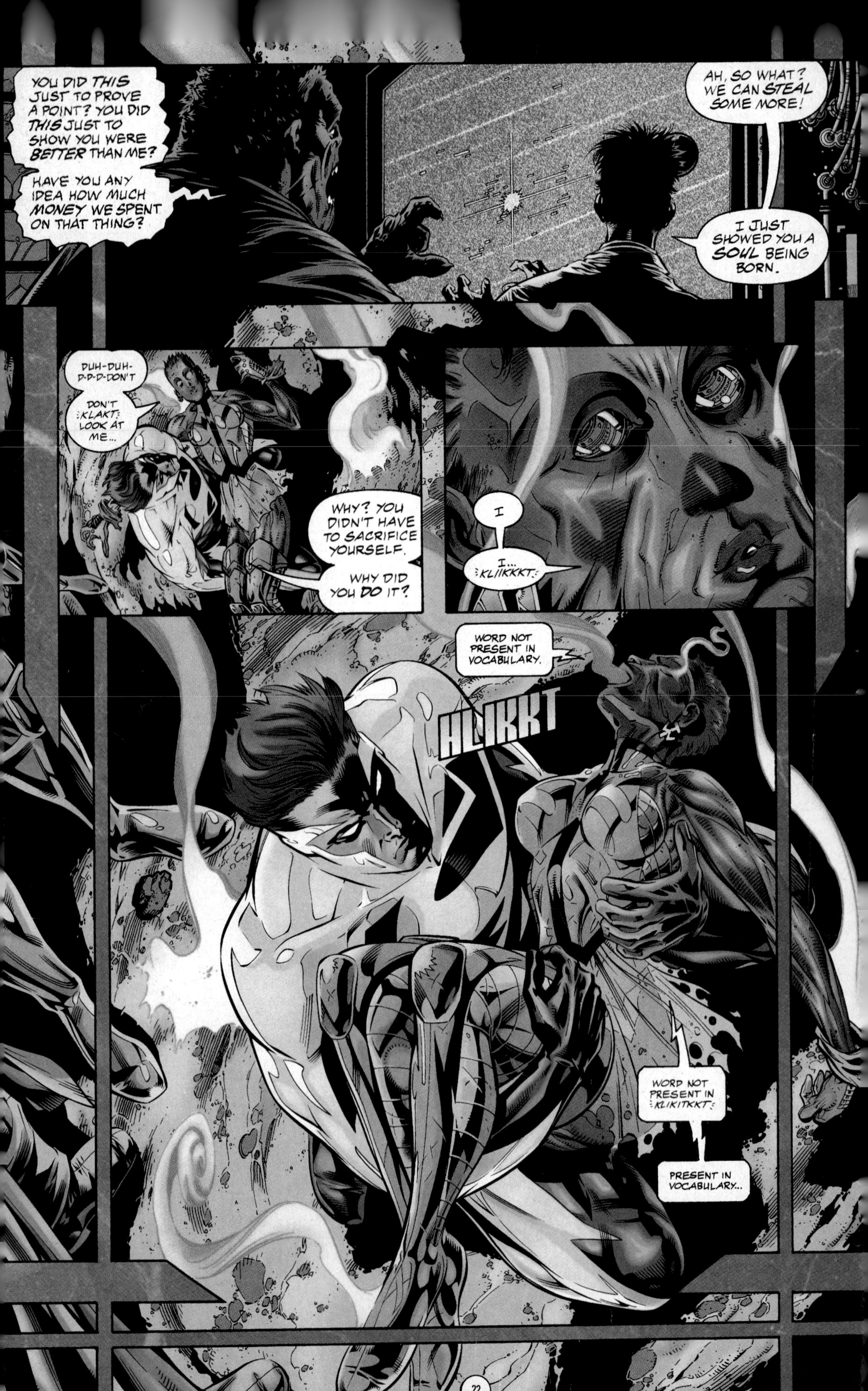
YOU DID THIS JUST TO PROVE A POINT? YOU DID THIS JUST TO SHOW YOU WERE BETTER THAN ME?
HAVE YOU ANY IDEA HOW MUCH MONEY WE SPENT ON THAT THING?
AH, SO WHAT? WE CAN STEAL SOME MORE!
I JUST SHOWED YOU A SOUL BEING BORN.
DUH-DUH-D-D-D-DON'T
DON'T KLAKT LOOK AT ME...
WHY? YOU DIDN'T HAVE TO SACRIFICE YOURSELF.
WHY DID YOU DO IT?
I
I... KLIIKKKT
WORD NOT PRESENT IN VOCABULARY.
KLIKKT
WORD NOT PRESENT IN KLIKITKKT
PRESENT IN VOCABULARY...

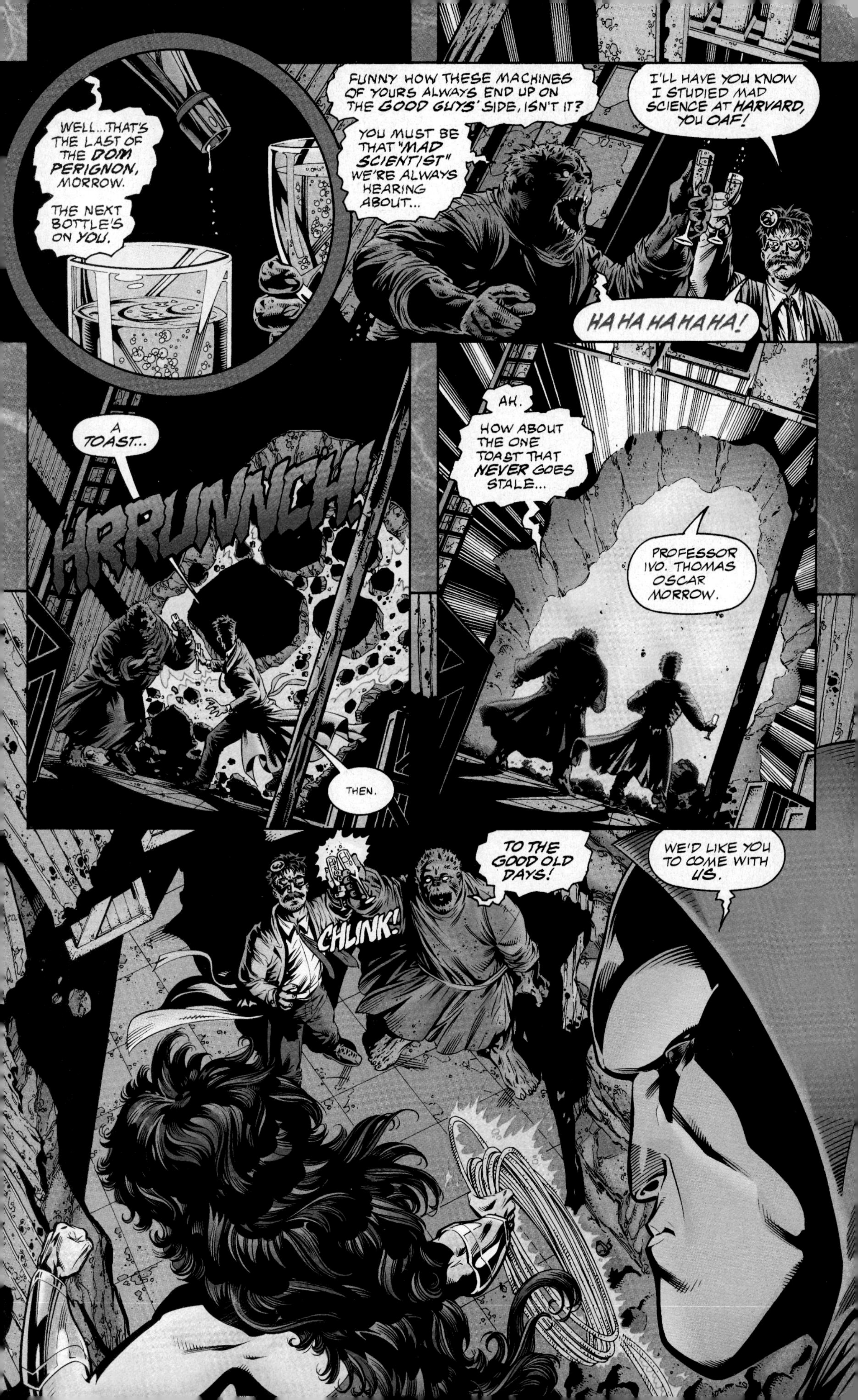
WELL...THAT'S THE LAST OF THE DOM PERIGNON, MORROW.
THE NEXT BOTTLE'S ON YOU.
FUNNY HOW THESE MACHINES OF YOURS ALWAYS END UP ON THE GOOD GUYS' SIDE, ISN'T IT?
YOU MUST BE THAT "MAD SCIENTIST" WE'RE ALWAYS HEARING ABOUT...
I'LL HAVE YOU KNOW I STUDIED MAD SCIENCE AT HARVARD, YOU OAF!
HA HA HA HA HA HA!
A TOAST...
HRRUNNCH!
THEN.
AH.
HOW ABOUT THE ONE TOAST THAT NEVER GOES STALE...
PROFESSOR IVO. THOMAS OSCAR MORROW.
TO THE GOOD OLD DAYS!
CHLINK!
WE'D LIKE YOU TO COME WITH US.

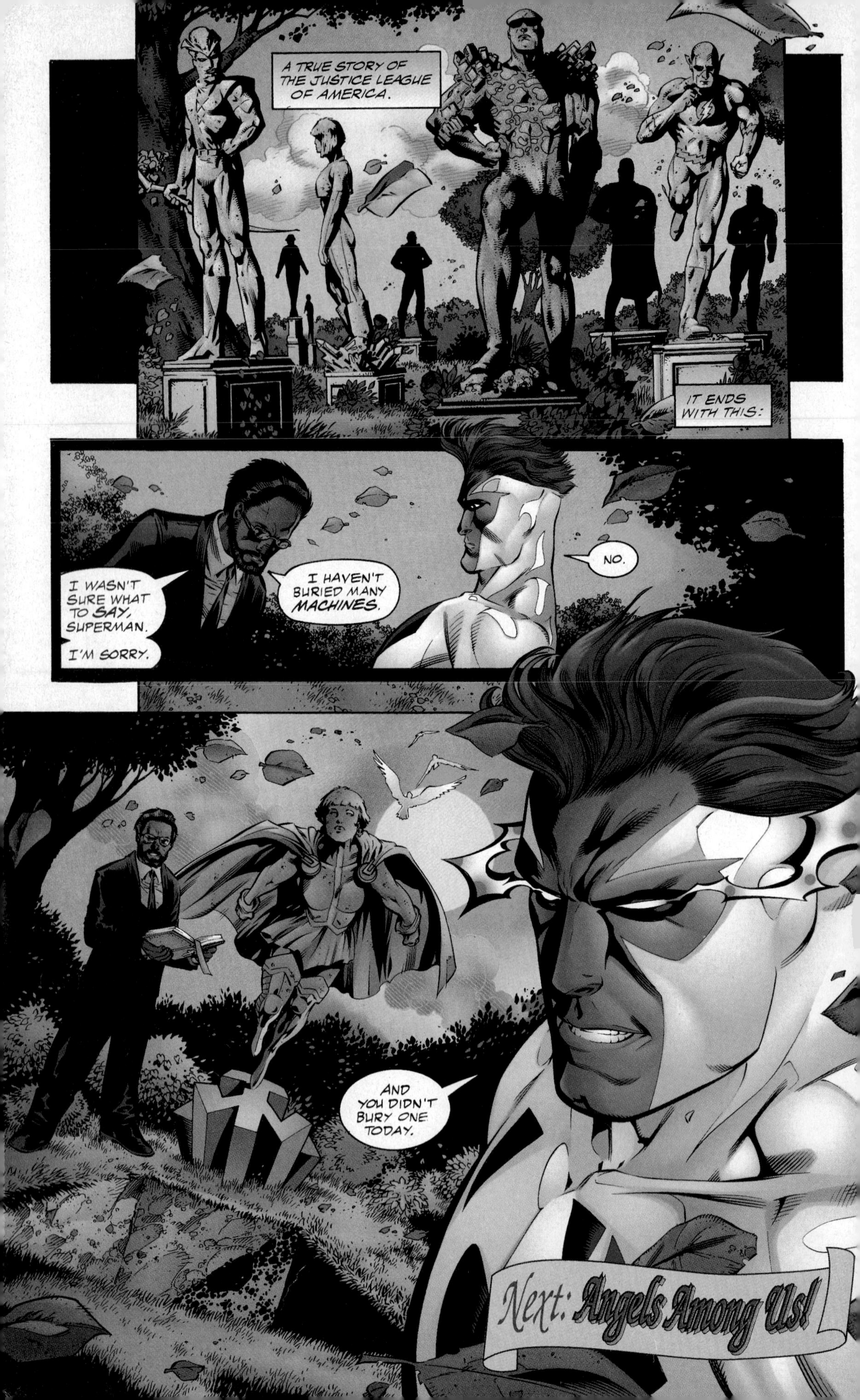
A TRUE STORY OF THE JUSTICE LEAGUE OF AMERICA.
IT ENDS WITH THIS:
I WASN'T SURE WHAT TO SAY, SUPERMAN.
I'M SORRY.
I HAVEN'T BURIED MANY MACHINES.
NO.
AND YOU DIDN'T BURY ONE TODAY.
Next: Angels Among Us!

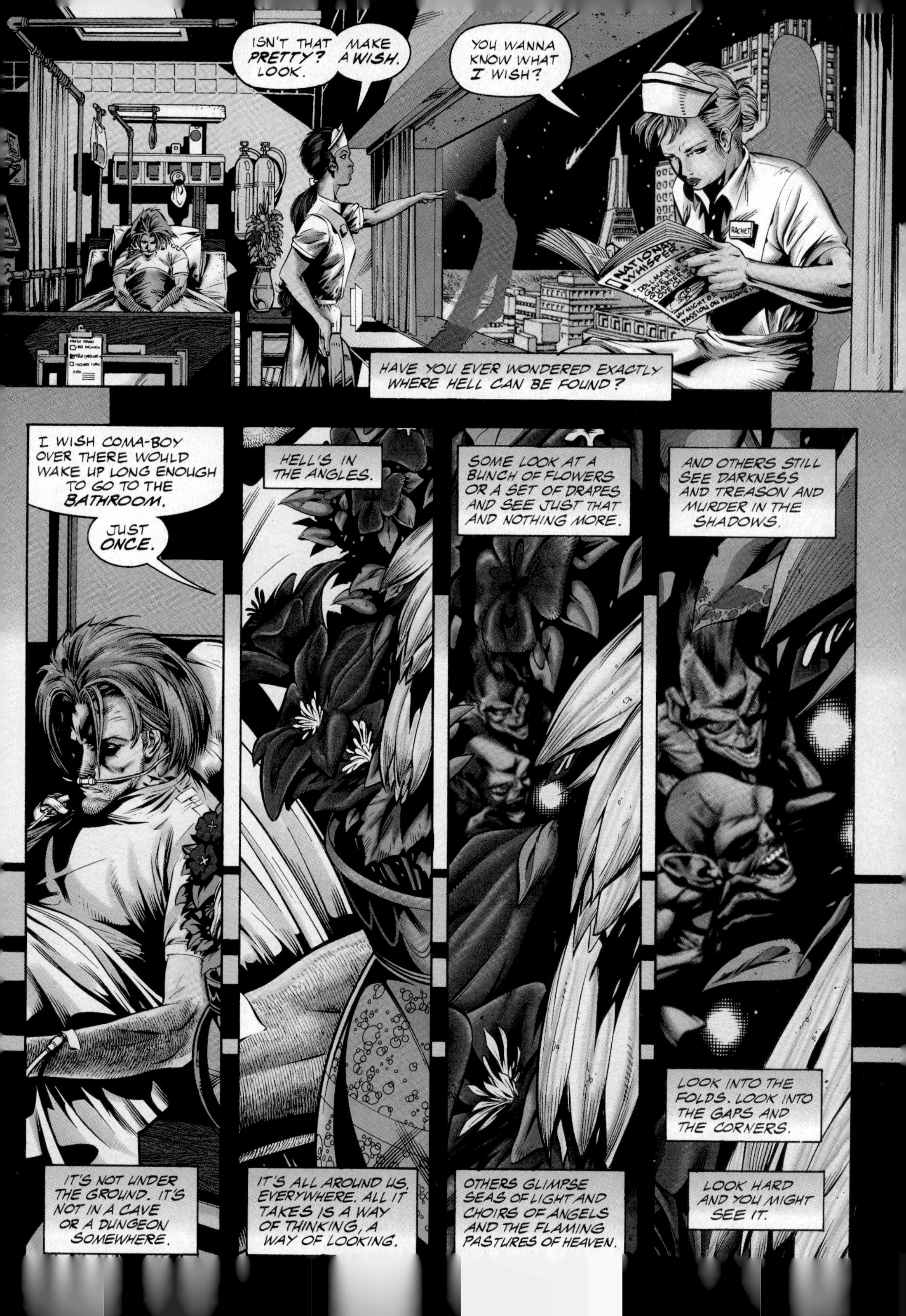

ISN'T THAT PRETTY? LOOK.
MAKE A WISH.
YOU WANNA KNOW WHAT I WISH?
RACHET
NATIONAL WHISPER
HAVE YOU EVER WONDERED EXACTLY WHERE HELL CAN BE FOUND?
I WISH COMA-BOY OVER THERE WOULD WAKE UP LONG ENOUGH TO GO TO THE BATHROOM.
JUST ONCE.
IT'S NOT UNDER THE GROUND. IT'S NOT IN A CAVE OR A DUNGEON SOMEWHERE.
HELL'S IN THE ANGLES.
IT'S ALL AROUND US. EVERYWHERE. ALL IT TAKES IS A WAY OF THINKING, A WAY OF LOOKING.
SOME LOOK AT A BUNCH OF FLOWERS OR A SET OF DRAPES AND SEE JUST THAT AND NOTHING MORE.
OTHERS GLIMPSE SEAS OF LIGHT AND CHOIRS OF ANGELS AND THE FLAMING PASTURES OF HEAVEN.
AND OTHERS STILL SEE DARKNESS AND TREASON AND MURDER IN THE SHADOWS.
LOOK INTO THE FOLDS. LOOK INTO THE GAPS AND THE CORNERS.
LOOK HARD AND YOU MIGHT SEE IT.

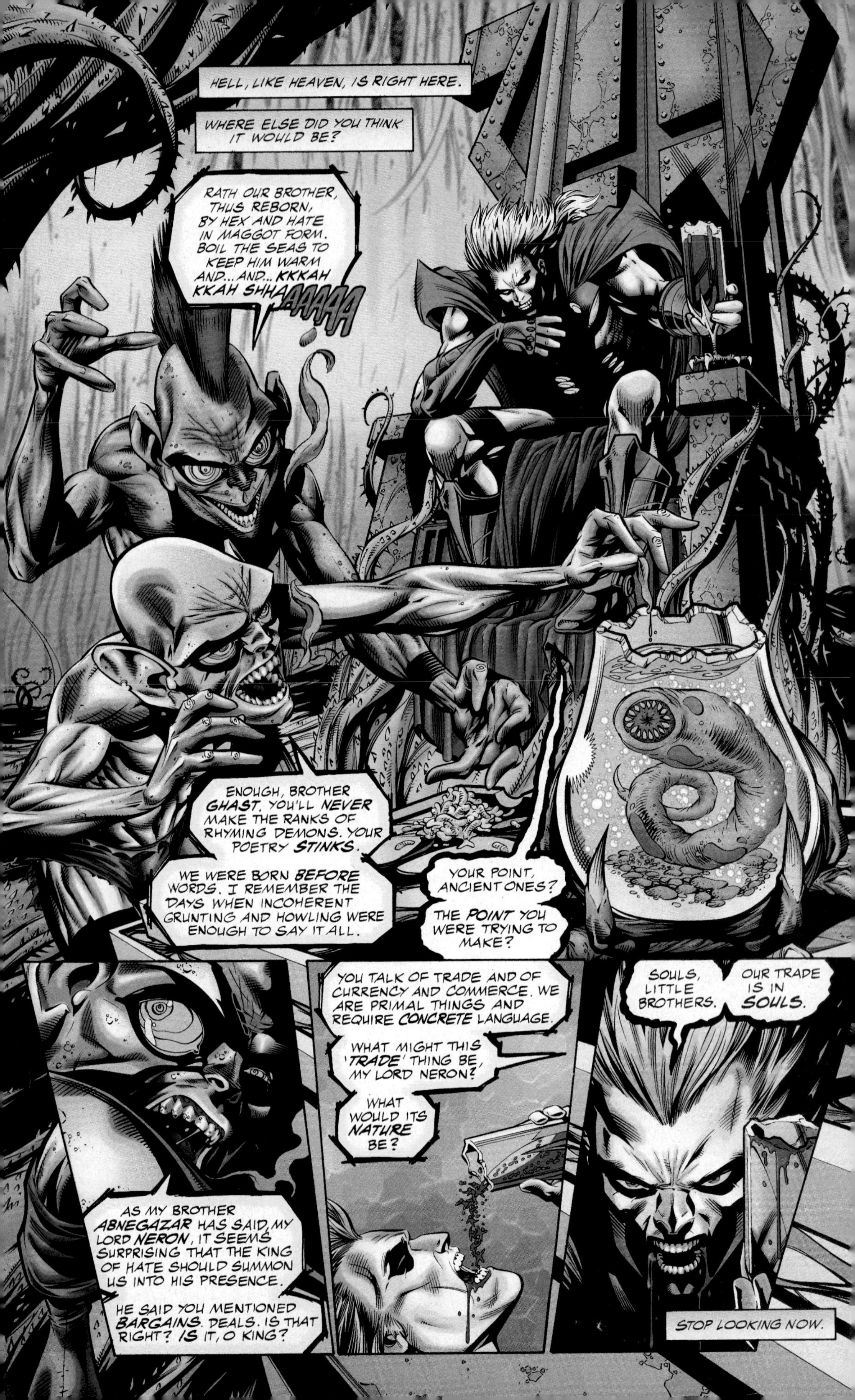
HELL, LIKE HEAVEN, IS RIGHT HERE.
WHERE ELSE DID YOU THINK IT WOULD BE?
RATH OUR BROTHER, THUS REBORN, BY HEX AND HATE IN MAGGOT FORM. BOIL THE SEAS TO KEEP HIM WARM AND... AND... KKKAH KKAH SHHAAAAAA
ENOUGH, BROTHER GHAST. YOU'LL NEVER MAKE THE RANKS OF RHYMING DEMONS. YOUR POETRY STINKS.
WE WERE BORN BEFORE WORDS. I REMEMBER THE DAYS WHEN INCOHERENT GRUNTING AND HOWLING WERE ENOUGH TO SAY IT ALL.
YOUR POINT, ANCIENT ONES?
THE POINT YOU WERE TRYING TO MAKE?
AS MY BROTHER ABNEGAZAR HAS SAID, MY LORD NERON, IT SEEMS SURPRISING THAT THE KING OF HATE SHOULD SUMMON US INTO HIS PRESENCE.
HE SAID YOU MENTIONED BARGAINS. DEALS. IS THAT RIGHT? IS IT, O KING?
YOU TALK OF TRADE AND OF CURRENCY AND COMMERCE. WE ARE PRIMAL THINGS AND REQUIRE CONCRETE LANGUAGE.
WHAT MIGHT THIS 'TRADE' THING BE, MY LORD NERON?
WHAT WOULD ITS NATURE BE?
SOULS, LITTLE BROTHERS.
OUR TRADE IS IN SOULS.
STOP LOOKING NOW.

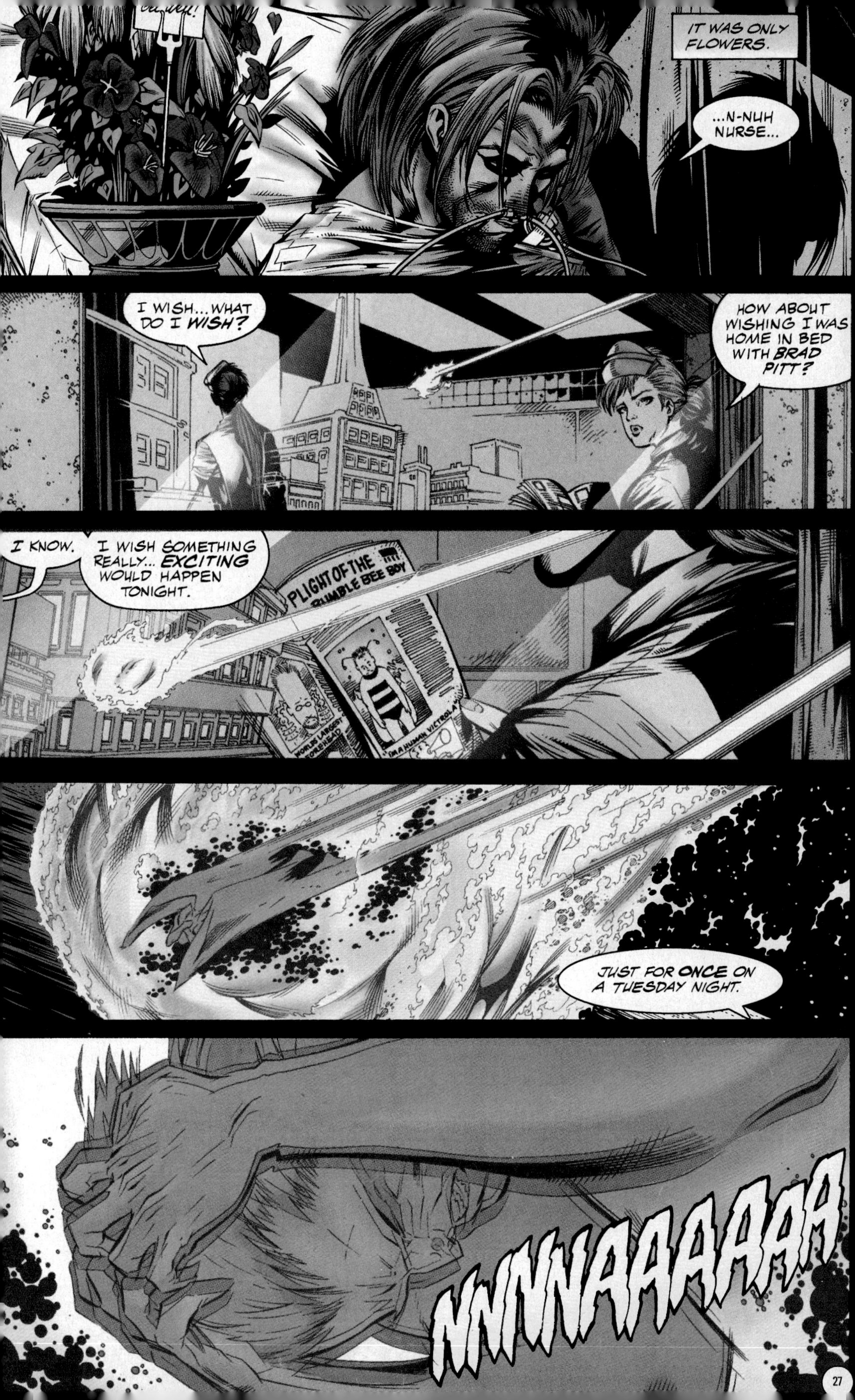
IT WAS ONLY FLOWERS.
...N-NUH NURSE...
I WISH... WHAT DO I WISH?
HOW ABOUT WISHING I WAS HOME IN BED WITH BRAD PITT?
I KNOW.
I WISH SOMETHING REALLY... EXCITING WOULD HAPPEN TONIGHT.
PLIGHT OF THE
BEE BOY
I'M A HUMAN VICTROLA
JUST FOR ONCE ON A TUESDAY NIGHT.
NNNNAAAAAAA

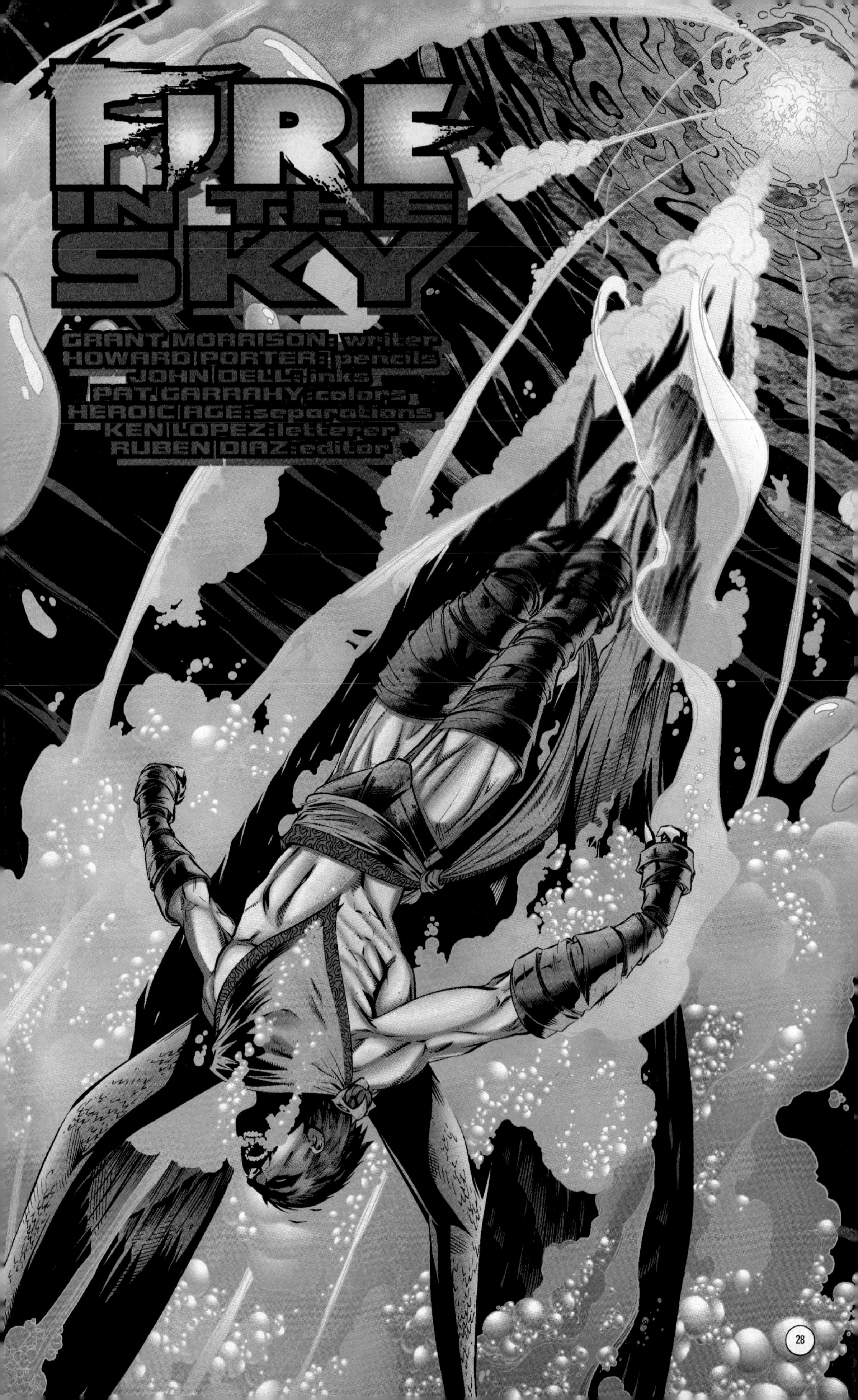
FIRE IN THE SKY
GRANT MORRISON: writer
HOWARD PORTER: pencils
JOHN DELL: inks
PAT GARRAHY: colors
HEROIC AGE: separations
KEN LOPEZ: letterer
RUBEN DIAZ: editor

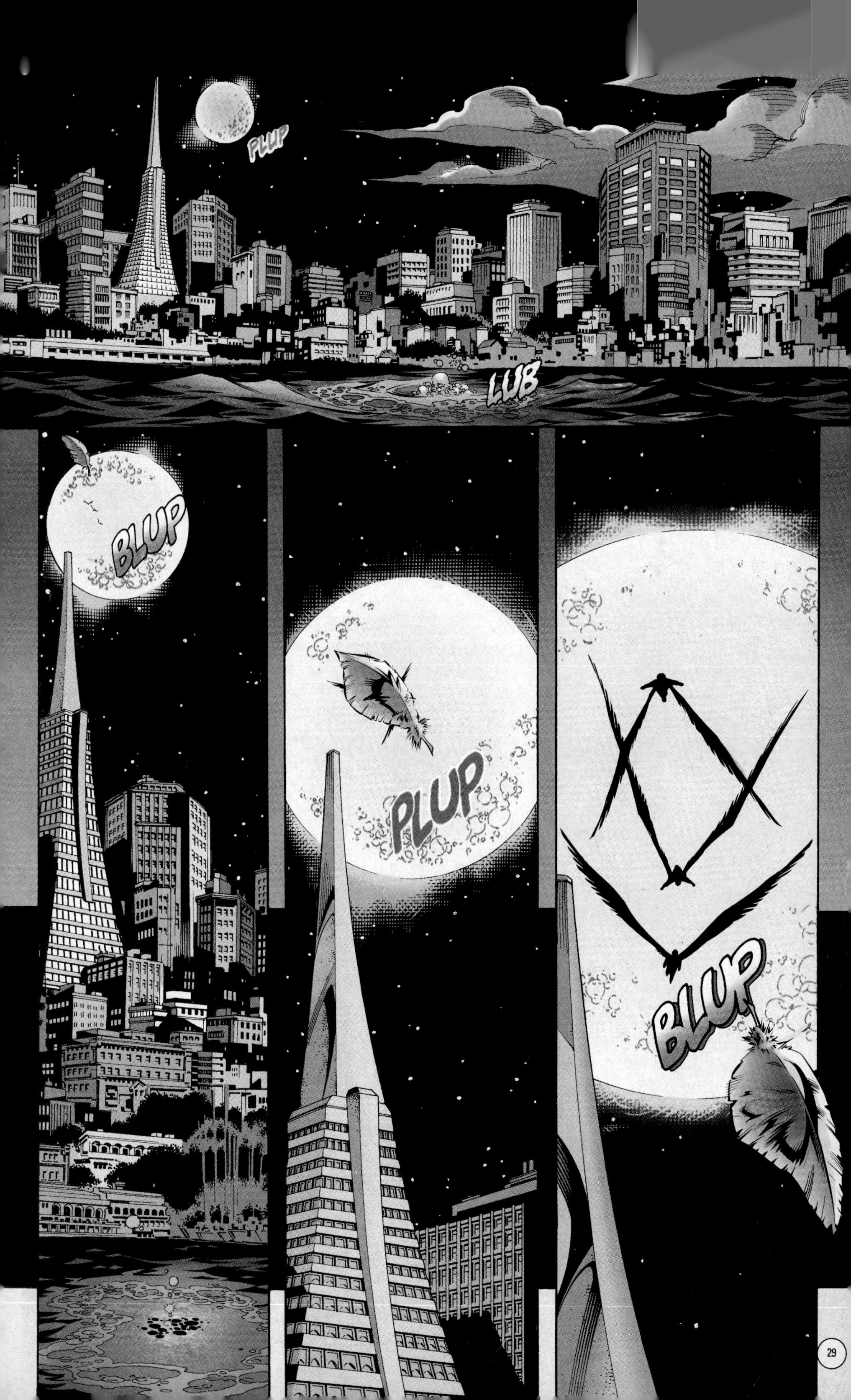
PLUP
LUB
BLUP
PLUP
BLUP

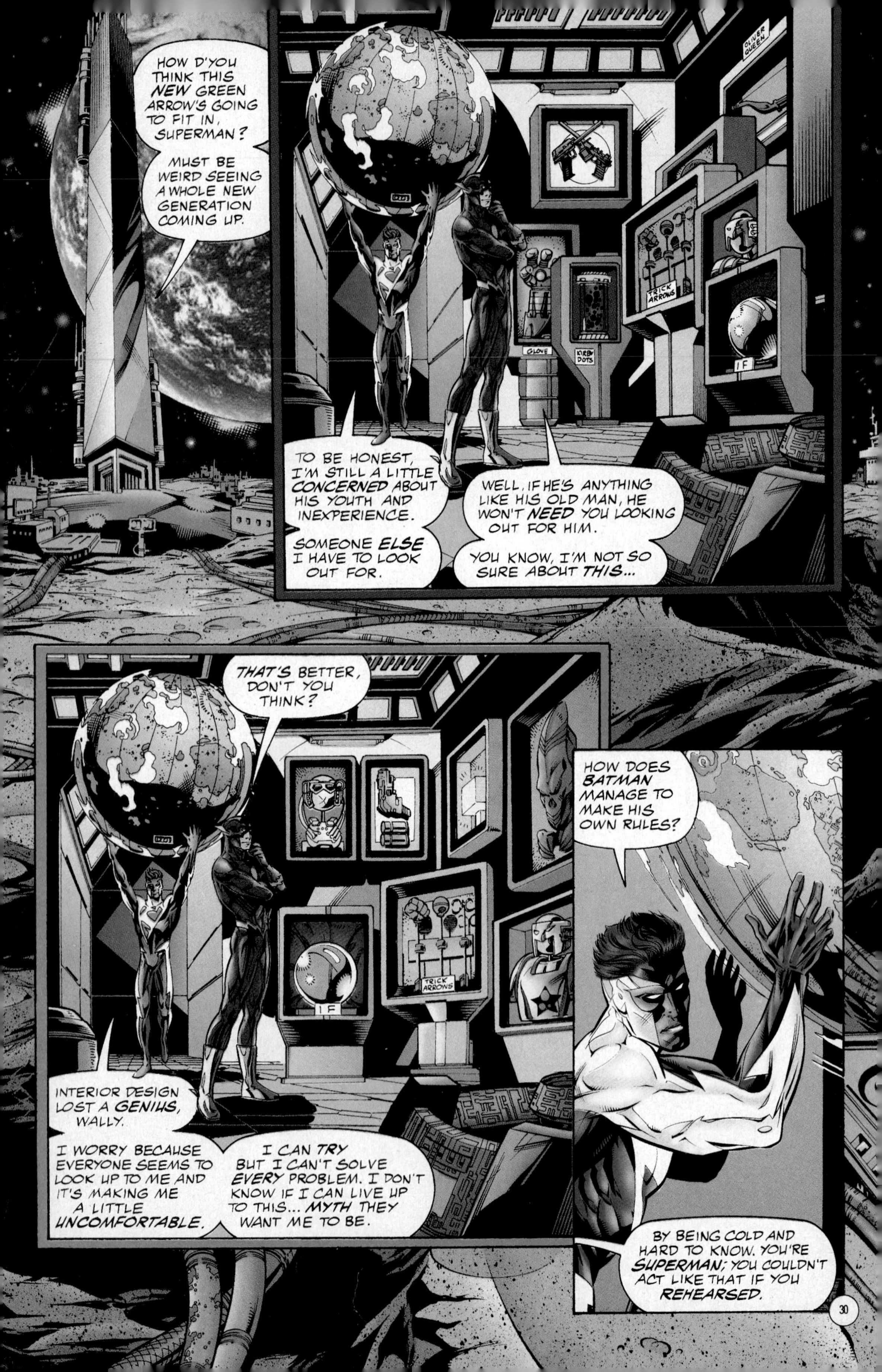
HOW D'YOU THINK THIS NEW GREEN ARROW'S GOING TO FIT IN, SUPERMAN?
MUST BE WEIRD SEEING A WHOLE NEW GENERATION COMING UP.
OLIVER QUEEN
GLOVE
KIRBY DOTS
TRICK ARROWS
I F
TO BE HONEST, I'M STILL A LITTLE CONCERNED ABOUT HIS YOUTH AND INEXPERIENCE.
SOMEONE ELSE I HAVE TO LOOK OUT FOR.
WELL, IF HE'S ANYTHING LIKE HIS OLD MAN, HE WON'T NEED YOU LOOKING OUT FOR HIM.
YOU KNOW, I'M NOT SO SURE ABOUT THIS...
THAT'S BETTER, DON'T YOU THINK?
I F
TRICK ARROWS
INTERIOR DESIGN LOST A GENIUS, WALLY.
I WORRY BECAUSE EVERYONE SEEMS TO LOOK UP TO ME AND IT'S MAKING ME A LITTLE UNCOMFORTABLE.
I CAN TRY BUT I CAN'T SOLVE EVERY PROBLEM. I DON'T KNOW IF I CAN LIVE UP TO THIS... MYTH THEY WANT ME TO BE.
HOW DOES BATMAN MANAGE TO MAKE HIS OWN RULES?
BY BEING COLD AND HARD TO KNOW. YOU'RE SUPERMAN; YOU COULDN'T ACT LIKE THAT IF YOU REHEARSED.

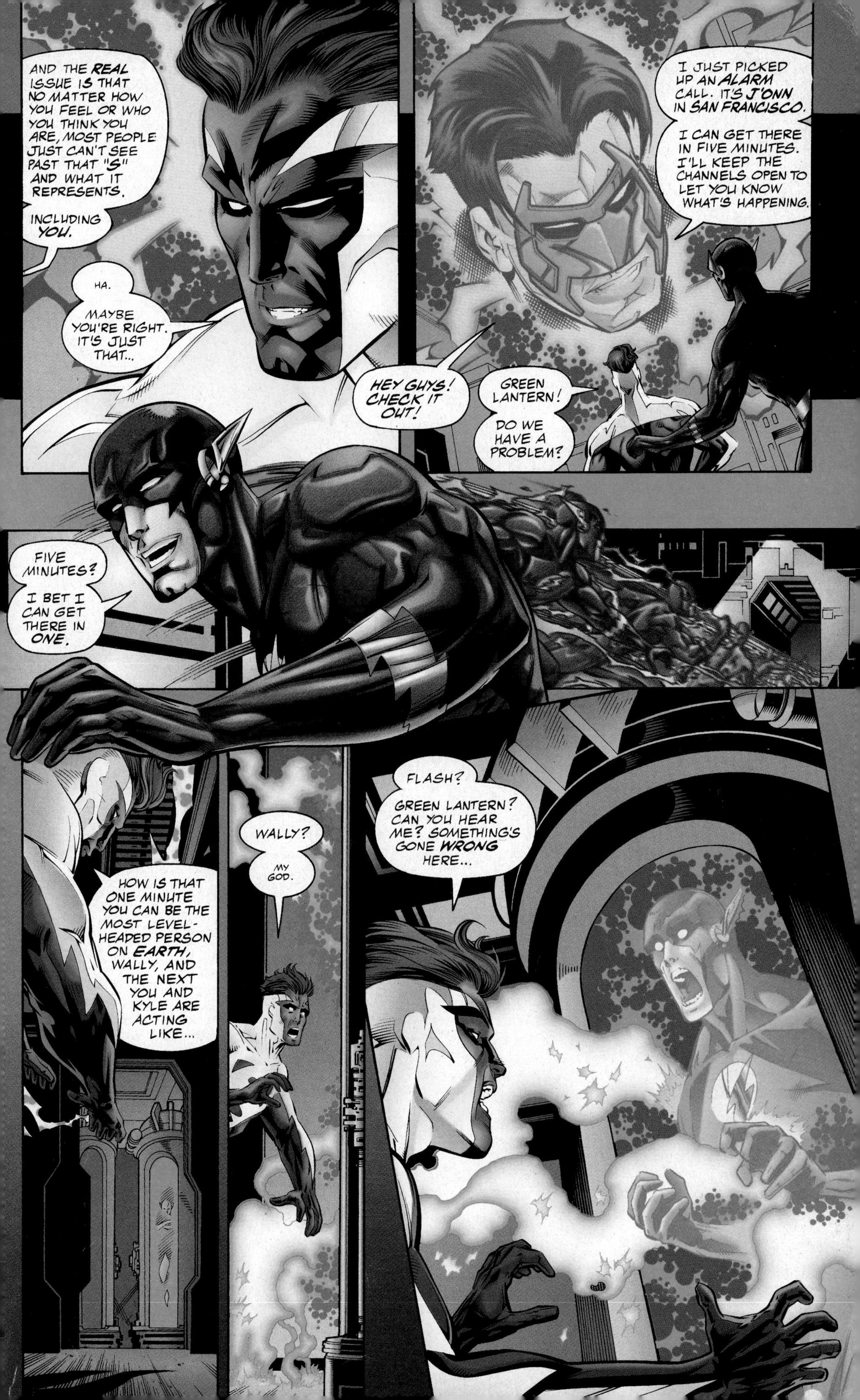
AND THE REAL ISSUE IS THAT NO MATTER HOW YOU FEEL OR WHO YOU THINK YOU ARE, MOST PEOPLE JUST CAN'T SEE PAST THAT "S" AND WHAT IT REPRESENTS.
INCLUDING YOU.
HA.
MAYBE YOU'RE RIGHT. IT'S JUST THAT...
I JUST PICKED UP AN ALARM CALL. IT'S J'ONN IN SAN FRANCISCO.
I CAN GET THERE IN FIVE MINUTES. I'LL KEEP THE CHANNELS OPEN TO LET YOU KNOW WHAT'S HAPPENING.
HEY GUYS! CHECK IT OUT!
GREEN LANTERN!
DO WE HAVE A PROBLEM?
FIVE MINUTES?
I BET I CAN GET THERE IN ONE.
HOW IS THAT ONE MINUTE YOU CAN BE THE MOST LEVEL-HEADED PERSON ON EARTH, WALLY, AND THE NEXT YOU AND KYLE ARE ACTING LIKE...
WALLY?
MY GOD.
FLASH?
GREEN LANTERN? CAN YOU HEAR ME? SOMETHING'S GONE WRONG HERE...

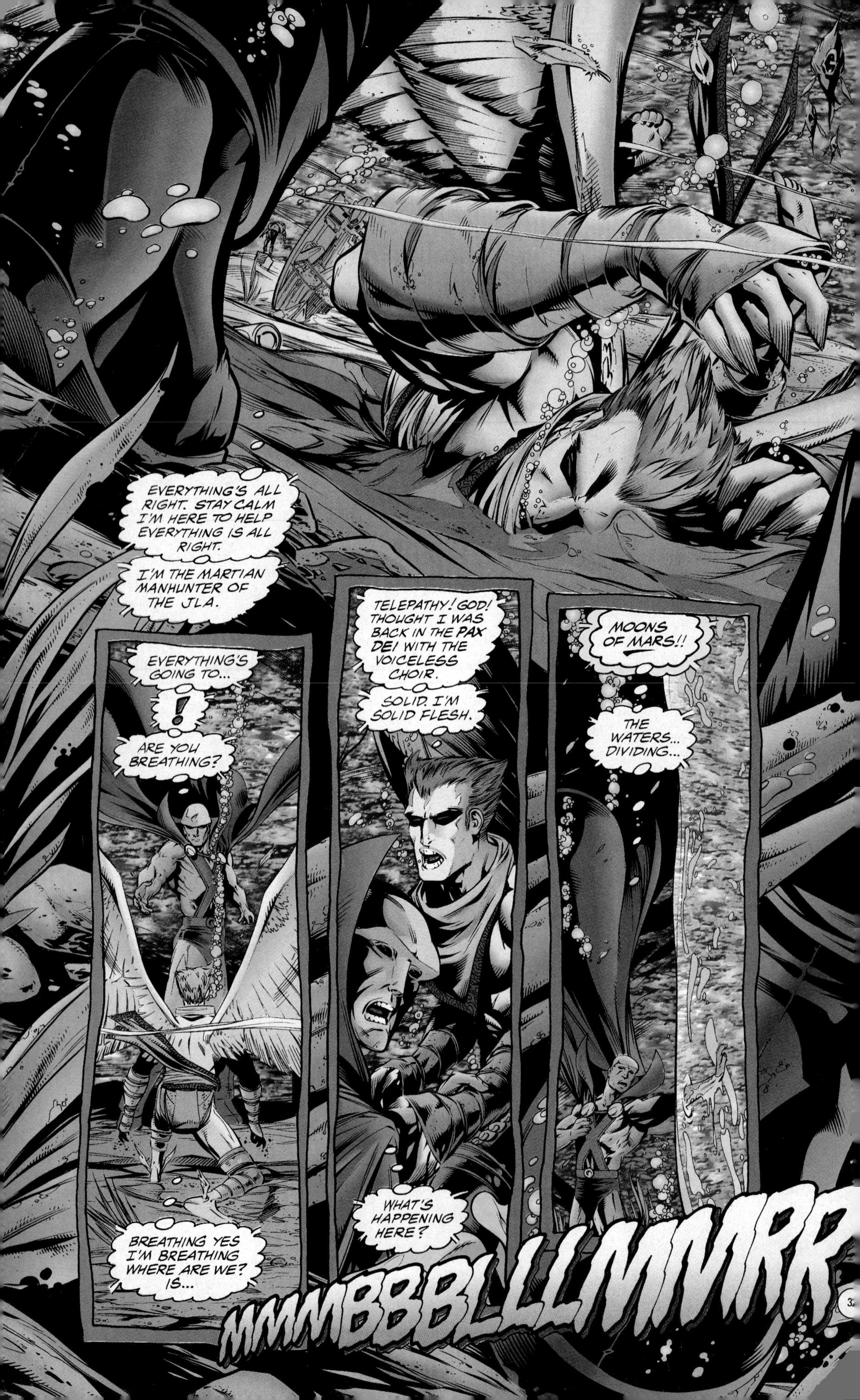
EVERYTHING'S ALL RIGHT. STAY CALM I'M HERE TO HELP EVERYTHING IS ALL RIGHT.
I'M THE MARTIAN MANHUNTER OF THE JLA.
EVERYTHING'S GOING TO...
!
ARE YOU BREATHING?
BREATHING YES I'M BREATHING WHERE ARE WE? IS...
TELEPATHY! GOD! THOUGHT I WAS BACK IN THE PAX DEI WITH THE VOICELESS CHOIR.
SOLID. I'M SOLID FLESH.
WHAT'S HAPPENING HERE?
MOONS OF MARS!!
THE WATERS... DIVIDING...
MMMBBBLLMMRR

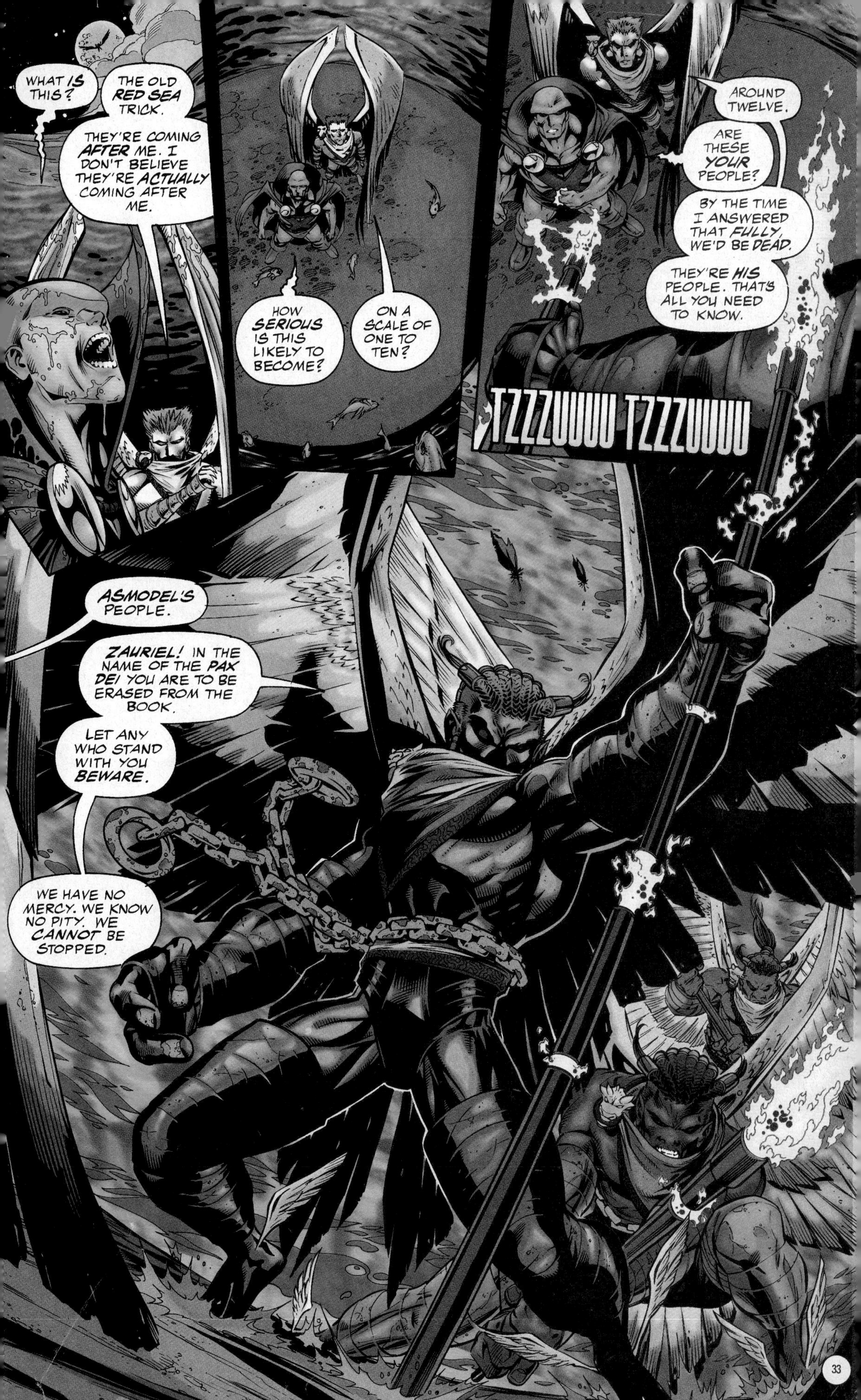
WHAT IS THIS?
THE OLD RED SEA TRICK.
THEY'RE COMING AFTER ME. I DON'T BELIEVE THEY'RE ACTUALLY COMING AFTER ME.
HOW SERIOUS IS THIS LIKELY TO BECOME?
ON A SCALE OF ONE TO TEN?
AROUND TWELVE.
ARE THESE YOUR PEOPLE?
BY THE TIME I ANSWERED THAT FULLY, WE'D BE DEAD.
THEY'RE HIS PEOPLE. THAT'S ALL YOU NEED TO KNOW.
TZZZUUUU TZZZUUUU
ASMODEL'S PEOPLE.
ZAURIEL! IN THE NAME OF THE PAX DEI YOU ARE TO BE ERASED FROM THE BOOK.
LET ANY WHO STAND WITH YOU BEWARE.
WE HAVE NO MERCY. WE KNOW NO PITY. WE CANNOT BE STOPPED.

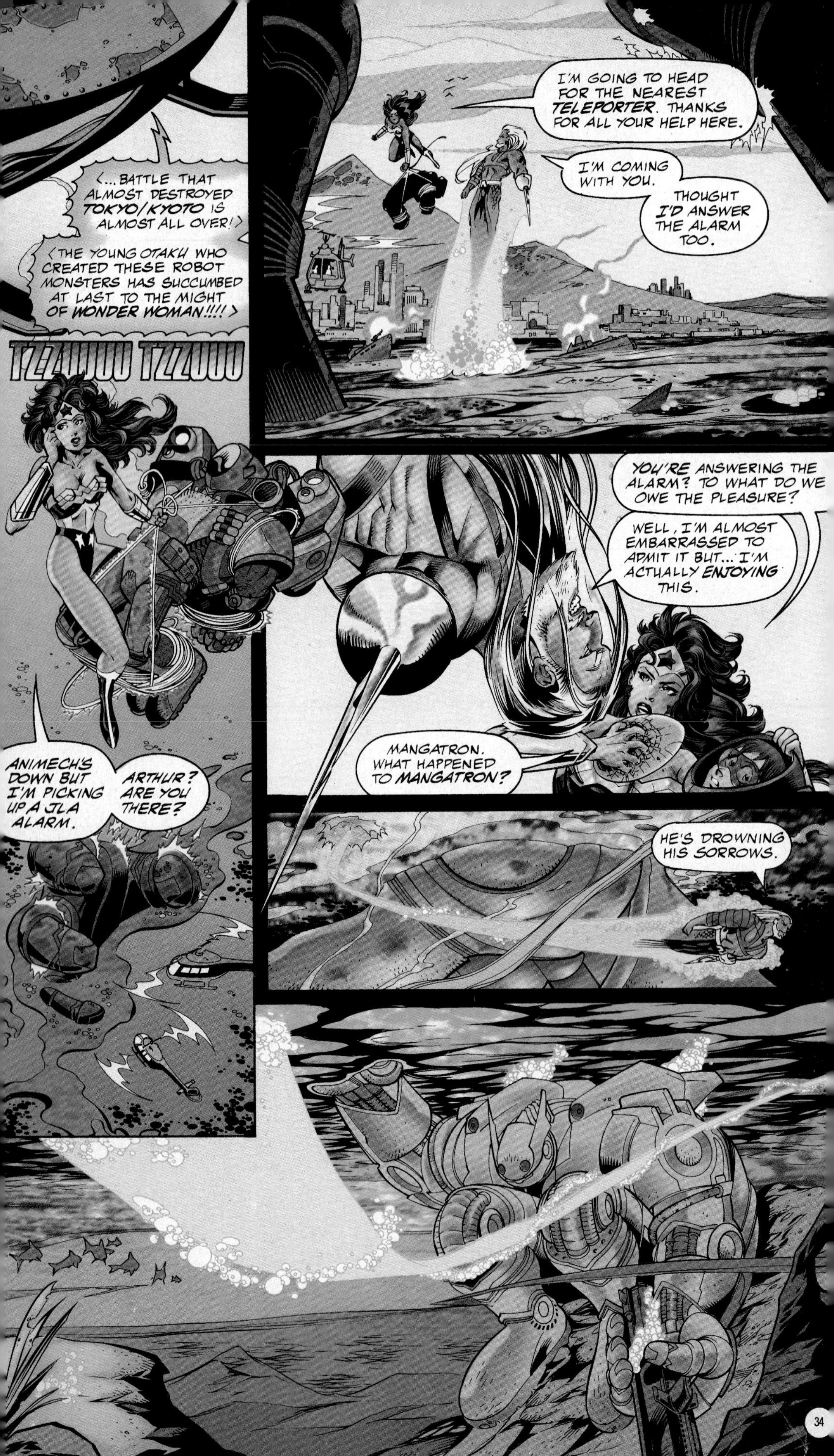

⟨...BATTLE THAT ALMOST DESTROYED TOKYO/KYOTO IS ALMOST ALL OVER!⟩
⟨THE YOUNG OTAKU WHO CREATED THESE ROBOT MONSTERS HAS SUCCUMBED AT LAST TO THE MIGHT OF WONDER WOMAN!!!!⟩
TZZUUUU TZZUUU
ANIMECH'S DOWN BUT I'M PICKING UP A JLA ALARM.
ARTHUR? ARE YOU THERE?
I'M GOING TO HEAD FOR THE NEAREST TELEPORTER. THANKS FOR ALL YOUR HELP HERE.
I'M COMING WITH YOU.
THOUGHT I'D ANSWER THE ALARM TOO.
YOU'RE ANSWERING THE ALARM? TO WHAT DO WE OWE THE PLEASURE?
WELL, I'M ALMOST EMBARRASSED TO ADMIT IT BUT... I'M ACTUALLY ENJOYING THIS.
MANGATRON. WHAT HAPPENED TO MANGATRON?
HE'S DROWNING HIS SORROWS.

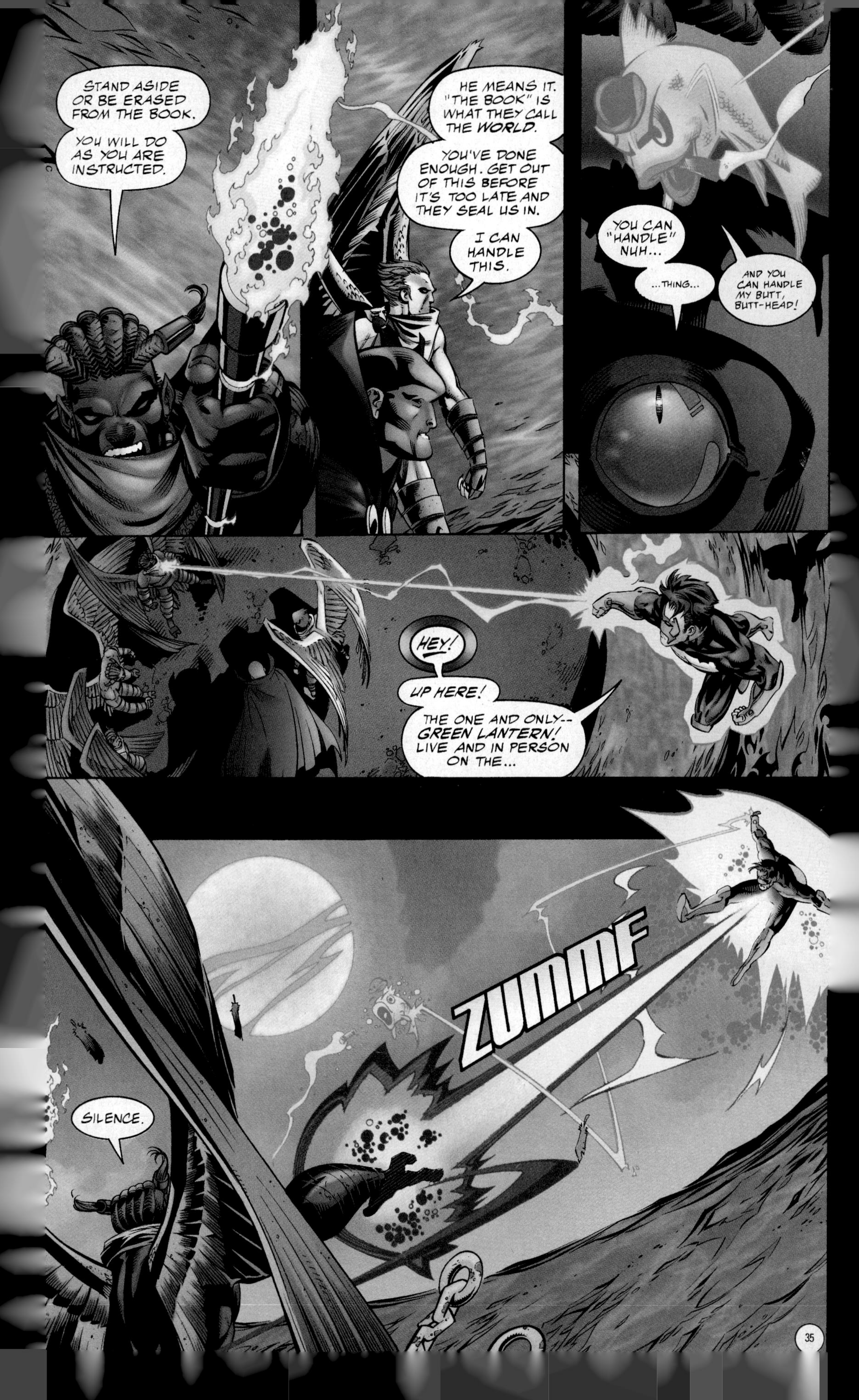
STAND ASIDE OR BE ERASED FROM THE BOOK.
YOU WILL DO AS YOU ARE INSTRUCTED.
HE MEANS IT. "THE BOOK" IS WHAT THEY CALL THE WORLD.
YOU'VE DONE ENOUGH. GET OUT OF THIS BEFORE IT'S TOO LATE AND THEY SEAL US IN.
I CAN HANDLE THIS.
YOU CAN "HANDLE" NUH...
...THING...
AND YOU CAN HANDLE MY BUTT, BUTT-HEAD!
HEY!
UP HERE!
THE ONE AND ONLY-- GREEN LANTERN! LIVE AND IN PERSON ON THE...
ZUMMF
SILENCE.

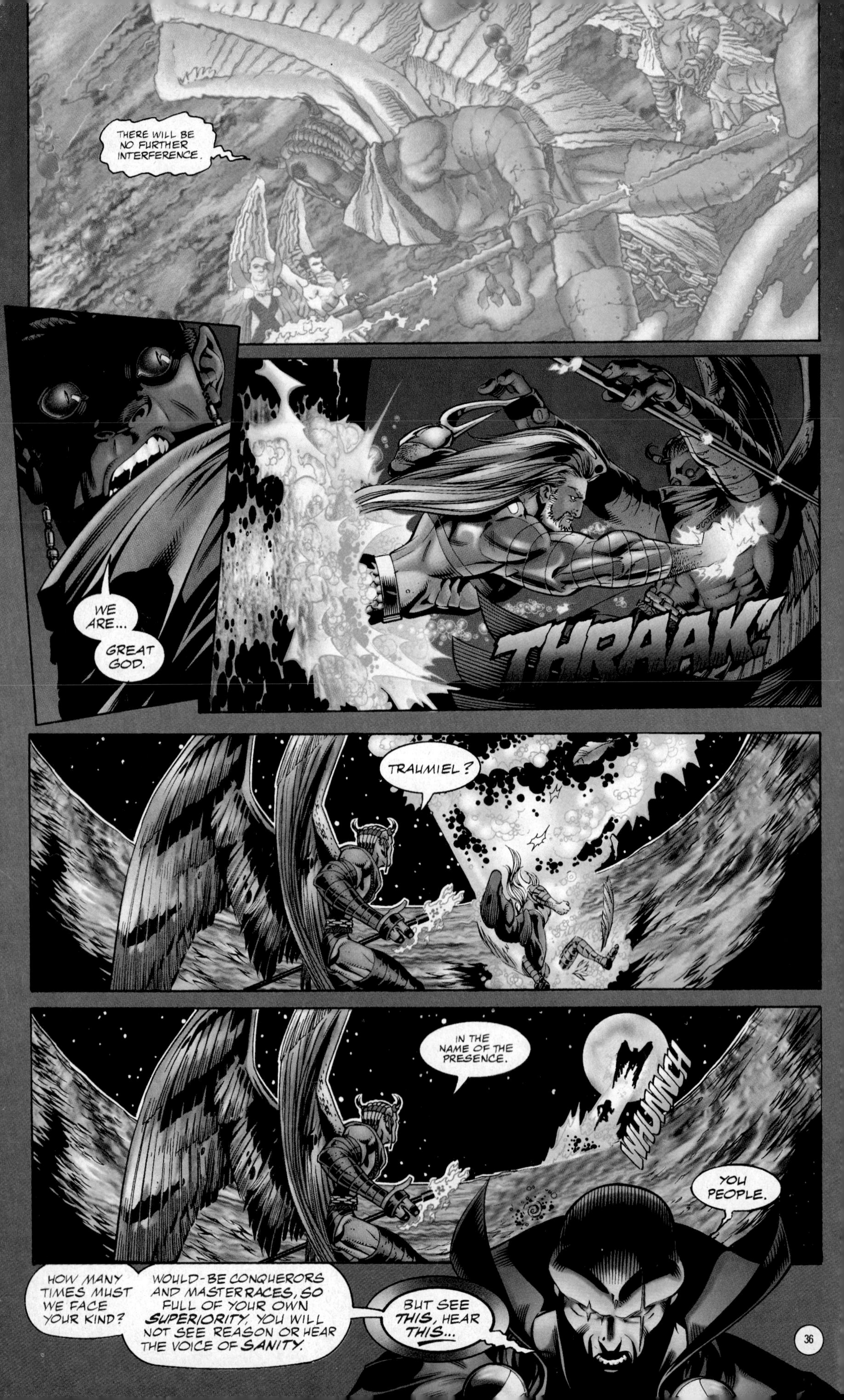
THERE WILL BE NO FURTHER INTERFERENCE.
WE ARE... GREAT GOD.
THRAAK!
TRAUMIEL?
IN THE NAME OF THE PRESENCE.
WHUNNCH
YOU PEOPLE.
HOW MANY TIMES MUST WE FACE YOUR KIND?
WOULD-BE CONQUERORS AND MASTER RACES, SO FULL OF YOUR OWN SUPERIORITY, YOU WILL NOT SEE REASON OR HEAR THE VOICE OF SANITY.
BUT SEE THIS, HEAR THIS...

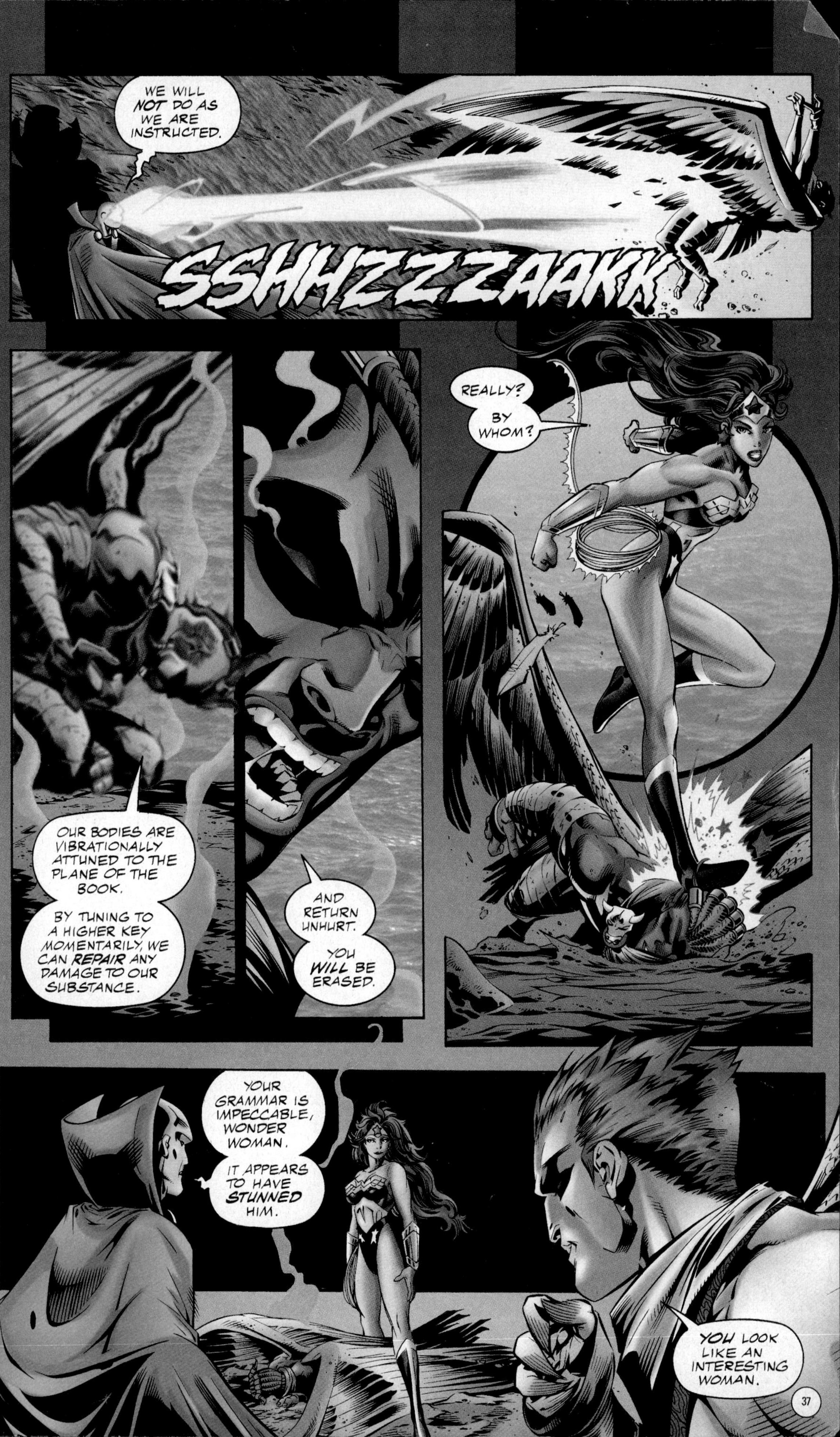

WE WILL NOT DO AS WE ARE INSTRUCTED.
SSHHZZZAAKK
REALLY? BY WHOM?
OUR BODIES ARE VIBRATIONALLY ATTUNED TO THE PLANE OF THE BOOK.
BY TUNING TO A HIGHER KEY MOMENTARILY, WE CAN REPAIR ANY DAMAGE TO OUR SUBSTANCE.
AND RETURN UNHURT.
YOU WILL BE ERASED.
YOUR GRAMMAR IS IMPECCABLE, WONDER WOMAN.
IT APPEARS TO HAVE STUNNED HIM.
YOU LOOK LIKE AN INTERESTING WOMAN.

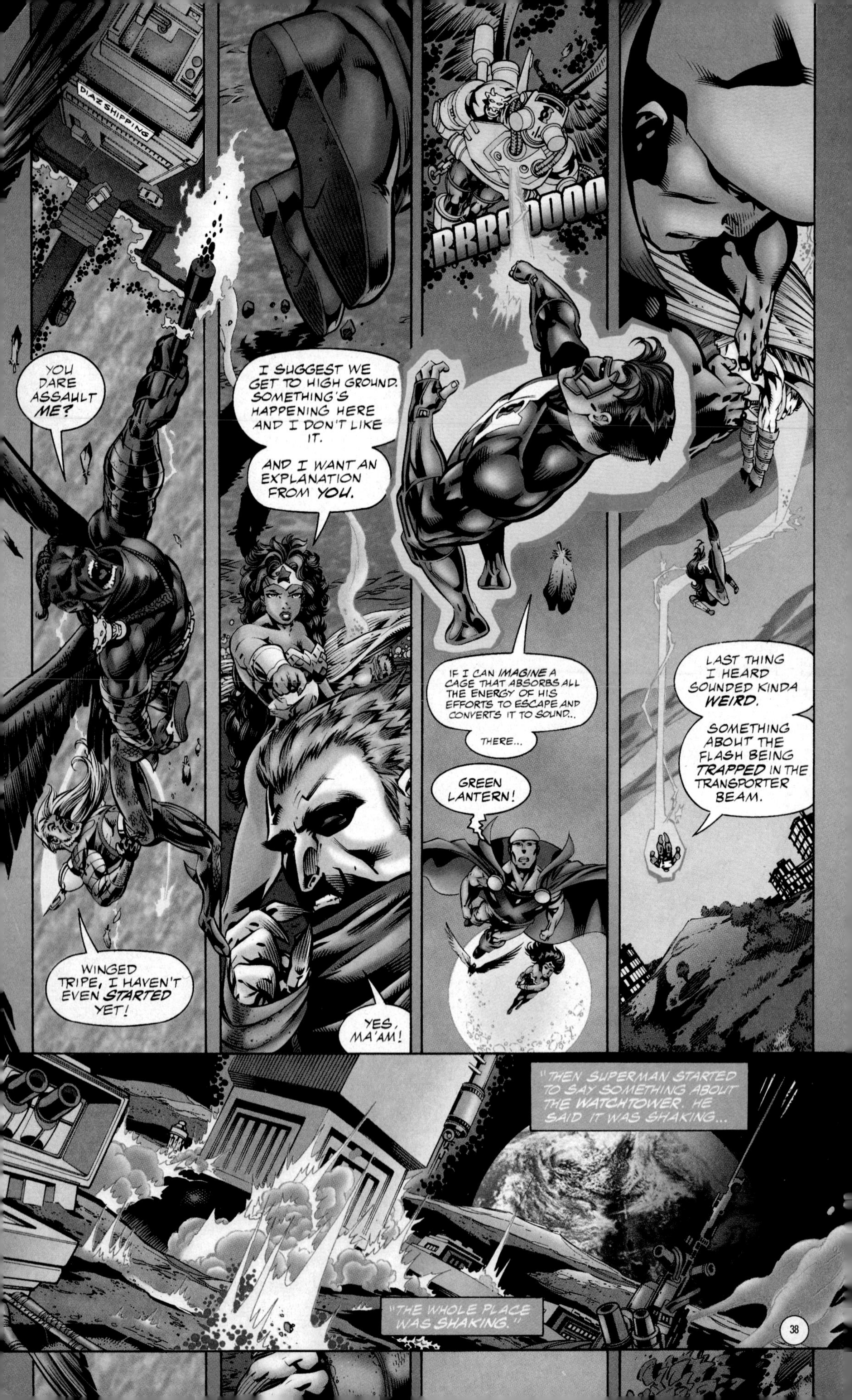
DIAZ SHIPPING
YOU DARE ASSAULT ME?
WINGED TRIPE, I HAVEN'T EVEN STARTED YET!
I SUGGEST WE GET TO HIGH GROUND. SOMETHING'S HAPPENING HERE AND I DON'T LIKE IT.
AND I WANT AN EXPLANATION FROM YOU.
YES, MA'AM!
BRRRROOOO
IF I CAN IMAGINE A CAGE THAT ABSORBS ALL THE ENERGY OF HIS EFFORTS TO ESCAPE AND CONVERTS IT TO SOUND...
THERE...
GREEN LANTERN!
LAST THING I HEARD SOUNDED KINDA WEIRD.
SOMETHING ABOUT THE FLASH BEING TRAPPED IN THE TRANSPORTER BEAM.
"THEN SUPERMAN STARTED TO SAY SOMETHING ABOUT THE WATCHTOWER. HE SAID IT WAS SHAKING...
"THE WHOLE PLACE WAS SHAKING."

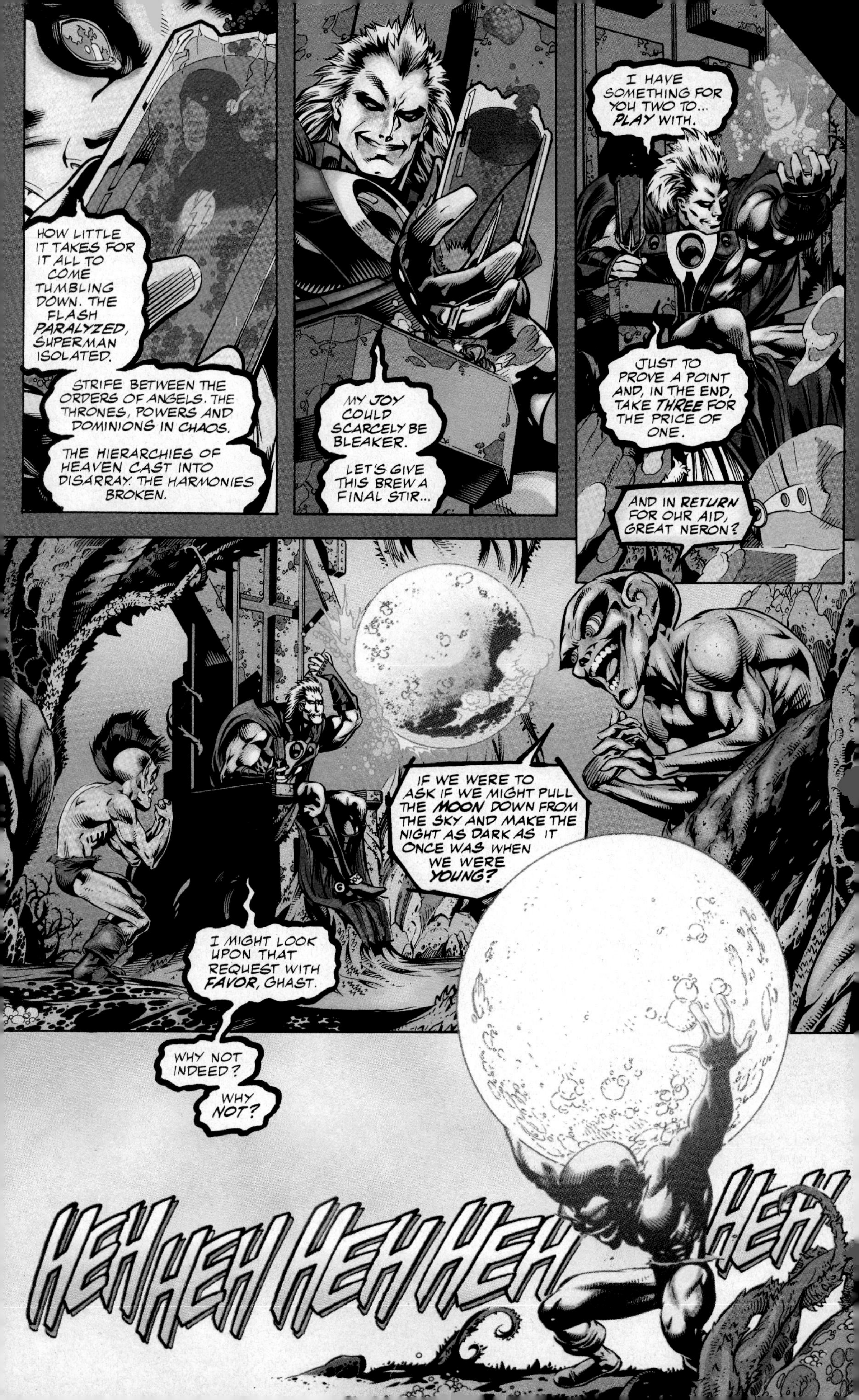
HOW LITTLE IT TAKES FOR IT ALL TO COME TUMBLING DOWN. THE FLASH PARALYZED, SUPERMAN ISOLATED.
STRIFE BETWEEN THE ORDERS OF ANGELS. THE THRONES, POWERS AND DOMINIONS IN CHAOS.
THE HIERARCHIES OF HEAVEN CAST INTO DISARRAY. THE HARMONIES BROKEN.
MY JOY COULD SCARCELY BE BLEAKER.
LET'S GIVE THIS BREW A FINAL STIR...
I HAVE SOMETHING FOR YOU TWO TO... PLAY WITH.
JUST TO PROVE A POINT AND, IN THE END, TAKE THREE FOR THE PRICE OF ONE.
AND IN RETURN FOR OUR AID, GREAT NERON?
IF WE WERE TO ASK IF WE MIGHT PULL THE MOON DOWN FROM THE SKY AND MAKE THE NIGHT AS DARK AS IT ONCE WAS WHEN WE WERE YOUNG?
I MIGHT LOOK UPON THAT REQUEST WITH FAVOR, GHAST.
WHY NOT INDEED?
WHY NOT?
HEH HEH HEH HEH HEH HEH

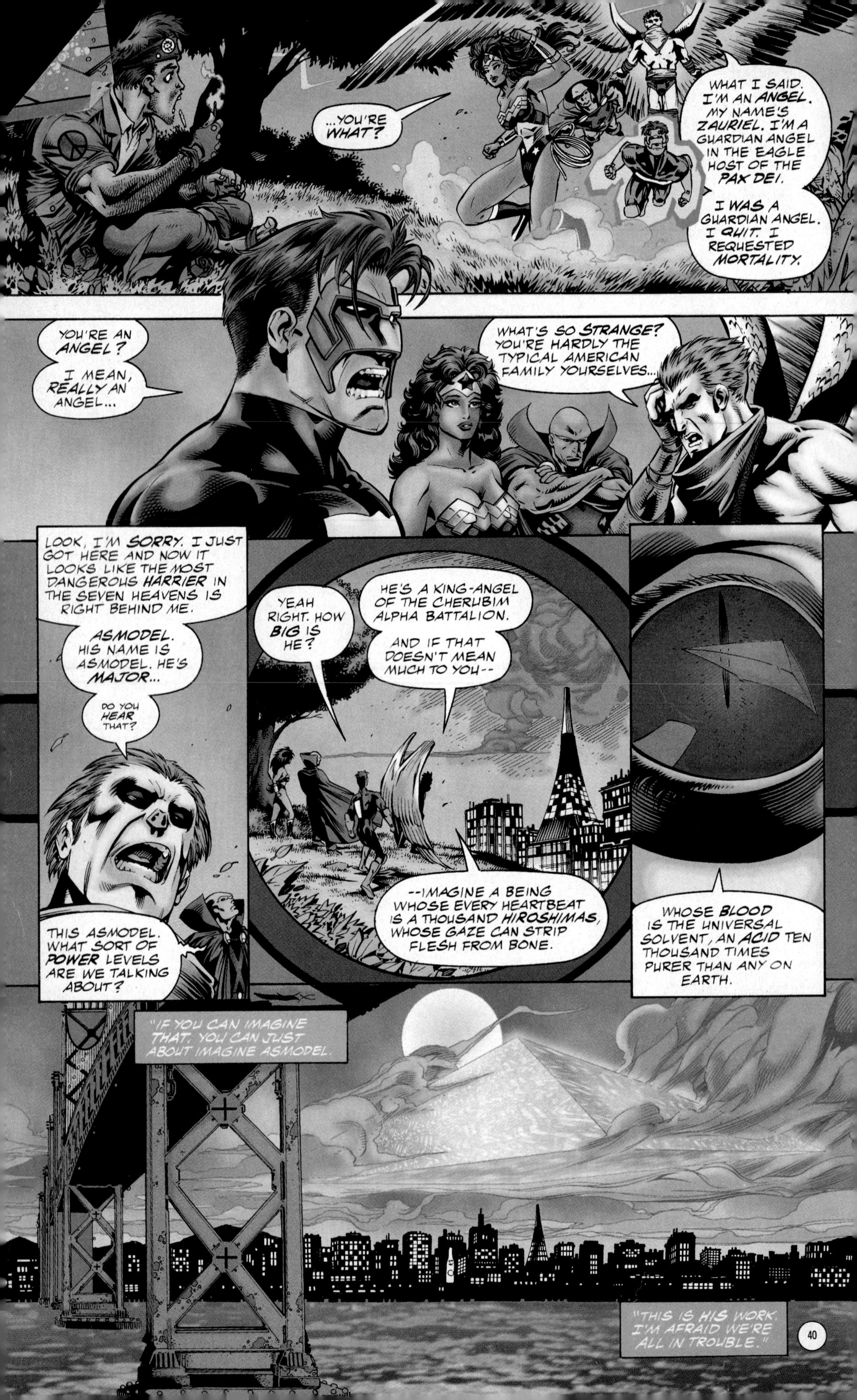
...YOU'RE WHAT?
WHAT I SAID. I'M AN ANGEL. MY NAME'S ZAURIEL. I'M A GUARDIAN ANGEL IN THE EAGLE HOST OF THE PAX DEI.
I WAS A GUARDIAN ANGEL. I QUIT. I REQUESTED MORTALITY.
YOU'RE AN ANGEL?
I MEAN, REALLY AN ANGEL...
WHAT'S SO STRANGE? YOU'RE HARDLY THE TYPICAL AMERICAN FAMILY YOURSELVES...
LOOK, I'M SORRY. I JUST GOT HERE AND NOW IT LOOKS LIKE THE MOST DANGEROUS HARRIER IN THE SEVEN HEAVENS IS RIGHT BEHIND ME.
ASMODEL. HIS NAME IS ASMODEL. HE'S MAJOR...
DO YOU HEAR THAT?
THIS ASMODEL. WHAT SORT OF POWER LEVELS ARE WE TALKING ABOUT?
YEAH RIGHT. HOW BIG IS HE?
HE'S A KING-ANGEL OF THE CHERUBIM ALPHA BATTALION.
AND IF THAT DOESN'T MEAN MUCH TO YOU--
--IMAGINE A BEING WHOSE EVERY HEARTBEAT IS A THOUSAND HIROSHIMAS, WHOSE GAZE CAN STRIP FLESH FROM BONE.
WHOSE BLOOD IS THE UNIVERSAL SOLVENT, AN ACID TEN THOUSAND TIMES PURER THAN ANY ON EARTH.
"IF YOU CAN IMAGINE THAT, YOU CAN JUST ABOUT IMAGINE ASMODEL.
"THIS IS HIS WORK. I'M AFRAID WE'RE ALL IN TROUBLE."

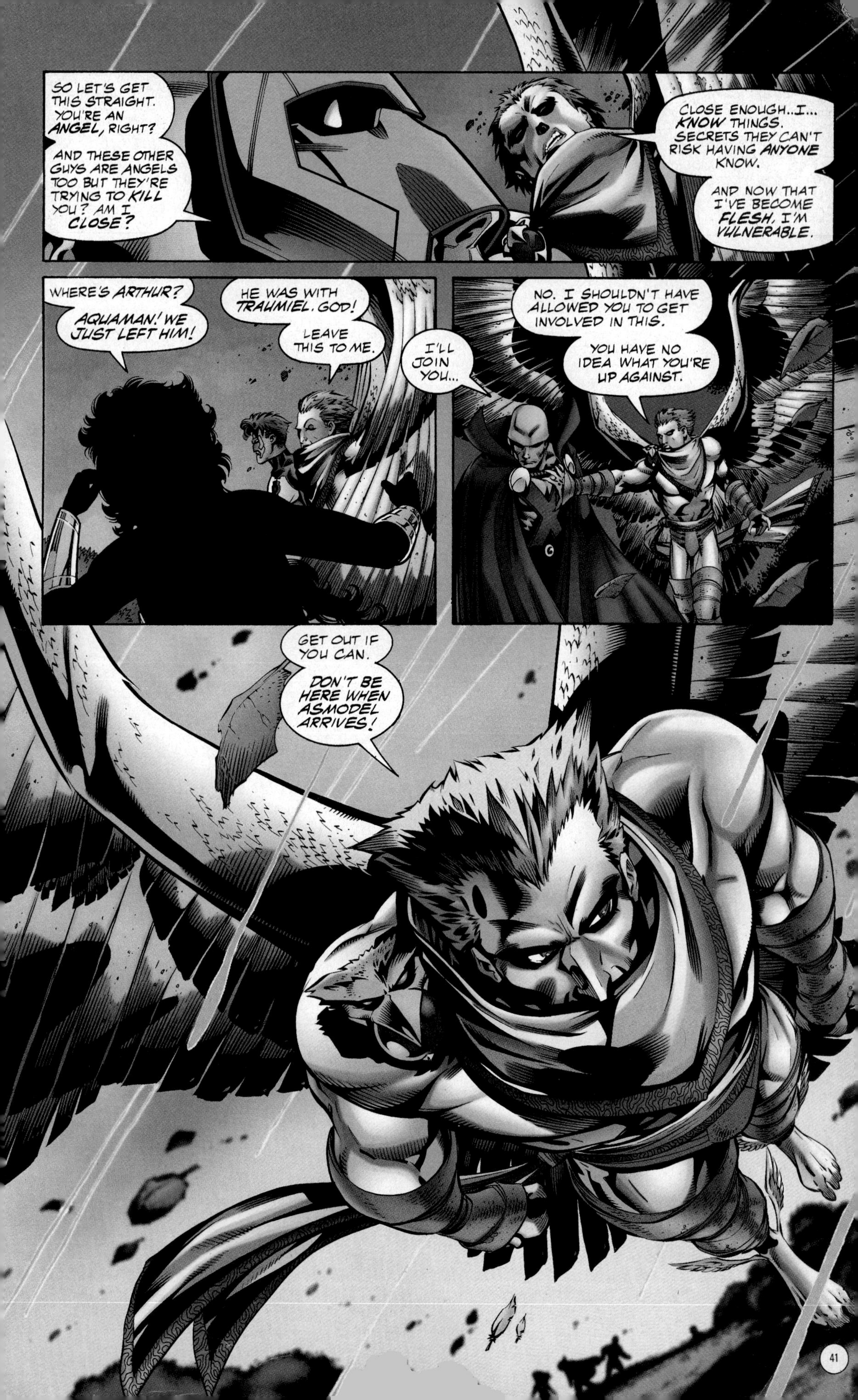

SO LET'S GET THIS STRAIGHT. YOU'RE AN ANGEL, RIGHT?
AND THESE OTHER GUYS ARE ANGELS TOO BUT THEY'RE TRYING TO KILL YOU? AM I CLOSE?
CLOSE ENOUGH...I... KNOW THINGS. SECRETS THEY CAN'T RISK HAVING ANYONE KNOW.
AND NOW THAT I'VE BECOME FLESH, I'M VULNERABLE.
WHERE'S ARTHUR?
AQUAMAN! WE JUST LEFT HIM!
HE WAS WITH TRAUMIEL. GOD!
LEAVE THIS TO ME.
I'LL JOIN YOU...
NO. I SHOULDN'T HAVE ALLOWED YOU TO GET INVOLVED IN THIS.
YOU HAVE NO IDEA WHAT YOU'RE UP AGAINST.
GET OUT IF YOU CAN.
DON'T BE HERE WHEN ASMODEL ARRIVES!

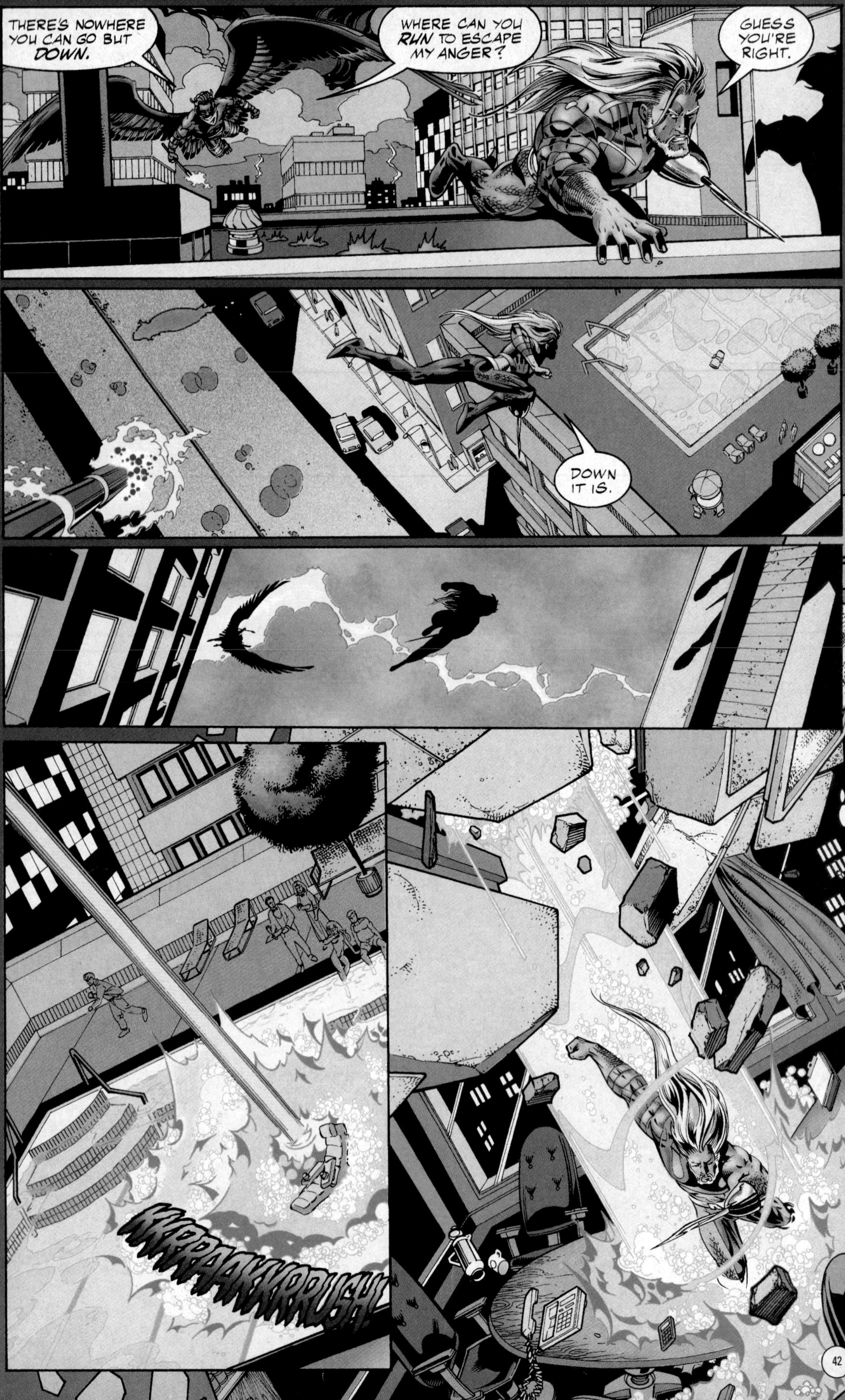
THERE'S NOWHERE YOU CAN GO BUT DOWN.
WHERE CAN YOU RUN TO ESCAPE MY ANGER?
GUESS YOU'RE RIGHT.
DOWN IT IS.
KKRRAAKKRRUSH!

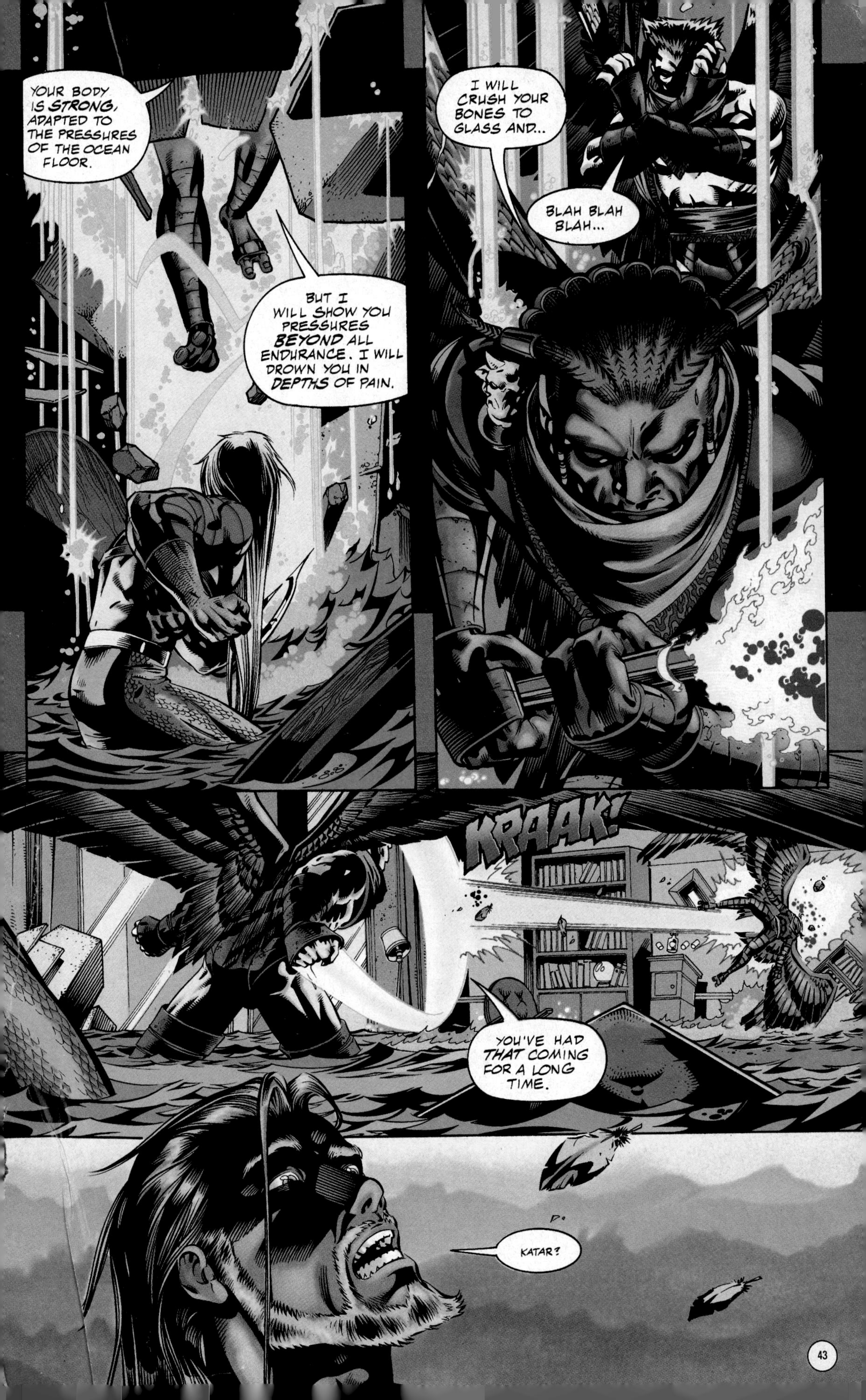
YOUR BODY IS STRONG, ADAPTED TO THE PRESSURES OF THE OCEAN FLOOR.
BUT I WILL SHOW YOU PRESSURES BEYOND ALL ENDURANCE. I WILL DROWN YOU IN DEPTHS OF PAIN.
I WILL CRUSH YOUR BONES TO GLASS AND...
BLAH BLAH BLAH...
KRAAK!
YOU'VE HAD THAT COMING FOR A LONG TIME.
KATAR?

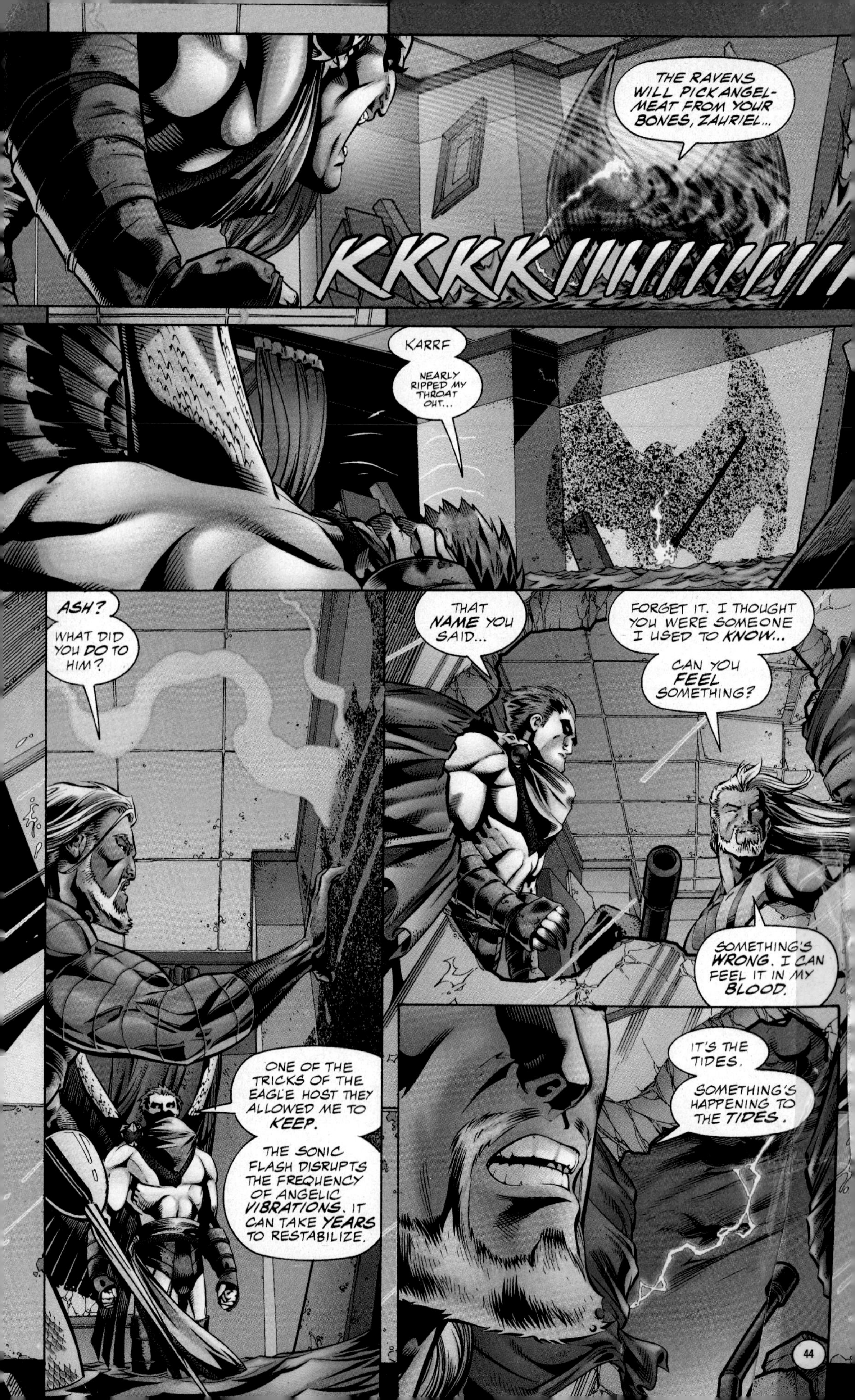
THE RAVENS WILL PICK ANGEL-MEAT FROM YOUR BONES, ZAURIEL...
KKKKIIIIIIIIIIIII
KARRF
NEARLY RIPPED MY THROAT OUT...
ASH? WHAT DID YOU DO TO HIM?
THAT NAME YOU SAID...
FORGET IT. I THOUGHT YOU WERE SOMEONE I USED TO KNOW...
CAN YOU FEEL SOMETHING?
SOMETHING'S WRONG. I CAN FEEL IT IN MY BLOOD.
ONE OF THE TRICKS OF THE EAGLE HOST THEY ALLOWED ME TO KEEP.
THE SONIC FLASH DISRUPTS THE FREQUENCY OF ANGELIC VIBRATIONS. IT CAN TAKE YEARS TO RESTABILIZE.
IT'S THE TIDES.
SOMETHING'S HAPPENING TO THE TIDES.

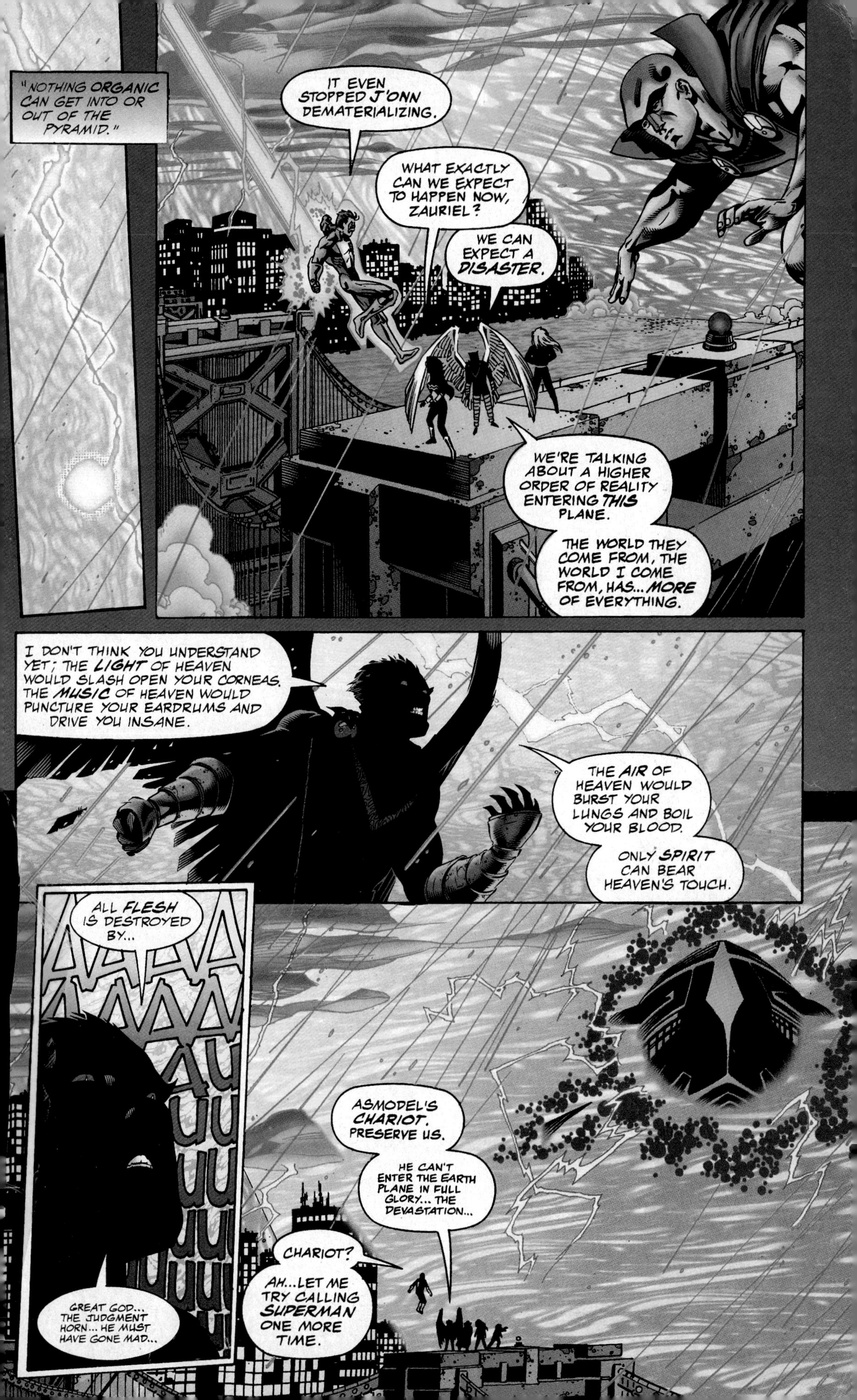
"NOTHING ORGANIC CAN GET INTO OR OUT OF THE PYRAMID."
IT EVEN STOPPED J'ONN DEMATERIALIZING.
WHAT EXACTLY CAN WE EXPECT TO HAPPEN NOW, ZAURIEL?
WE CAN EXPECT A DISASTER.
WE'RE TALKING ABOUT A HIGHER ORDER OF REALITY ENTERING THIS PLANE.
THE WORLD THEY COME FROM, THE WORLD I COME FROM, HAS... MORE OF EVERYTHING.
I DON'T THINK YOU UNDERSTAND YET; THE LIGHT OF HEAVEN WOULD SLASH OPEN YOUR CORNEAS. THE MUSIC OF HEAVEN WOULD PUNCTURE YOUR EARDRUMS AND DRIVE YOU INSANE.
THE AIR OF HEAVEN WOULD BURST YOUR LUNGS AND BOIL YOUR BLOOD.
ONLY SPIRIT CAN BEAR HEAVEN'S TOUCH.
ALL FLESH IS DESTROYED BY...
AAAAAAAAUUUUUUUU
GREAT GOD... THE JUDGMENT HORN... HE MUST HAVE GONE MAD...
ASMODEL'S CHARIOT. PRESERVE US.
HE CAN'T ENTER THE EARTH PLANE IN FULL GLORY... THE DEVASTATION...
CHARIOT?
AH... LET ME TRY CALLING SUPERMAN ONE MORE TIME.

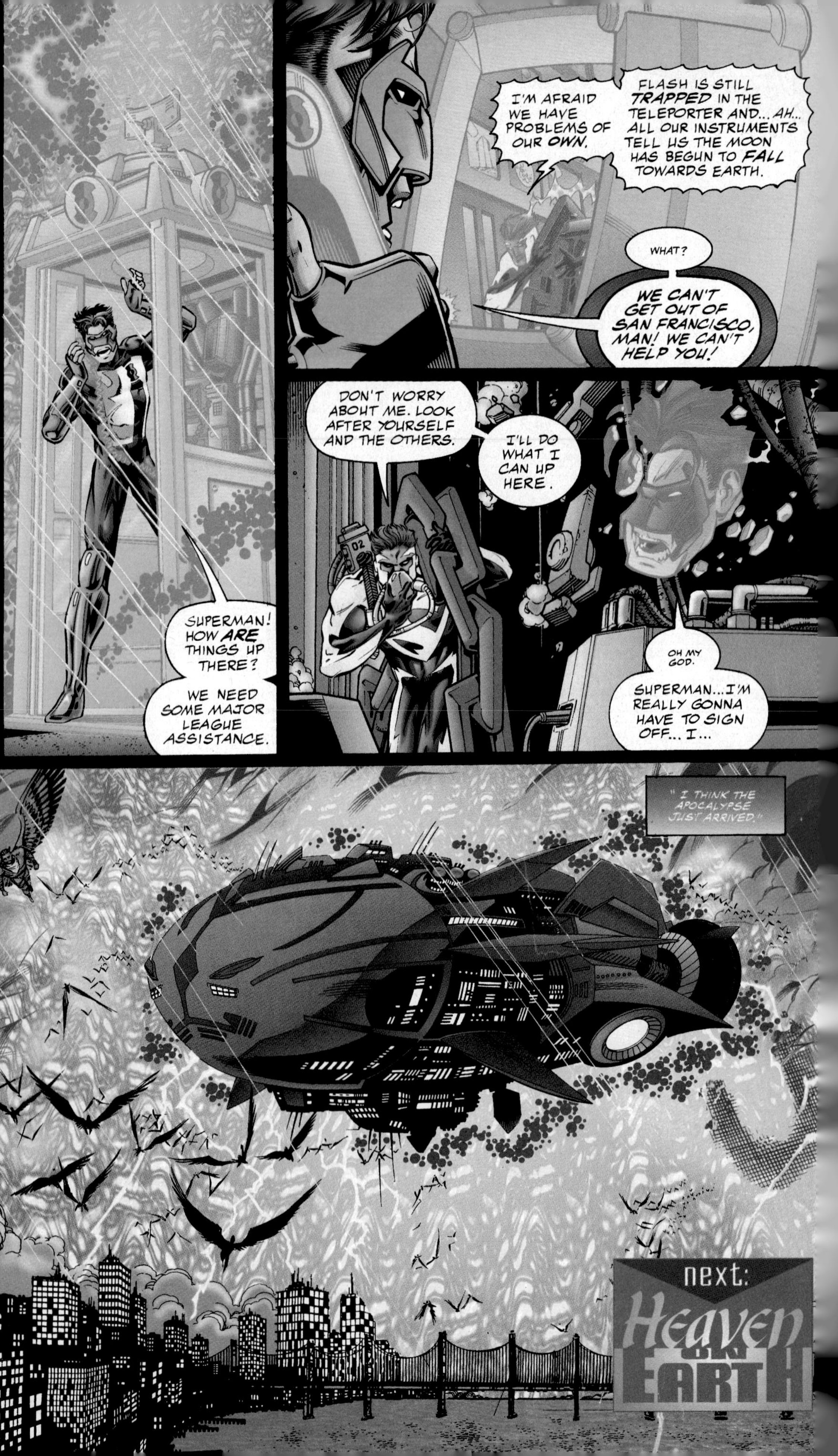
I'M AFRAID WE HAVE PROBLEMS OF OUR OWN.
FLASH IS STILL TRAPPED IN THE TELEPORTER AND... AH... ALL OUR INSTRUMENTS TELL US THE MOON HAS BEGUN TO FALL TOWARDS EARTH.
WHAT?
WE CAN'T GET OUT OF SAN FRANCISCO, MAN! WE CAN'T HELP YOU!
SUPERMAN! HOW ARE THINGS UP THERE?
WE NEED SOME MAJOR LEAGUE ASSISTANCE.
DON'T WORRY ABOUT ME. LOOK AFTER YOURSELF AND THE OTHERS.
I'LL DO WHAT I CAN UP HERE.
OH MY GOD.
SUPERMAN...I'M REALLY GONNA HAVE TO SIGN OFF... I...
"I THINK THE APOCALYPSE JUST ARRIVED."
next:
Heaven ON EARTH

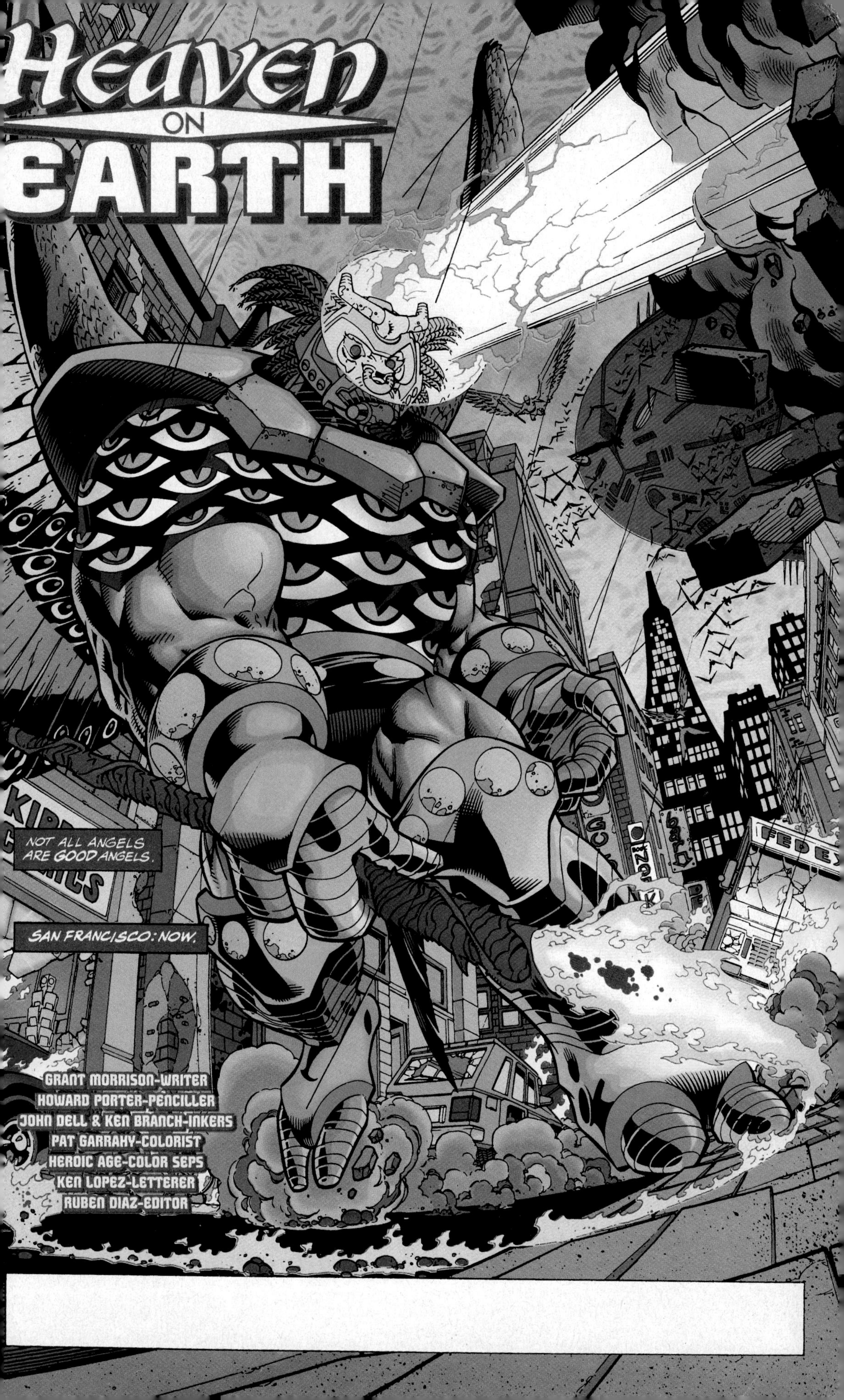
HEAVEN ON EARTH
NOT ALL ANGELS ARE GOOD ANGELS.
SAN FRANCISCO: NOW.
GRANT MORRISON-WRITER
HOWARD PORTER-PENCILLER
JOHN DELL & KEN BRANCH-INKERS
PAT GARRAHY-COLORIST
HEROIC AGE-COLOR SEPS
KEN LOPEZ-LETTERER
RUBEN DIAZ-EDITOR

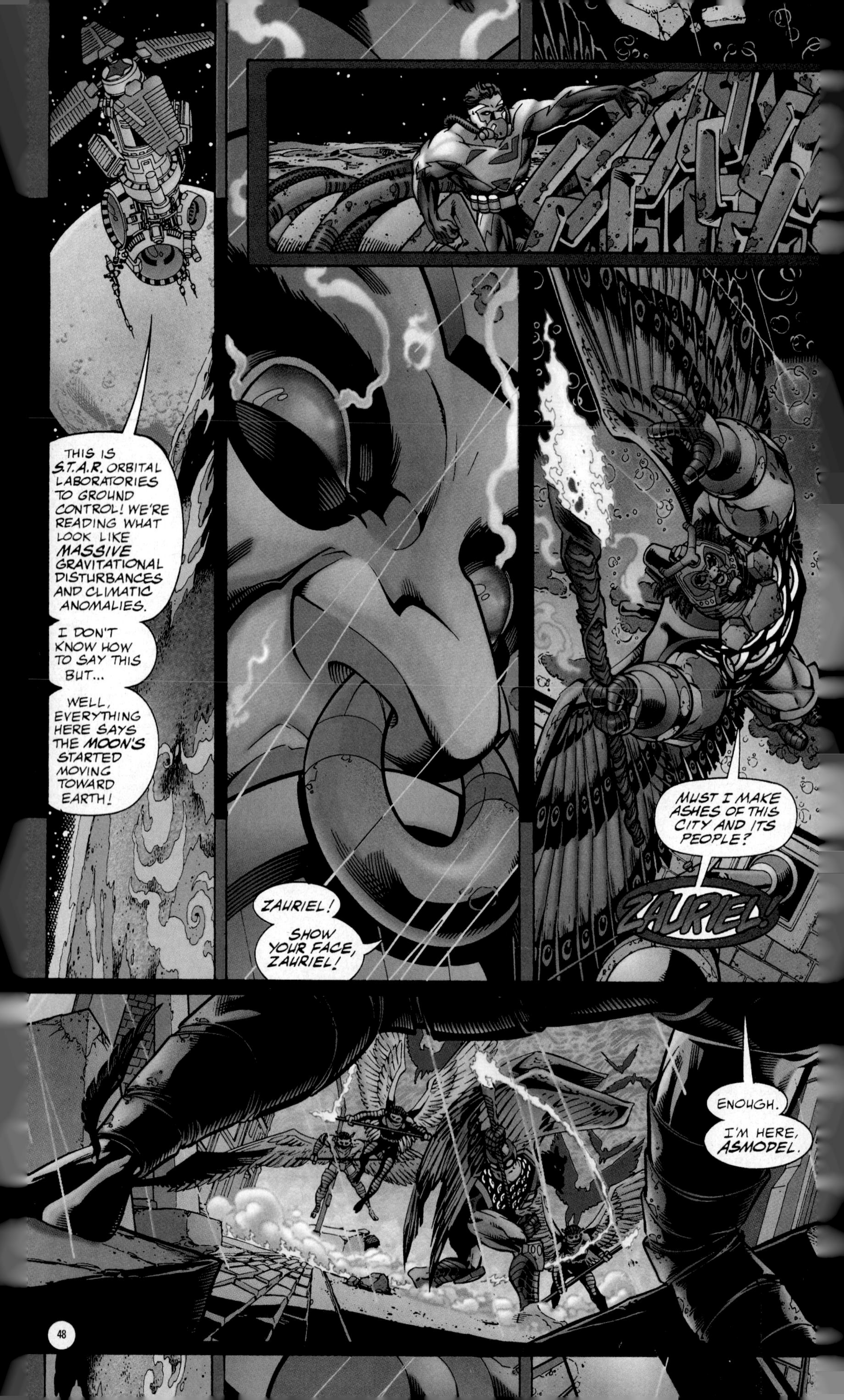

THIS IS S.T.A.R. ORBITAL LABORATORIES TO GROUND CONTROL! WE'RE READING WHAT LOOK LIKE MASSIVE GRAVITATIONAL DISTURBANCES AND CLIMATIC ANOMALIES.
I DON'T KNOW HOW TO SAY THIS BUT...
WELL, EVERYTHING HERE SAYS THE MOON'S STARTED MOVING TOWARD EARTH!
ZAURIEL!
SHOW YOUR FACE, ZAURIEL!
MUST I MAKE ASHES OF THIS CITY AND ITS PEOPLE?
ZAURIEL!
ENOUGH.
I'M HERE, ASMODEL.

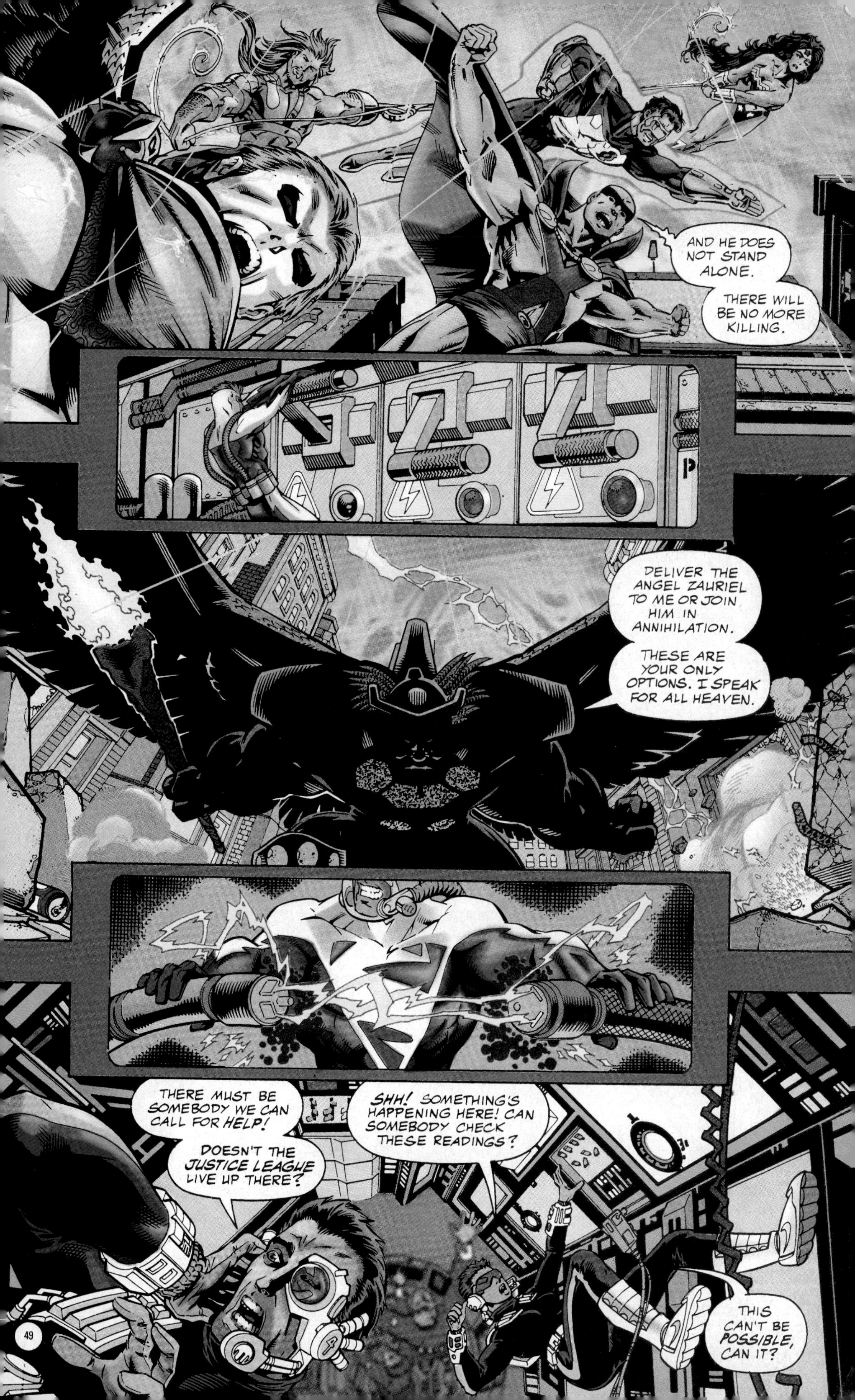
AND HE DOES NOT STAND ALONE.
THERE WILL BE NO MORE KILLING.
DELIVER THE ANGEL ZAURIEL TO ME OR JOIN HIM IN ANNIHILATION.
THESE ARE YOUR ONLY OPTIONS. I SPEAK FOR ALL HEAVEN.
THERE MUST BE SOMEBODY WE CAN CALL FOR *HELP!*
DOESN'T THE *JUSTICE LEAGUE* LIVE UP THERE?
SHH! SOMETHING'S HAPPENING HERE! CAN SOMEBODY CHECK THESE READINGS?
THIS CAN'T BE *POSSIBLE*, CAN IT?

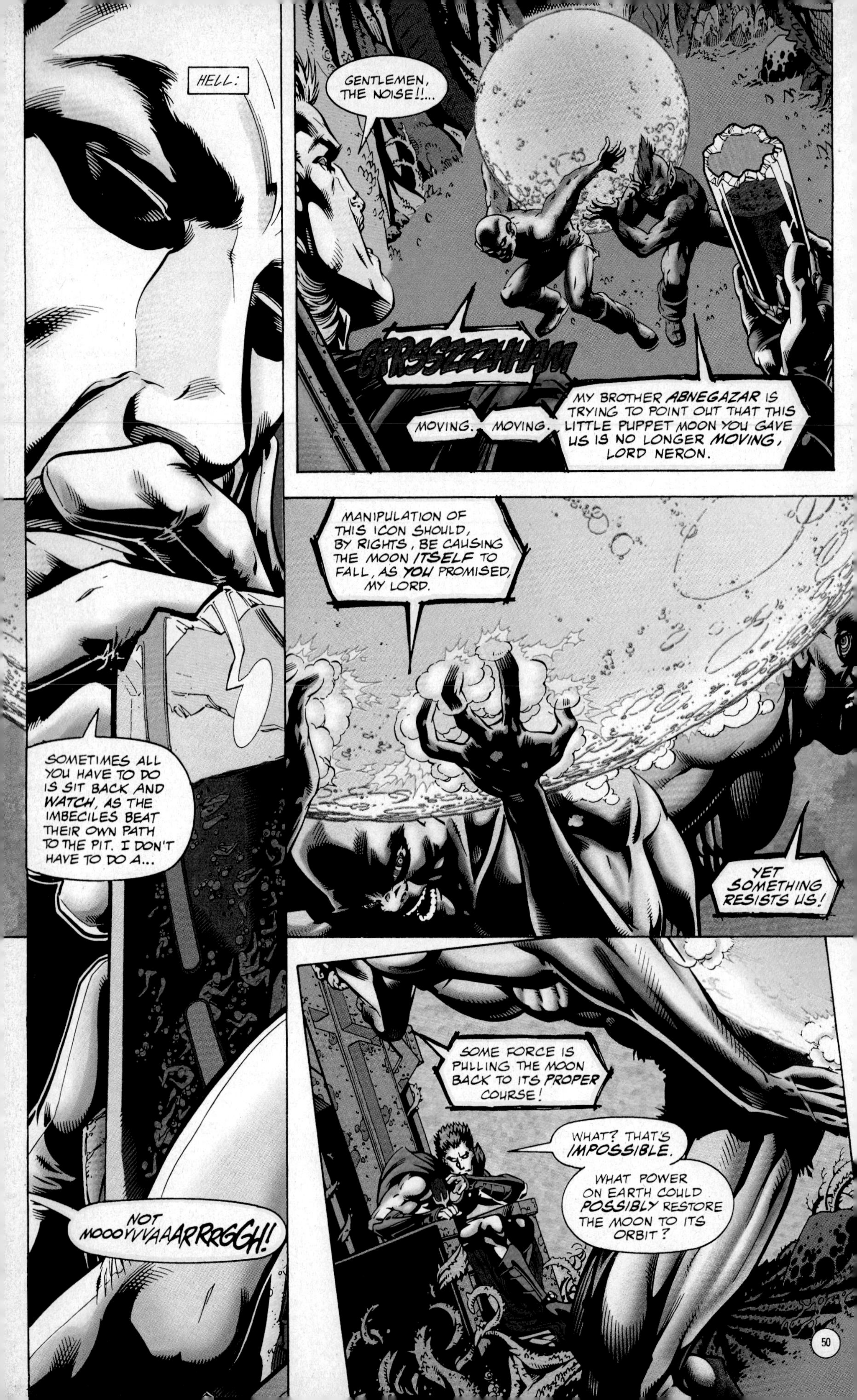
HELL:
GENTLEMEN, THE NOISE!!...
GRRSSZZZHHAM
MOVING.
MOVING.
MY BROTHER ABNEGAZAR IS TRYING TO POINT OUT THAT THIS LITTLE PUPPET MOON YOU GAVE US IS NO LONGER MOVING, LORD NERON.
MANIPULATION OF THIS ICON SHOULD, BY RIGHTS, BE CAUSING THE MOON ITSELF TO FALL, AS YOU PROMISED, MY LORD.
SOMETIMES ALL YOU HAVE TO DO IS SIT BACK AND WATCH, AS THE IMBECILES BEAT THEIR OWN PATH TO THE PIT. I DON'T HAVE TO DO A...
YET SOMETHING RESISTS US!
NOT MOOOVVVAAARRRGGH!
SOME FORCE IS PULLING THE MOON BACK TO ITS PROPER COURSE!
WHAT? THAT'S IMPOSSIBLE.
WHAT POWER ON EARTH COULD POSSIBLY RESTORE THE MOON TO ITS ORBIT?

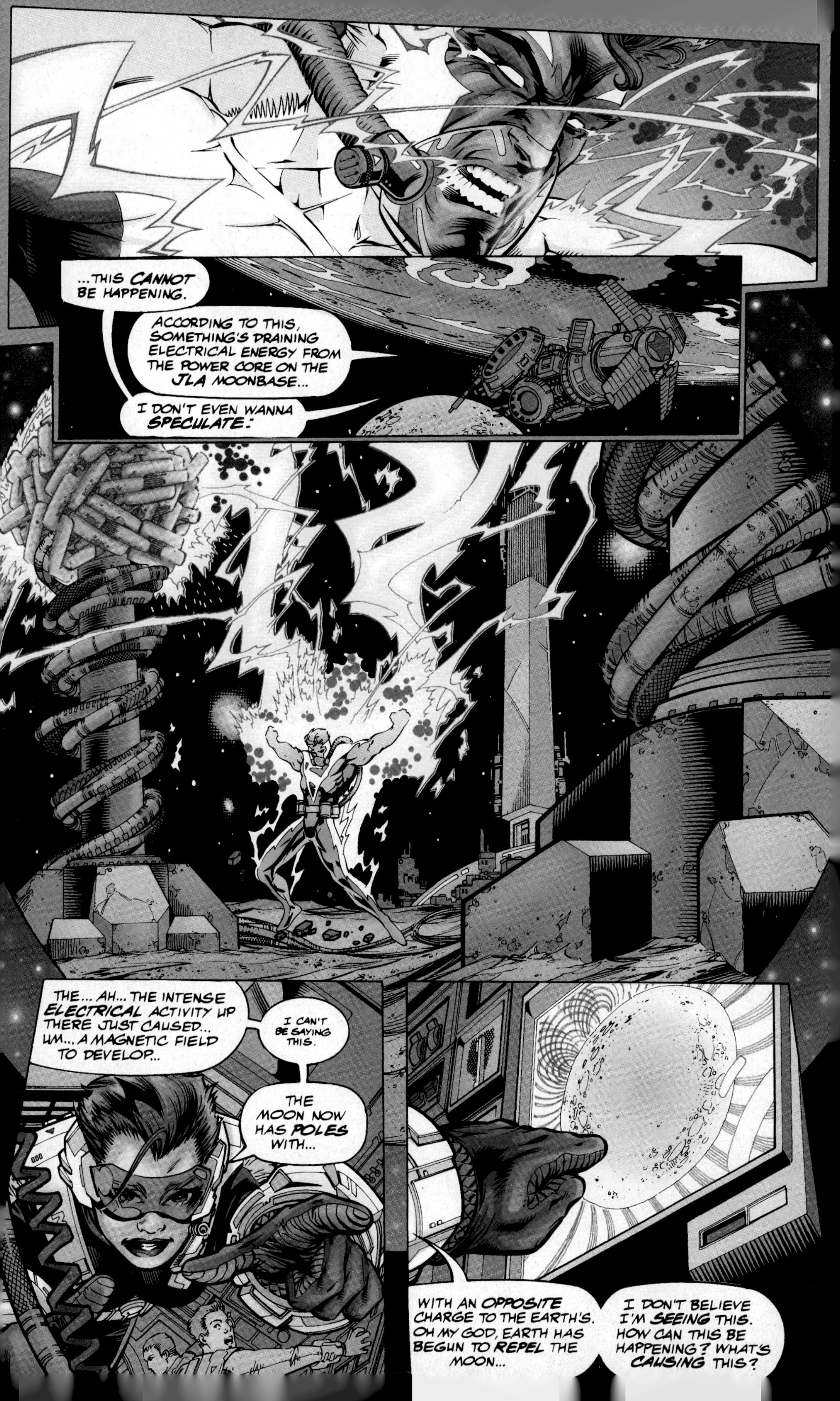
...THIS CANNOT BE HAPPENING.
ACCORDING TO THIS, SOMETHING'S DRAINING ELECTRICAL ENERGY FROM THE POWER CORE ON THE JLA MOONBASE...
I DON'T EVEN WANNA SPECULATE:
THE... AH... THE INTENSE ELECTRICAL ACTIVITY UP THERE JUST CAUSED... UM... A MAGNETIC FIELD TO DEVELOP...
I CAN'T BE SAYING THIS.
THE MOON NOW HAS POLES WITH...
WITH AN OPPOSITE CHARGE TO THE EARTH'S. OH MY GOD, EARTH HAS BEGUN TO REPEL THE MOON...
I DON'T BELIEVE I'M SEEING THIS. HOW CAN THIS BE HAPPENING? WHAT'S CAUSING THIS?

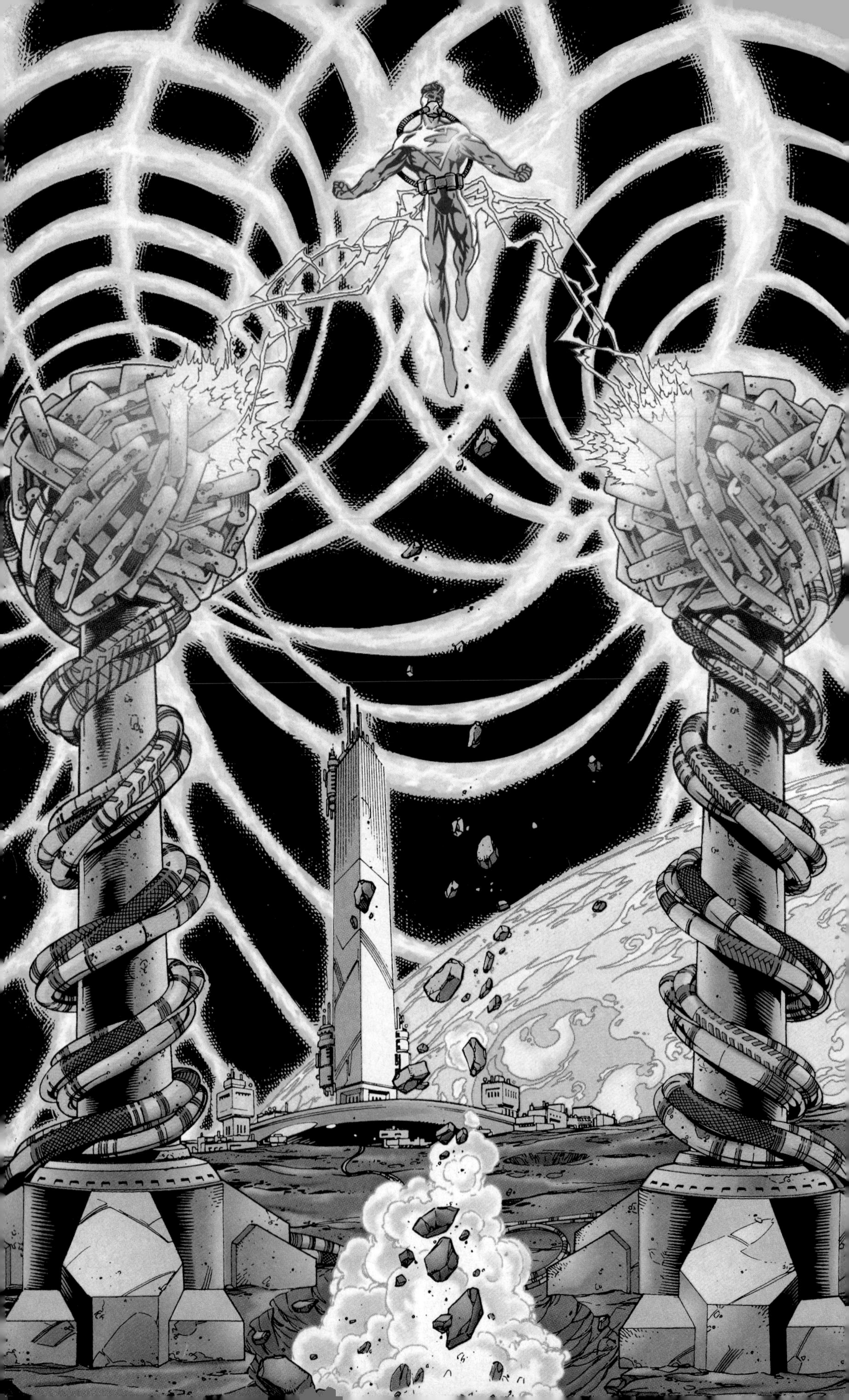

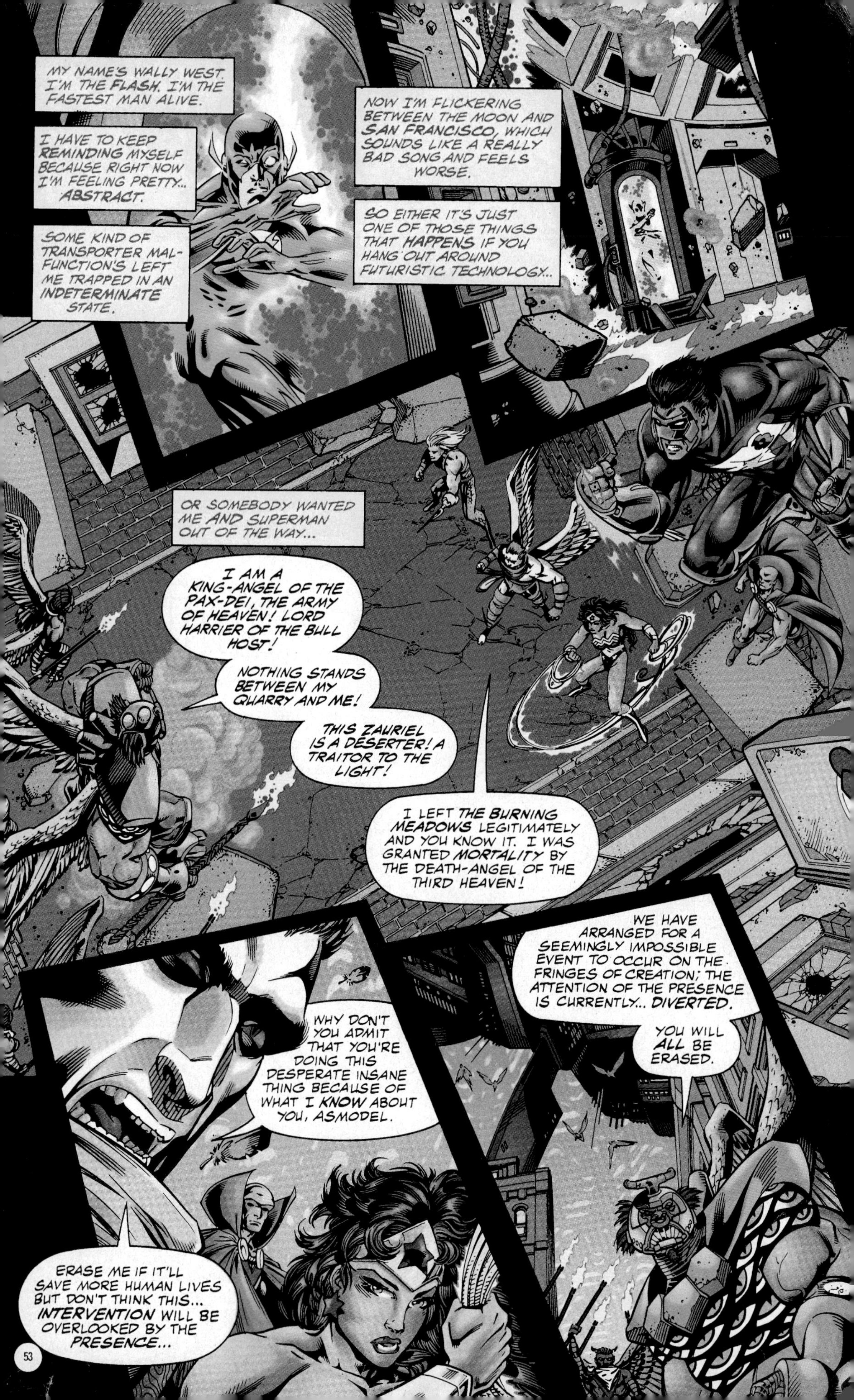
MY NAME'S WALLY WEST. I'M THE FLASH. I'M THE FASTEST MAN ALIVE.
I HAVE TO KEEP REMINDING MYSELF BECAUSE RIGHT NOW I'M FEELING PRETTY... ABSTRACT.
SOME KIND OF TRANSPORTER MAL-FUNCTION'S LEFT ME TRAPPED IN AN INDETERMINATE STATE.
NOW I'M FLICKERING BETWEEN THE MOON AND SAN FRANCISCO, WHICH SOUNDS LIKE A REALLY BAD SONG AND FEELS WORSE.
SO EITHER IT'S JUST ONE OF THOSE THINGS THAT HAPPENS IF YOU HANG OUT AROUND FUTURISTIC TECHNOLOGY...
OR SOMEBODY WANTED ME AND SUPERMAN OUT OF THE WAY...
I AM A KING-ANGEL OF THE PAX-DEI, THE ARMY OF HEAVEN! LORD HARRIER OF THE BULL HOST!
NOTHING STANDS BETWEEN MY QUARRY AND ME!
THIS ZAURIEL IS A DESERTER! A TRAITOR TO THE LIGHT!
I LEFT THE BURNING MEADOWS LEGITIMATELY AND YOU KNOW IT. I WAS GRANTED MORTALITY BY THE DEATH-ANGEL OF THE THIRD HEAVEN!
WHY DON'T YOU ADMIT THAT YOU'RE DOING THIS DESPERATE INSANE THING BECAUSE OF WHAT I KNOW ABOUT YOU, ASMODEL.
WE HAVE ARRANGED FOR A SEEMINGLY IMPOSSIBLE EVENT TO OCCUR ON THE FRINGES OF CREATION; THE ATTENTION OF THE PRESENCE IS CURRENTLY... DIVERTED.
YOU WILL ALL BE ERASED.
ERASE ME IF IT'LL SAVE MORE HUMAN LIVES BUT DON'T THINK THIS... INTERVENTION WILL BE OVERLOOKED BY THE PRESENCE...

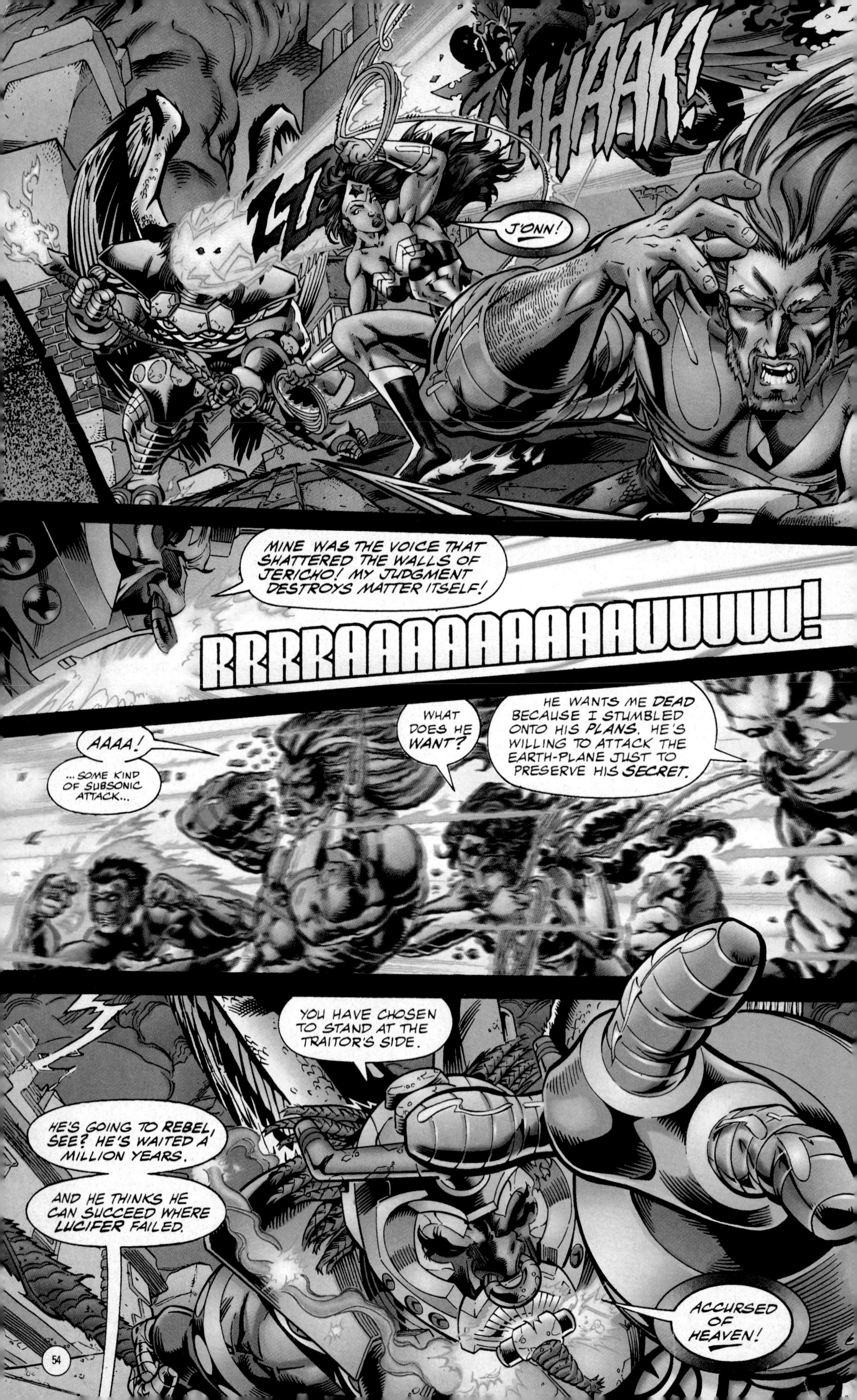
ZZZ
HHAAK!
J'ONN!
MINE WAS THE VOICE THAT SHATTERED THE WALLS OF JERICHO! MY JUDGMENT DESTROYS MATTER ITSELF!
RRRRAAAAAAAAAAAVUUUUU!
AAAA!
...SOME KIND OF SUBSONIC ATTACK...
WHAT DOES HE WANT?
HE WANTS ME DEAD BECAUSE I STUMBLED ONTO HIS PLANS. HE'S WILLING TO ATTACK THE EARTH-PLANE JUST TO PRESERVE HIS SECRET.
YOU HAVE CHOSEN TO STAND AT THE TRAITOR'S SIDE.
HE'S GOING TO REBEL, SEE? HE'S WAITED A MILLION YEARS.
AND HE THINKS HE CAN SUCCEED WHERE LUCIFER FAILED.
ACCURSED OF HEAVEN!

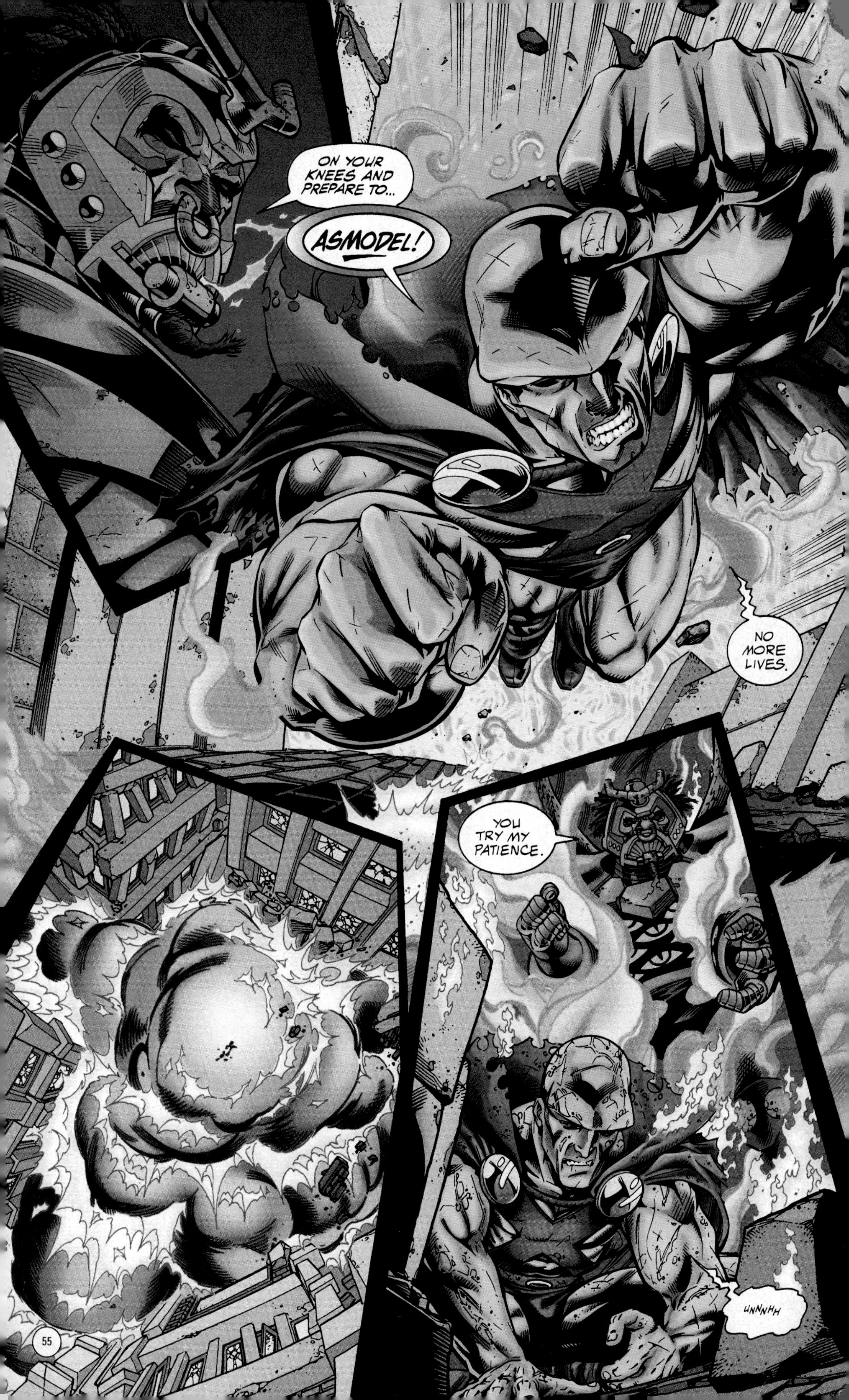
ON YOUR KNEES AND PREPARE TO...
ASMODEL!
NO MORE LIVES.
YOU TRY MY PATIENCE.
UNNNHH

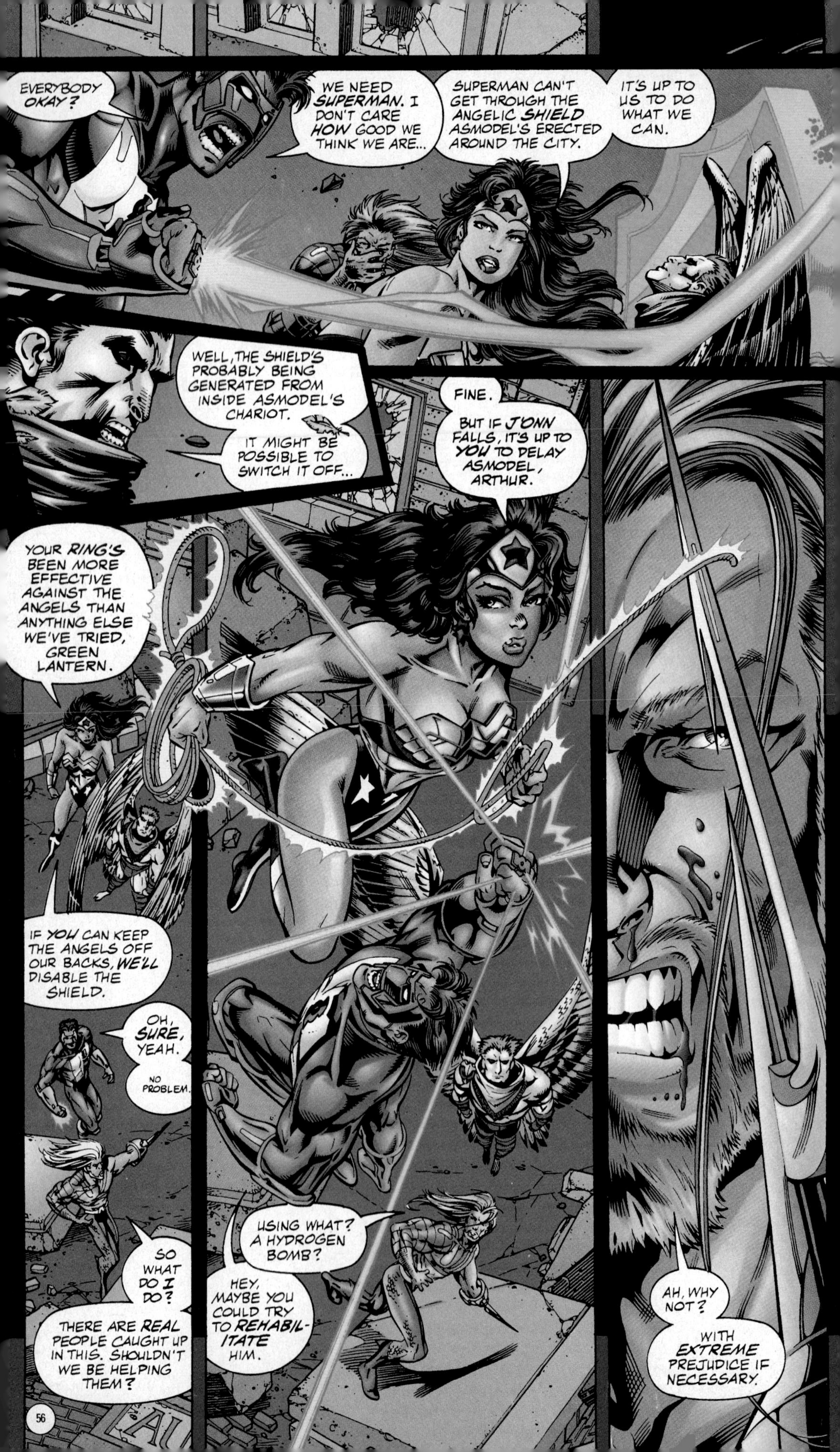
EVERYBODY OKAY?
WE NEED SUPERMAN. I DON'T CARE HOW GOOD WE THINK WE ARE...
SUPERMAN CAN'T GET THROUGH THE ANGELIC SHIELD ASMODEL'S ERECTED AROUND THE CITY.
IT'S UP TO US TO DO WHAT WE CAN.
WELL, THE SHIELD'S PROBABLY BEING GENERATED FROM INSIDE ASMODEL'S CHARIOT.
IT MIGHT BE POSSIBLE TO SWITCH IT OFF...
FINE.
BUT IF J'ONN FALLS, IT'S UP TO YOU TO DELAY ASMODEL, ARTHUR.
YOUR RING'S BEEN MORE EFFECTIVE AGAINST THE ANGELS THAN ANYTHING ELSE WE'VE TRIED, GREEN LANTERN.
IF YOU CAN KEEP THE ANGELS OFF OUR BACKS, WE'LL DISABLE THE SHIELD.
OH, SURE, YEAH.
NO PROBLEM.
SO WHAT DO I DO?
THERE ARE REAL PEOPLE CAUGHT UP IN THIS. SHOULDN'T WE BE HELPING THEM?
USING WHAT? A HYDROGEN BOMB?
HEY, MAYBE YOU COULD TRY TO REHABIL-ITATE HIM.
AH, WHY NOT?
WITH EXTREME PREJUDICE IF NECESSARY.

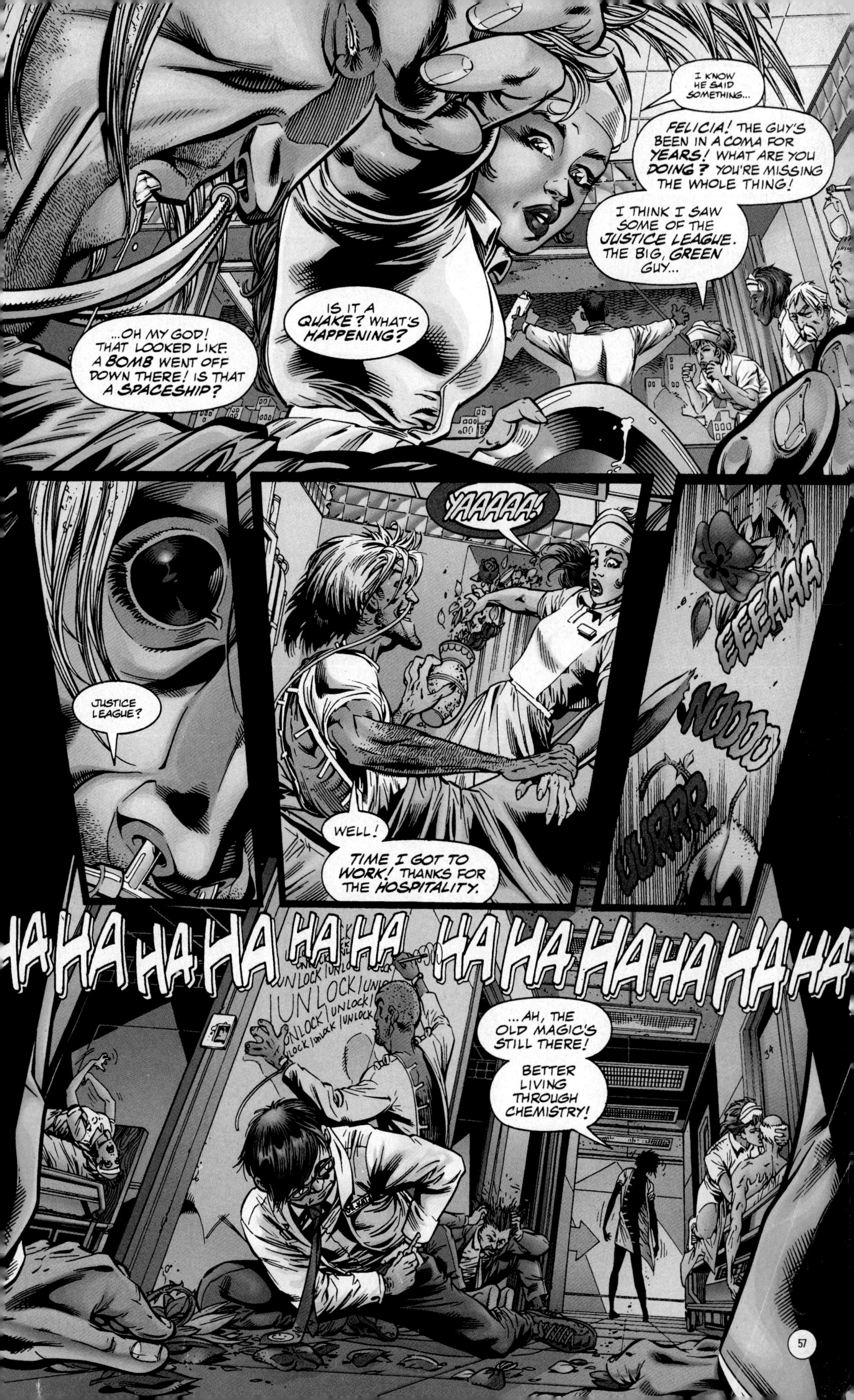
I KNOW HE SAID SOMETHING...
FELICIA! THE GUY'S BEEN IN A COMA FOR YEARS! WHAT ARE YOU DOING? YOU'RE MISSING THE WHOLE THING!
I THINK I SAW SOME OF THE JUSTICE LEAGUE. THE BIG, GREEN GUY...
IS IT A QUAKE? WHAT'S HAPPENING?
...OH MY GOD! THAT LOOKED LIKE A BOMB WENT OFF DOWN THERE! IS THAT A SPACESHIP?
JUSTICE LEAGUE?
YAAAAA!
WELL!
TIME I GOT TO WORK! THANKS FOR THE HOSPITALITY.
EEEAAA
NOOOO
UURRR
HA HA HA HA HA HA HA HA HA HA HA HA HA HA HA
UNLOCK UNLOCK UNLOCK UNLOCK UNLOCK UNLOCK
...AH, THE OLD MAGIC'S STILL THERE!
BETTER LIVING THROUGH CHEMISTRY!

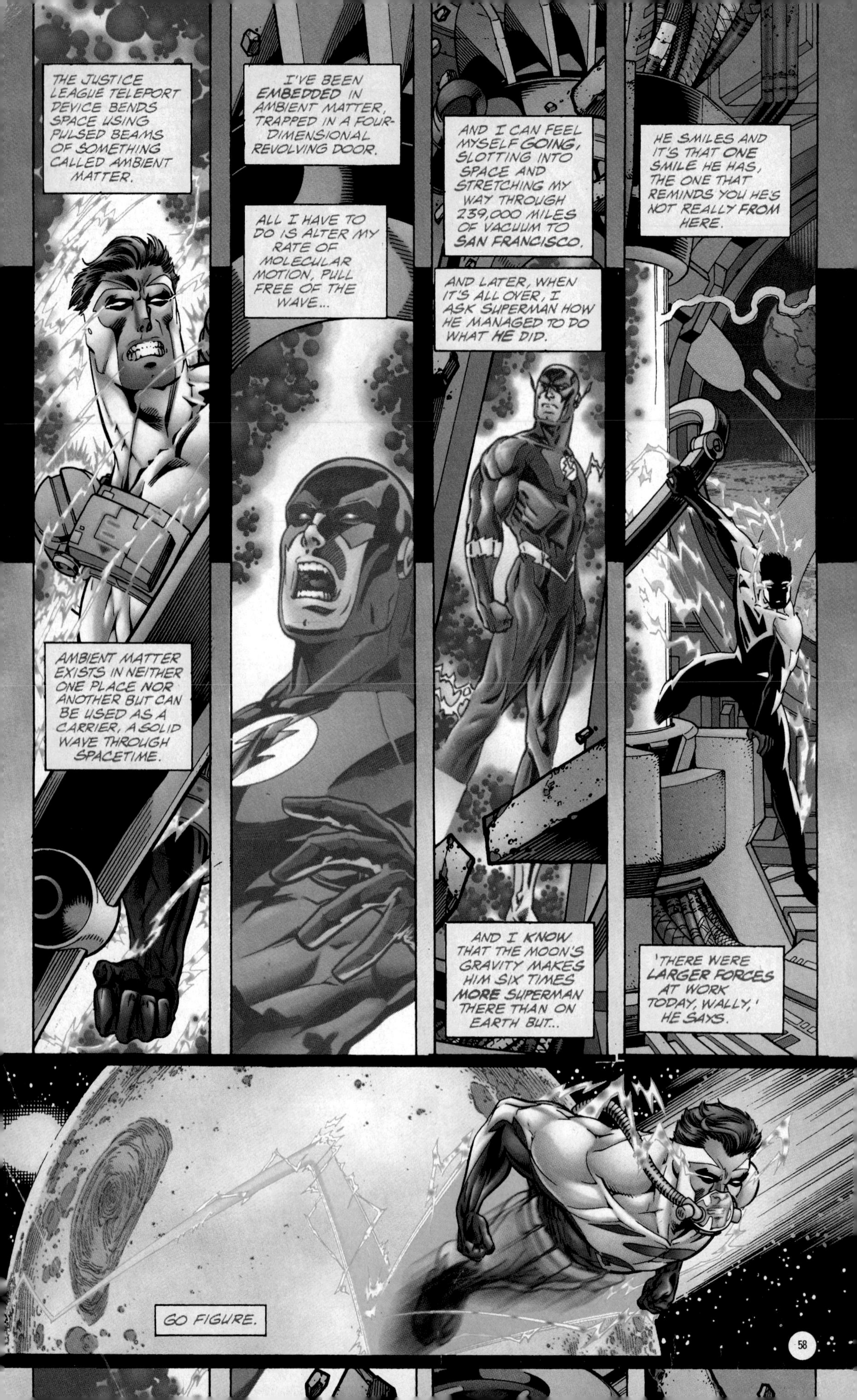
THE JUSTICE LEAGUE TELEPORT DEVICE BENDS SPACE USING PULSED BEAMS OF SOMETHING CALLED AMBIENT MATTER.
AMBIENT MATTER EXISTS IN NEITHER ONE PLACE NOR ANOTHER BUT CAN BE USED AS A CARRIER, A SOLID WAVE THROUGH SPACETIME.
I'VE BEEN EMBEDDED IN AMBIENT MATTER, TRAPPED IN A FOUR-DIMENSIONAL REVOLVING DOOR.
ALL I HAVE TO DO IS ALTER MY RATE OF MOLECULAR MOTION, PULL FREE OF THE WAVE...
AND I CAN FEEL MYSELF GOING, SLOTTING INTO SPACE AND STRETCHING MY WAY THROUGH 239,000 MILES OF VACUUM TO SAN FRANCISCO.
AND LATER, WHEN IT'S ALL OVER, I ASK SUPERMAN HOW HE MANAGED TO DO WHAT HE DID.
AND I KNOW THAT THE MOON'S GRAVITY MAKES HIM SIX TIMES MORE SUPERMAN THERE THAN ON EARTH BUT...
HE SMILES AND IT'S THAT ONE SMILE HE HAS, THE ONE THAT REMINDS YOU HE'S NOT REALLY FROM HERE.
'THERE WERE LARGER FORCES AT WORK TODAY, WALLY,' HE SAYS.
GO FIGURE.

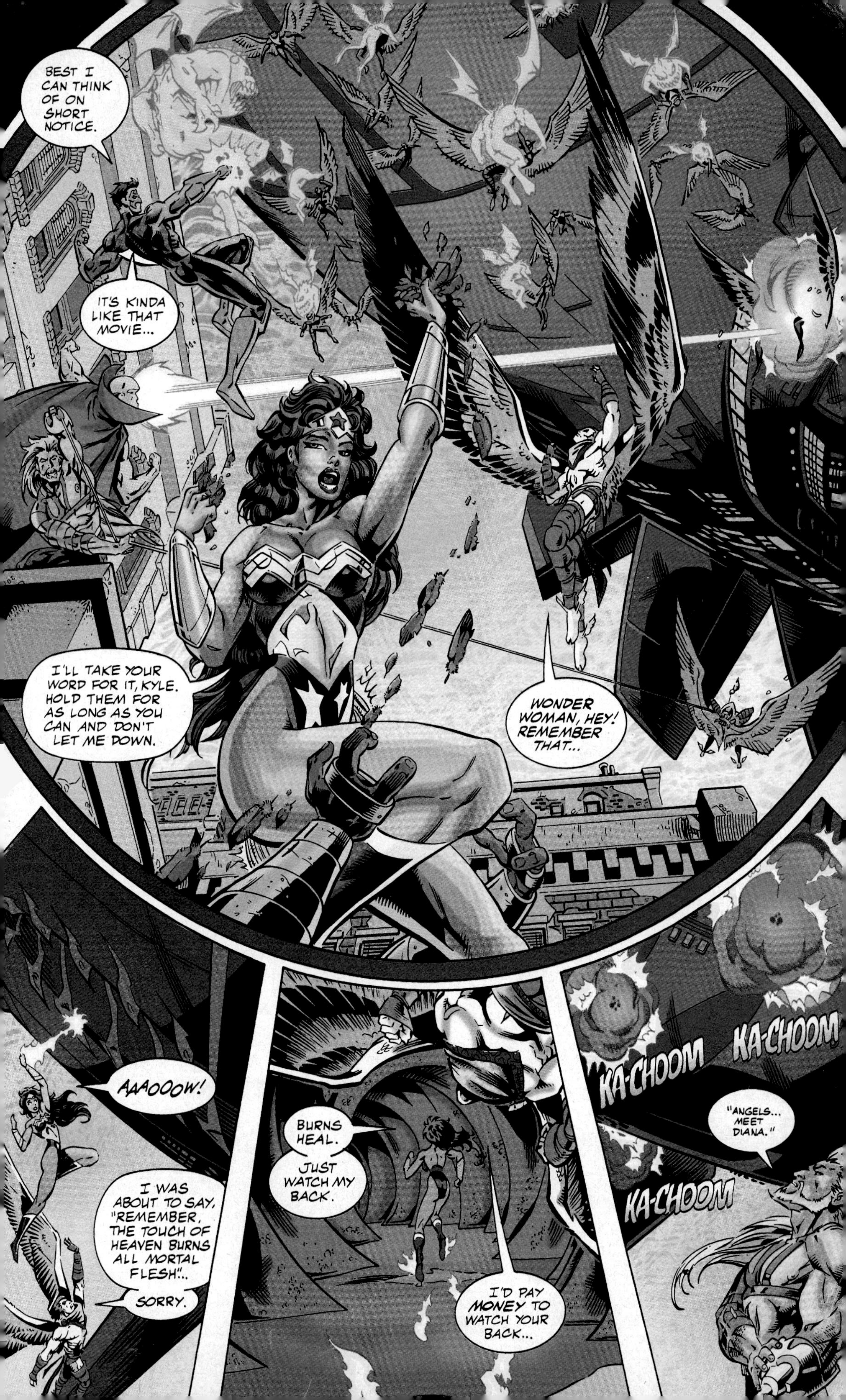
BEST I CAN THINK OF ON SHORT NOTICE.
IT'S KINDA LIKE THAT MOVIE...
I'LL TAKE YOUR WORD FOR IT, KYLE. HOLD THEM FOR AS LONG AS YOU CAN AND DON'T LET ME DOWN.
WONDER WOMAN, HEY! REMEMBER THAT...
AAAOOOW!
I WAS ABOUT TO SAY, "REMEMBER, THE TOUCH OF HEAVEN BURNS ALL MORTAL FLESH"...
SORRY.
BURNS HEAL.
JUST WATCH MY BACK.
I'D PAY MONEY TO WATCH YOUR BACK...
KA-CHOOM
KA-CHOOM
KA-CHOOM
"ANGELS... MEET DIANA."

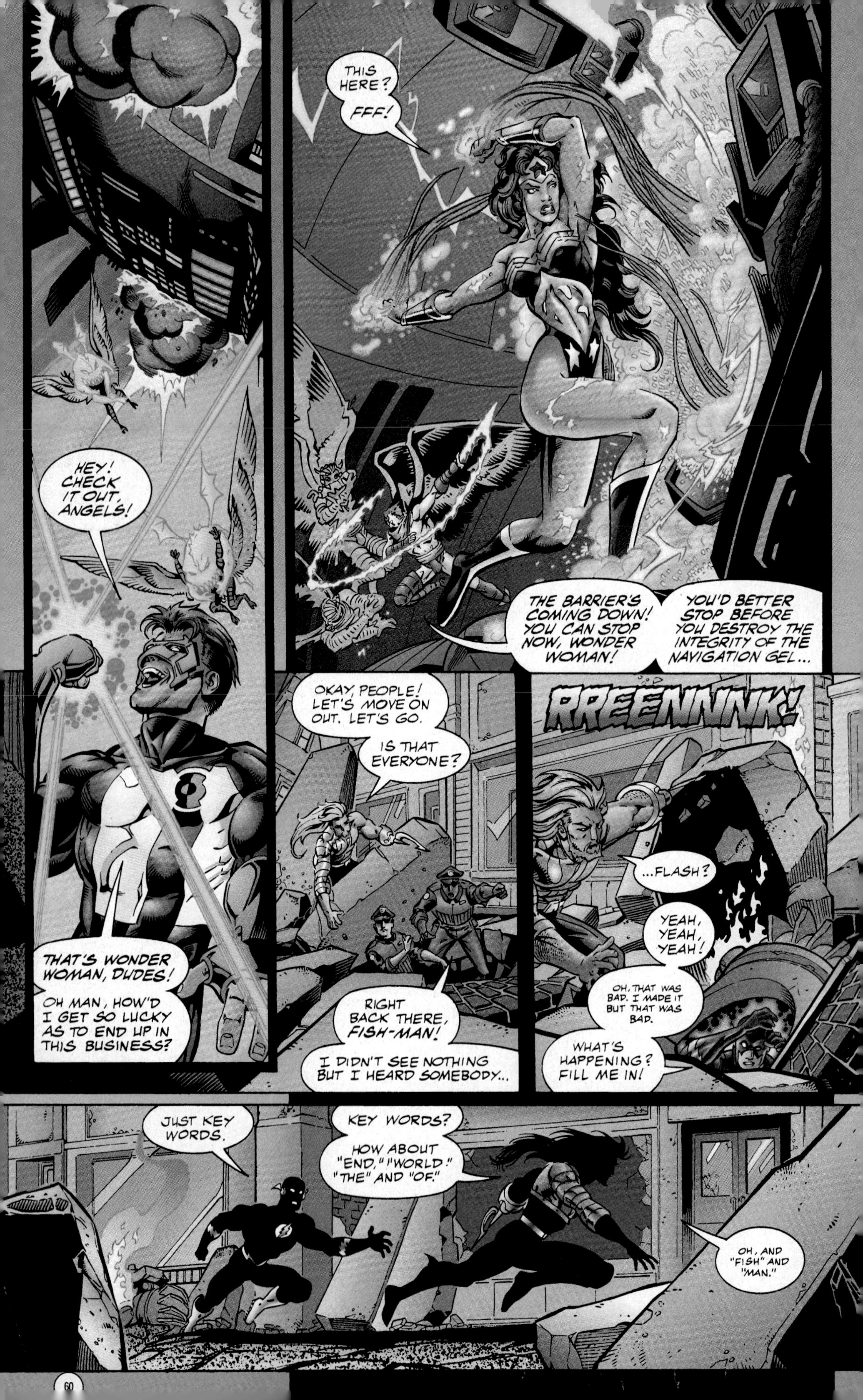
THIS HERE? FFF!
HEY! CHECK IT OUT, ANGELS!
THE BARRIER'S COMING DOWN! YOU CAN STOP NOW, WONDER WOMAN!
YOU'D BETTER STOP BEFORE YOU DESTROY THE INTEGRITY OF THE NAVIGATION GEL...
THAT'S WONDER WOMAN, DUDES!
OH MAN, HOW'D I GET SO LUCKY AS TO END UP IN THIS BUSINESS?
OKAY, PEOPLE! LET'S MOVE ON OUT. LET'S GO.
IS THAT EVERYONE?
RIGHT BACK THERE, FISH-MAN!
I DIDN'T SEE NOTHING BUT I HEARD SOMEBODY...
RREENNNNK!
...FLASH?
YEAH, YEAH, YEAH!
OH, THAT WAS BAD. I MADE IT BUT THAT WAS BAD.
WHAT'S HAPPENING? FILL ME IN!
JUST KEY WORDS.
KEY WORDS?
HOW ABOUT "END," "WORLD," "THE" AND "OF."
OH, AND "FISH" AND "MAN."

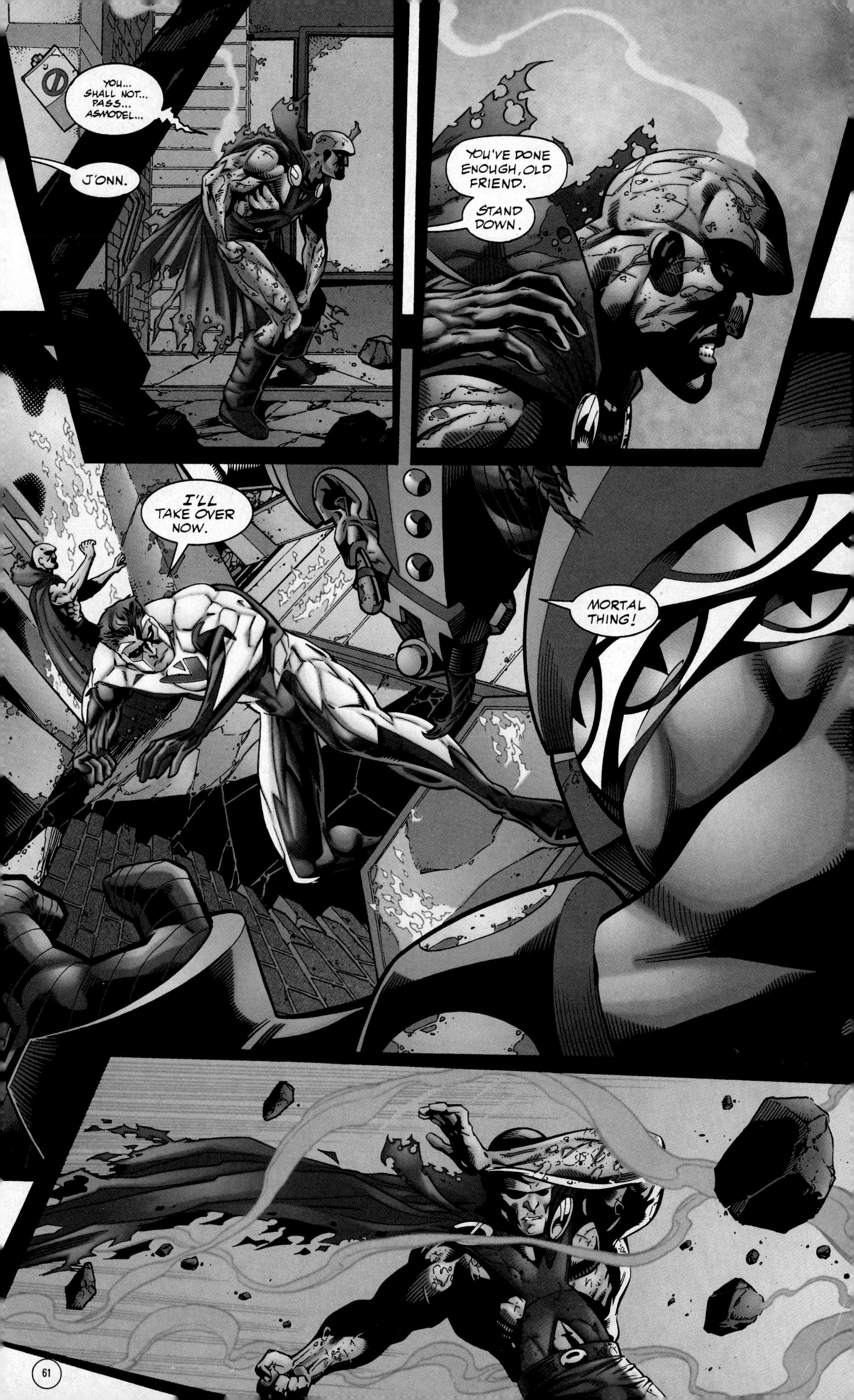
YOU... SHALL NOT... PASS... ASMODEL...
J'ONN.
YOU'VE DONE ENOUGH, OLD FRIEND.
STAND DOWN.
I'LL TAKE OVER NOW.
MORTAL THING!

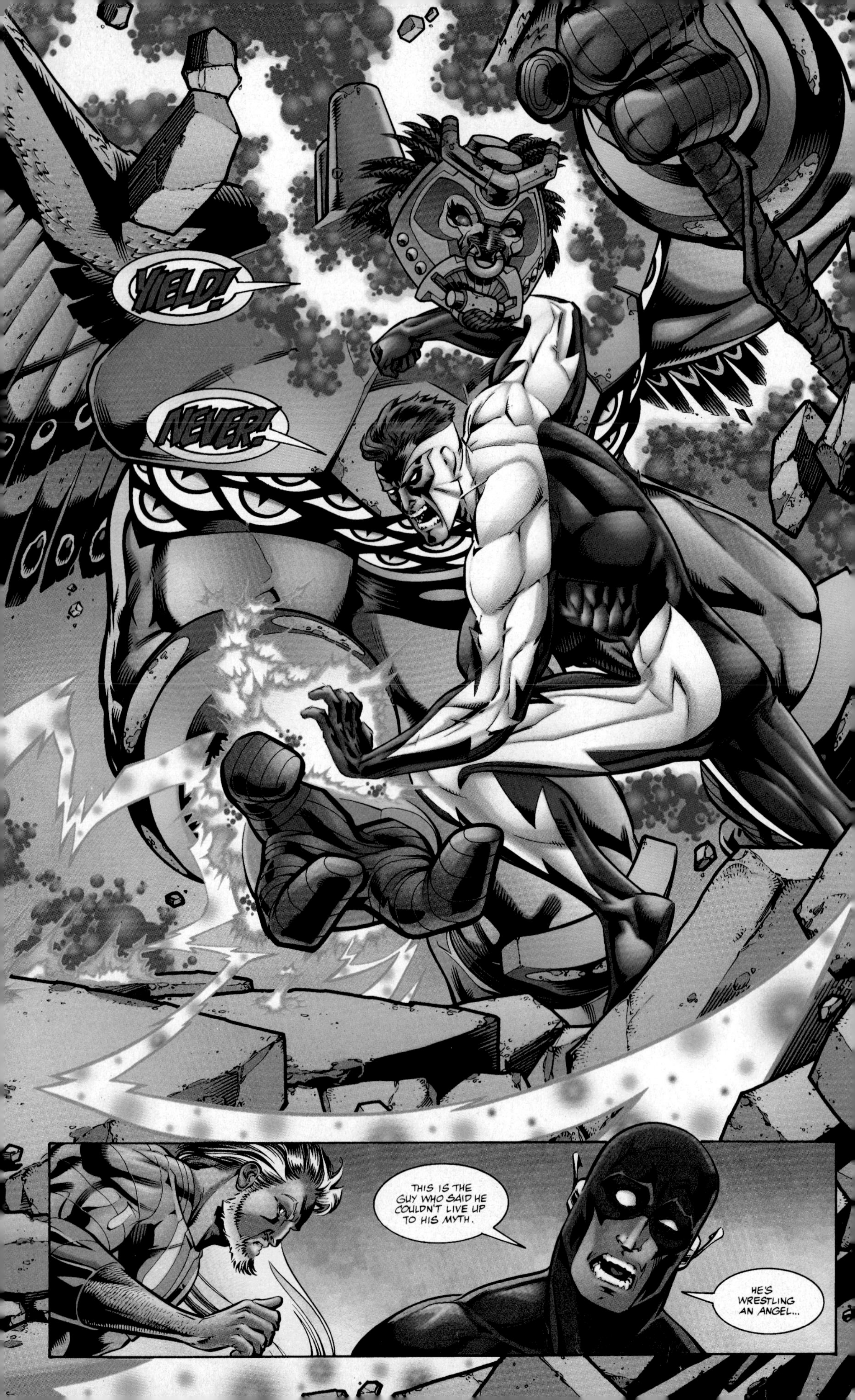
YIELD!
NEVER!
THIS IS THE GUY WHO SAID HE COULDN'T LIVE UP TO HIS MYTH.
HE'S WRESTLING AN ANGEL...

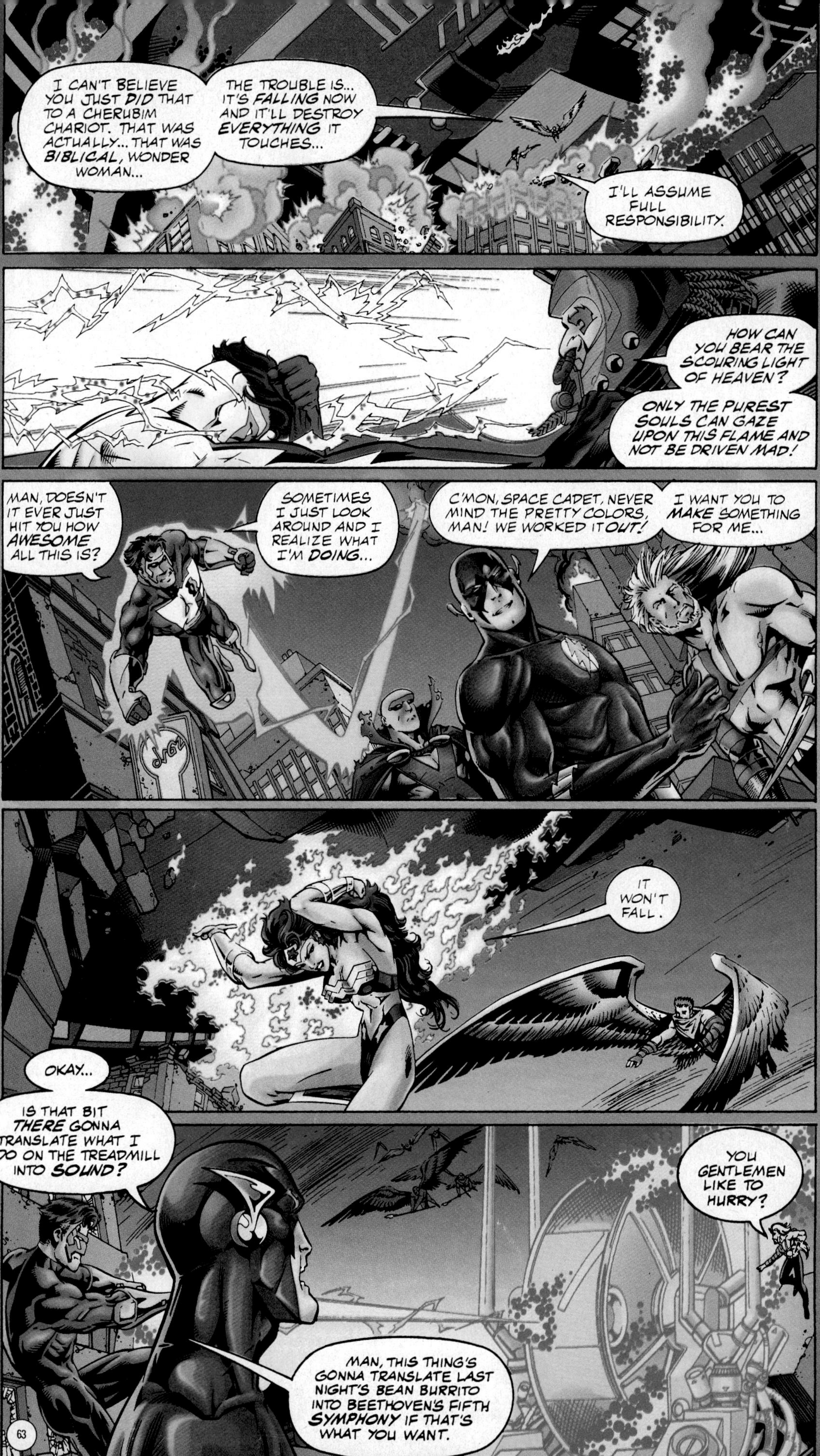

I CAN'T BELIEVE YOU JUST DID THAT TO A CHERUBIM CHARIOT. THAT WAS ACTUALLY... THAT WAS BIBLICAL, WONDER WOMAN...
THE TROUBLE IS... IT'S FALLING NOW AND IT'LL DESTROY EVERYTHING IT TOUCHES...
I'LL ASSUME FULL RESPONSIBILITY.
HOW CAN YOU BEAR THE SCOURING LIGHT OF HEAVEN?
ONLY THE PUREST SOULS CAN GAZE UPON THIS FLAME AND NOT BE DRIVEN MAD!
MAN, DOESN'T IT EVER JUST HIT YOU HOW AWESOME ALL THIS IS?
SOMETIMES I JUST LOOK AROUND AND I REALIZE WHAT I'M DOING...
C'MON, SPACE CADET, NEVER MIND THE PRETTY COLORS, MAN! WE WORKED IT OUT!
I WANT YOU TO MAKE SOMETHING FOR ME...
IT WON'T FALL.
OKAY...
IS THAT BIT THERE GONNA TRANSLATE WHAT I DO ON THE TREADMILL INTO SOUND?
YOU GENTLEMEN LIKE TO HURRY?
MAN, THIS THING'S GONNA TRANSLATE LAST NIGHT'S BEAN BURRITO INTO BEETHOVEN'S FIFTH SYMPHONY IF THAT'S WHAT YOU WANT.

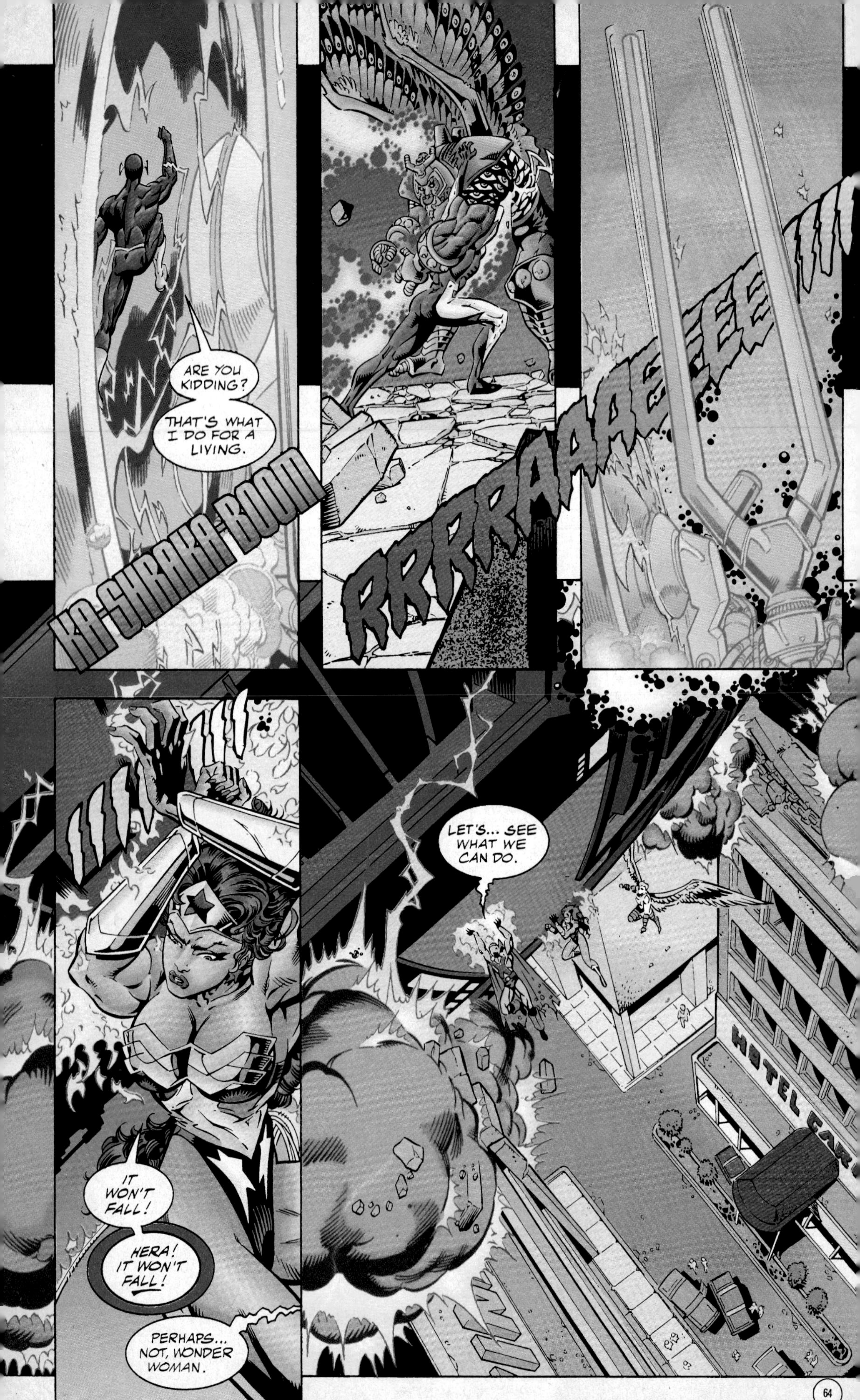
ARE YOU KIDDING?
THAT'S WHAT I DO FOR A LIVING.
KA-SHRAKA-BOOM
RRRRAAAAEEEEE
LET'S... SEE WHAT WE CAN DO.
IT WON'T FALL!
HERA! IT WON'T FALL!
PERHAPS... NOT, WONDER WOMAN.

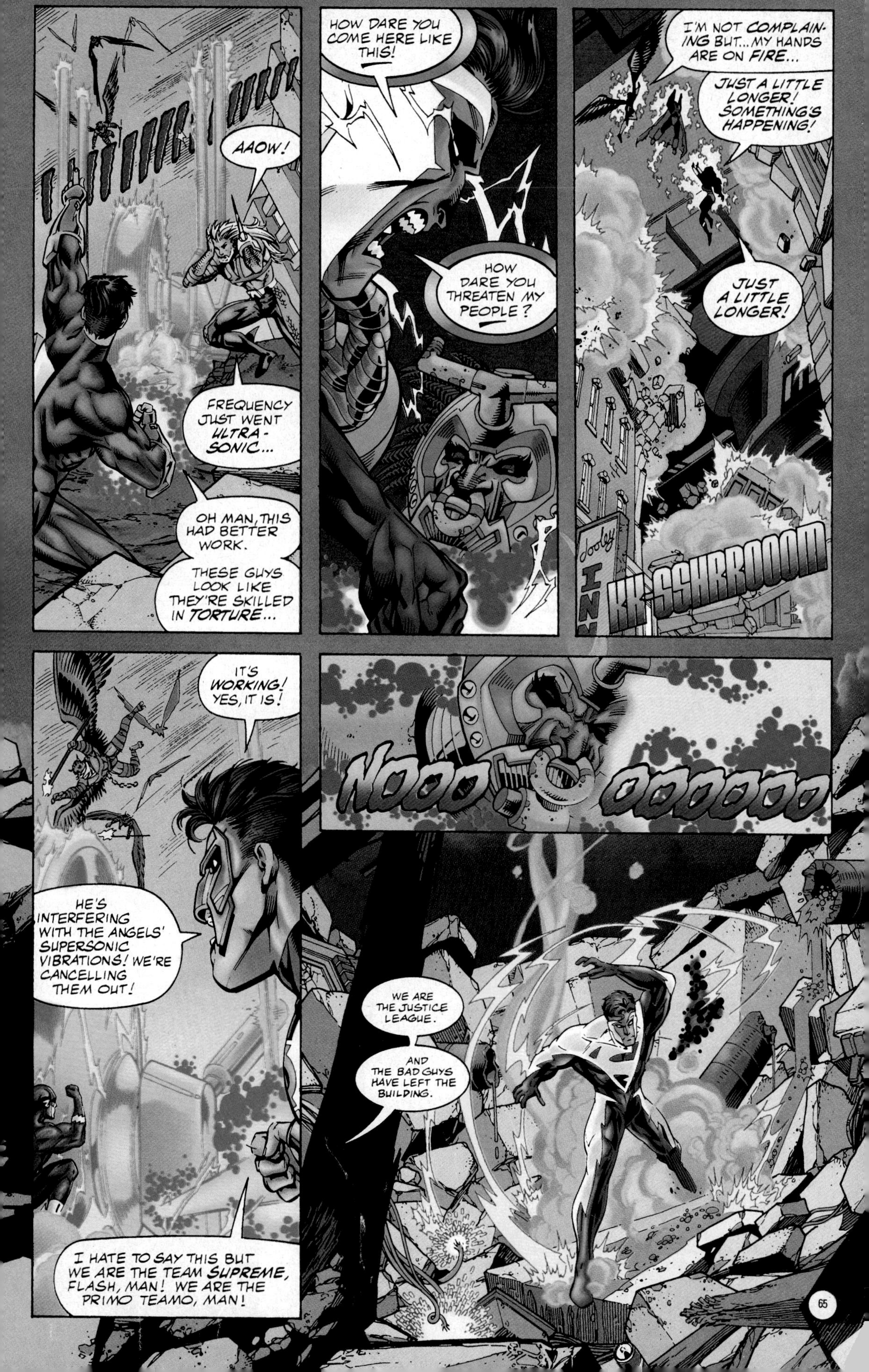
AAOW!
FREQUENCY JUST WENT ULTRA-SONIC...
OH MAN, THIS HAD BETTER WORK.
THESE GUYS LOOK LIKE THEY'RE SKILLED IN TORTURE...
HOW DARE YOU COME HERE LIKE THIS!
HOW DARE YOU THREATEN MY PEOPLE?
I'M NOT COMPLAINING BUT... MY HANDS ARE ON FIRE...
JUST A LITTLE LONGER! SOMETHING'S HAPPENING!
JUST A LITTLE LONGER!
dooley INN
KK-SSHBROOOM
IT'S WORKING! YES, IT IS!
HE'S INTERFERING WITH THE ANGELS' SUPERSONIC VIBRATIONS! WE'RE CANCELLING THEM OUT!
I HATE TO SAY THIS BUT WE ARE THE TEAM SUPREME, FLASH, MAN! WE ARE THE PRIMO TEAMO, MAN!
NOOO-OOOOOO
WE ARE THE JUSTICE LEAGUE.
AND THE BAD GUYS HAVE LEFT THE BUILDING.

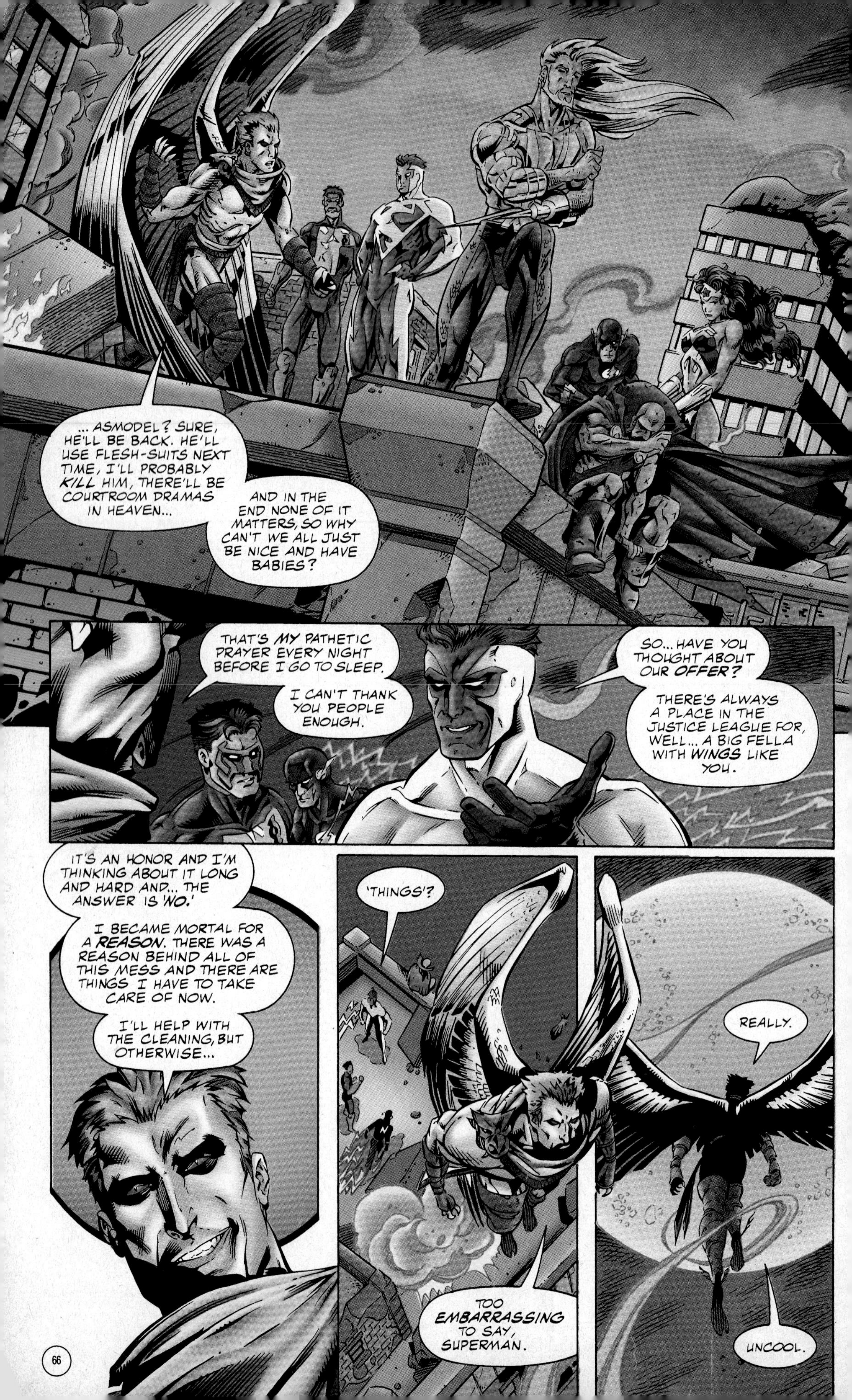
... ASMODEL? SURE, HE'LL BE BACK. HE'LL USE FLESH-SUITS NEXT TIME, I'LL PROBABLY KILL HIM, THERE'LL BE COURTROOM DRAMAS IN HEAVEN...
AND IN THE END NONE OF IT MATTERS, SO WHY CAN'T WE ALL JUST BE NICE AND HAVE BABIES?
THAT'S MY PATHETIC PRAYER EVERY NIGHT BEFORE I GO TO SLEEP.
I CAN'T THANK YOU PEOPLE ENOUGH.
SO... HAVE YOU THOUGHT ABOUT OUR OFFER?
THERE'S ALWAYS A PLACE IN THE JUSTICE LEAGUE FOR, WELL... A BIG FELLA WITH WINGS LIKE YOU.
IT'S AN HONOR AND I'M THINKING ABOUT IT LONG AND HARD AND... THE ANSWER IS 'NO.'
I BECAME MORTAL FOR A REASON. THERE WAS A REASON BEHIND ALL OF THIS MESS AND THERE ARE THINGS I HAVE TO TAKE CARE OF NOW.
I'LL HELP WITH THE CLEANING, BUT OTHERWISE...
'THINGS'?
TOO EMBARRASSING TO SAY, SUPERMAN.
REALLY.
UNCOOL.

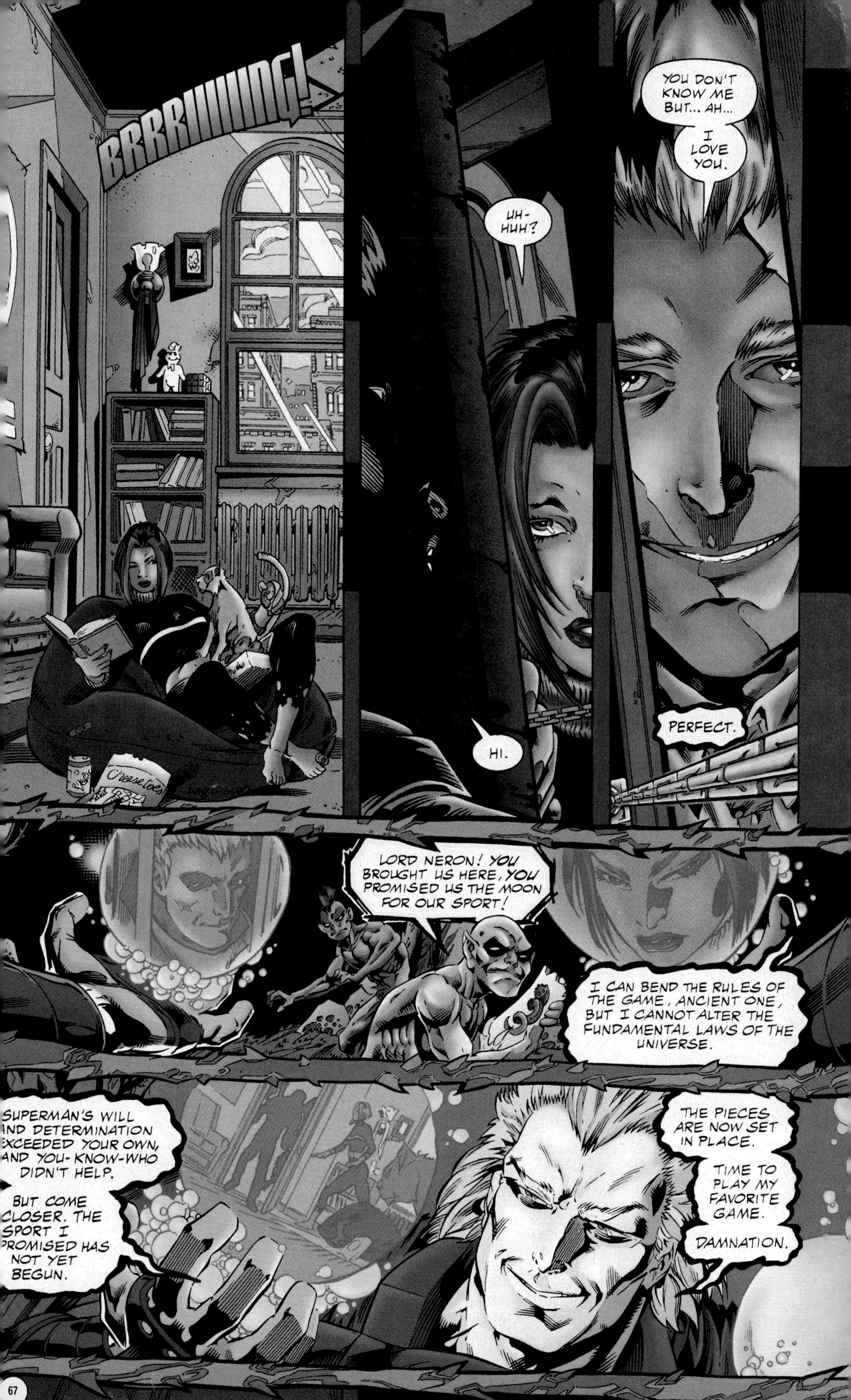
BRRRIIIIIING!
UH-HUH?
YOU DON'T KNOW ME BUT... AH...
I LOVE YOU.
HI.
PERFECT.
LORD NERON! YOU BROUGHT US HERE, YOU PROMISED US THE MOON FOR OUR SPORT!
I CAN BEND THE RULES OF THE GAME, ANCIENT ONE, BUT I CANNOT ALTER THE FUNDAMENTAL LAWS OF THE UNIVERSE.
SUPERMAN'S WILL AND DETERMINATION EXCEEDED YOUR OWN, AND YOU-KNOW-WHO DIDN'T HELP.
BUT COME CLOSER. THE SPORT I PROMISED HAS NOT YET BEGUN.
THE PIECES ARE NOW SET IN PLACE.
TIME TO PLAY MY FAVORITE GAME.
DAMNATION.

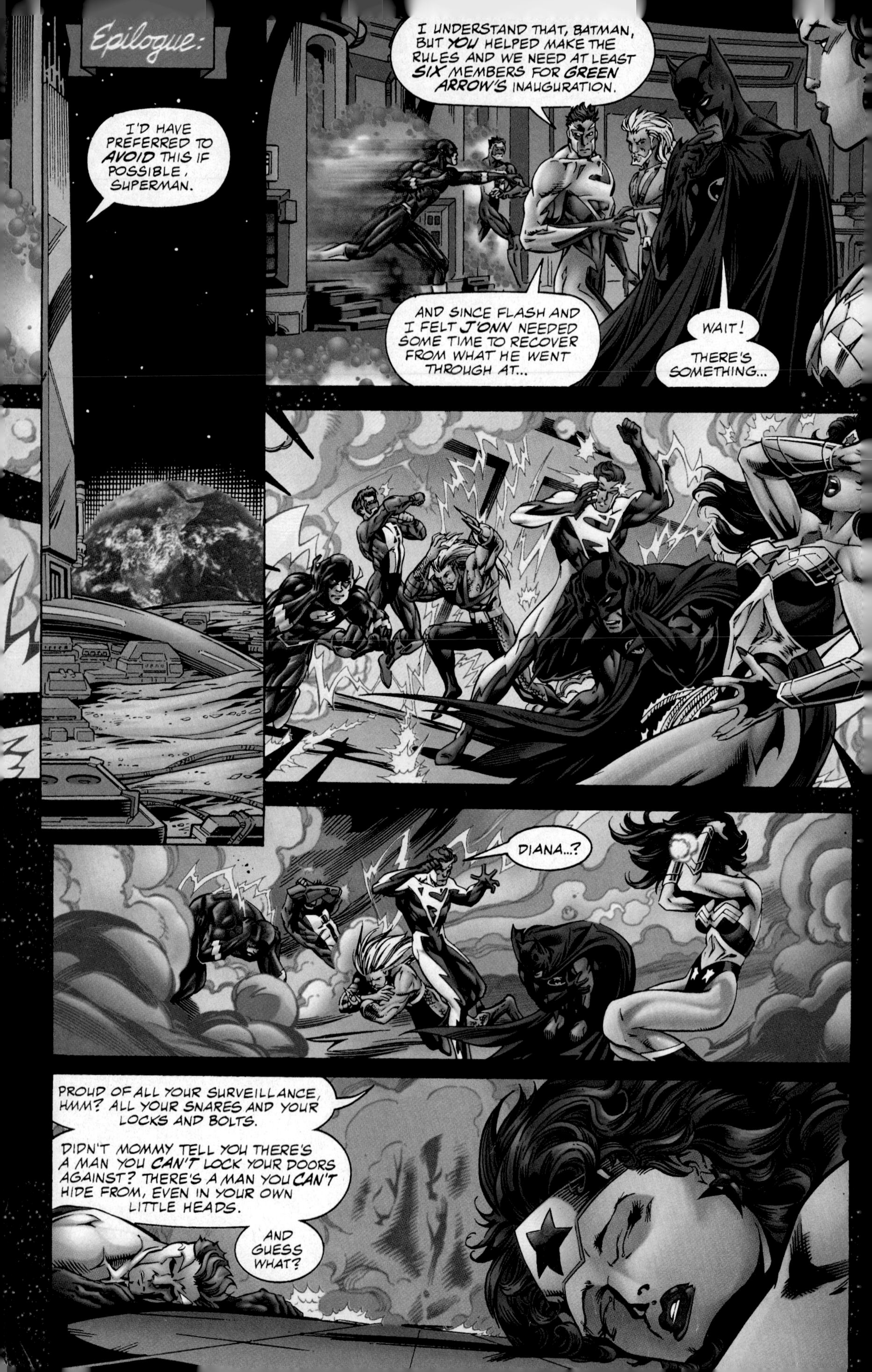
Epilogue:
I'D HAVE PREFERRED TO AVOID THIS IF POSSIBLE, SUPERMAN.
I UNDERSTAND THAT, BATMAN, BUT YOU HELPED MAKE THE RULES AND WE NEED AT LEAST SIX MEMBERS FOR GREEN ARROW'S INAUGURATION.
AND SINCE FLASH AND I FELT J'ONN NEEDED SOME TIME TO RECOVER FROM WHAT HE WENT THROUGH AT...
WAIT!
THERE'S SOMETHING...
DIANA...?
PROUD OF ALL YOUR SURVEILLANCE, HMM? ALL YOUR SNARES AND YOUR LOCKS AND BOLTS.
DIDN'T MOMMY TELL YOU THERE'S A MAN YOU CAN'T LOCK YOUR DOORS AGAINST? THERE'S A MAN YOU CAN'T HIDE FROM, EVEN IN YOUR OWN LITTLE HEADS.
AND GUESS WHAT?

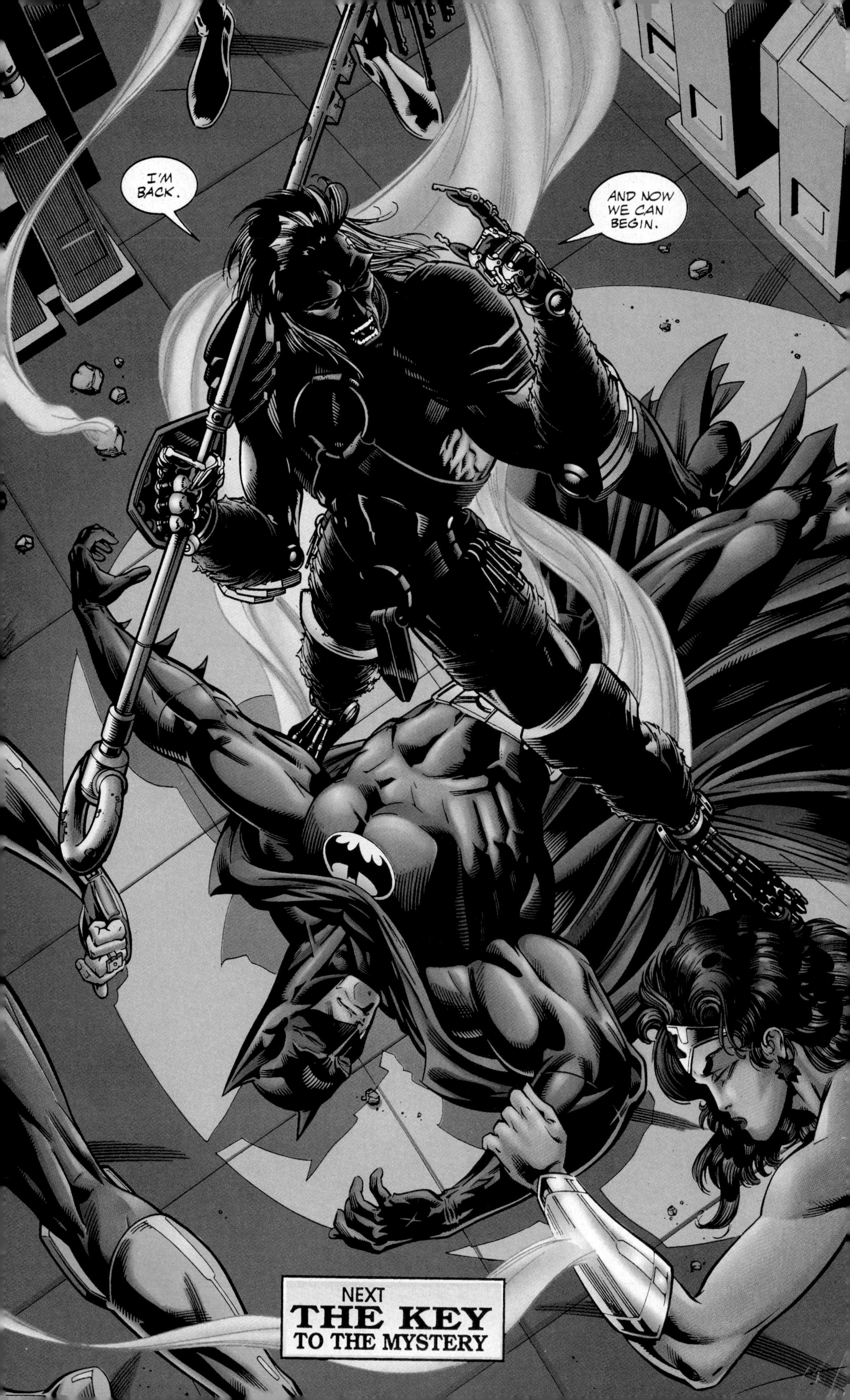
I'M BACK.
AND NOW WE CAN BEGIN.
NEXT
THE KEY
TO THE MYSTERY

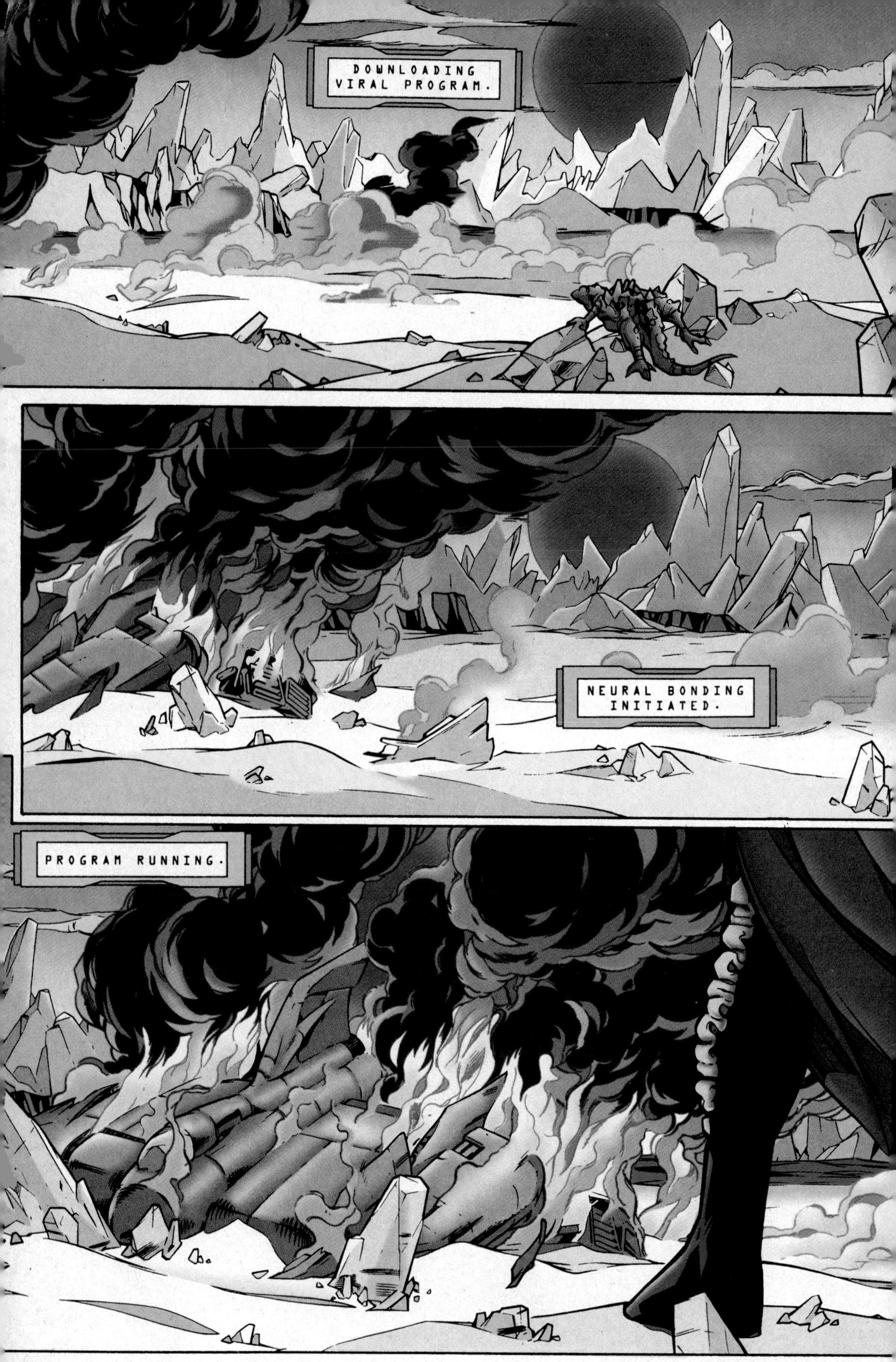
DOWNLOADING VIRAL PROGRAM.
NEURAL BONDING INITIATED.
PROGRAM RUNNING.

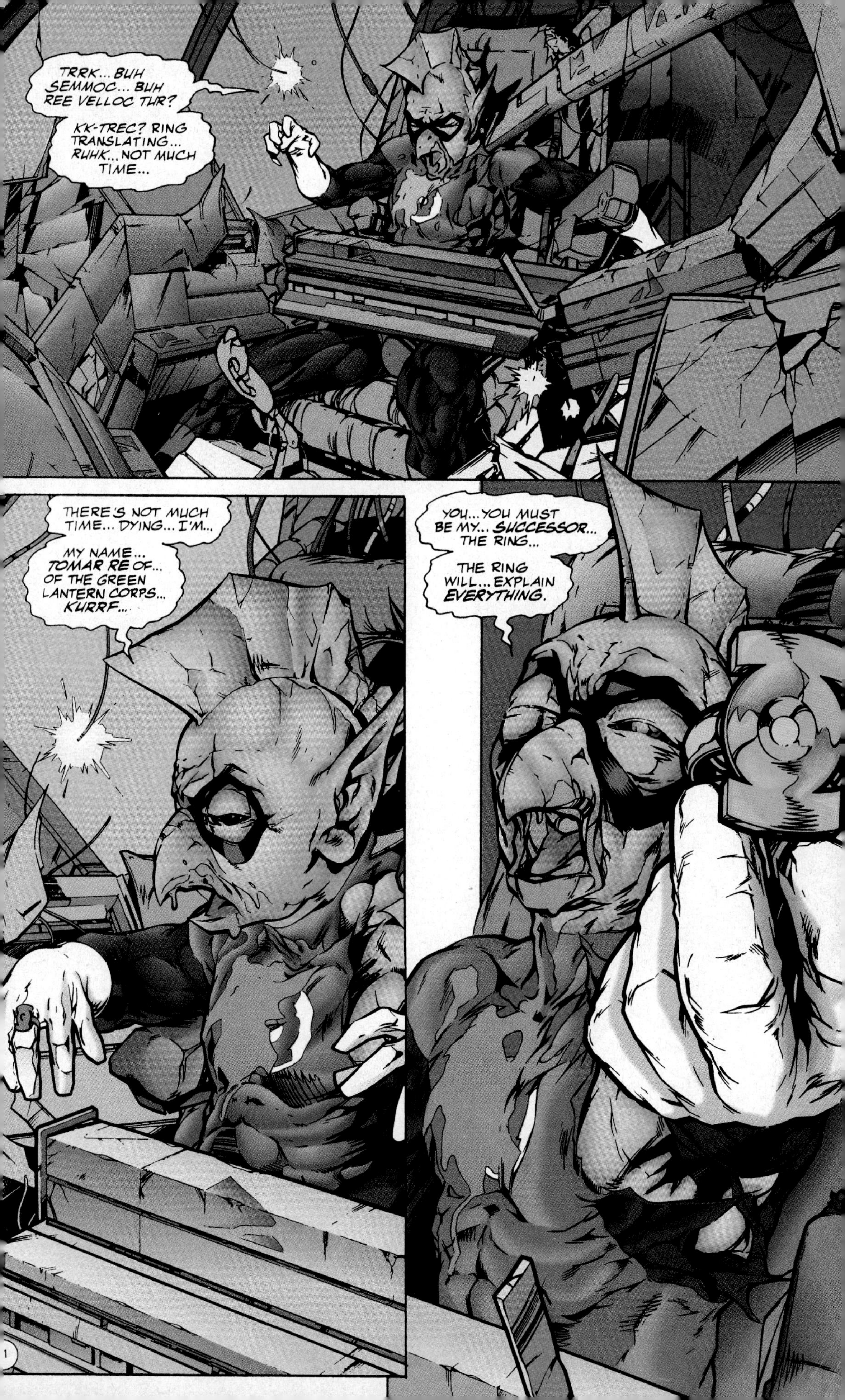
TRRK... BUH SEMMOC... BUH REE VELLOC TUR?
KK-TREC? RING TRANSLATING... RUHK... NOT MUCH TIME...
THERE'S NOT MUCH TIME... DYING... I'M...
MY NAME... TOMAR RE OF... OF THE GREEN LANTERN CORPS... KURRF...
YOU... YOU MUST BE MY... SUCCESSOR... THE RING...
THE RING WILL... EXPLAIN EVERYTHING.

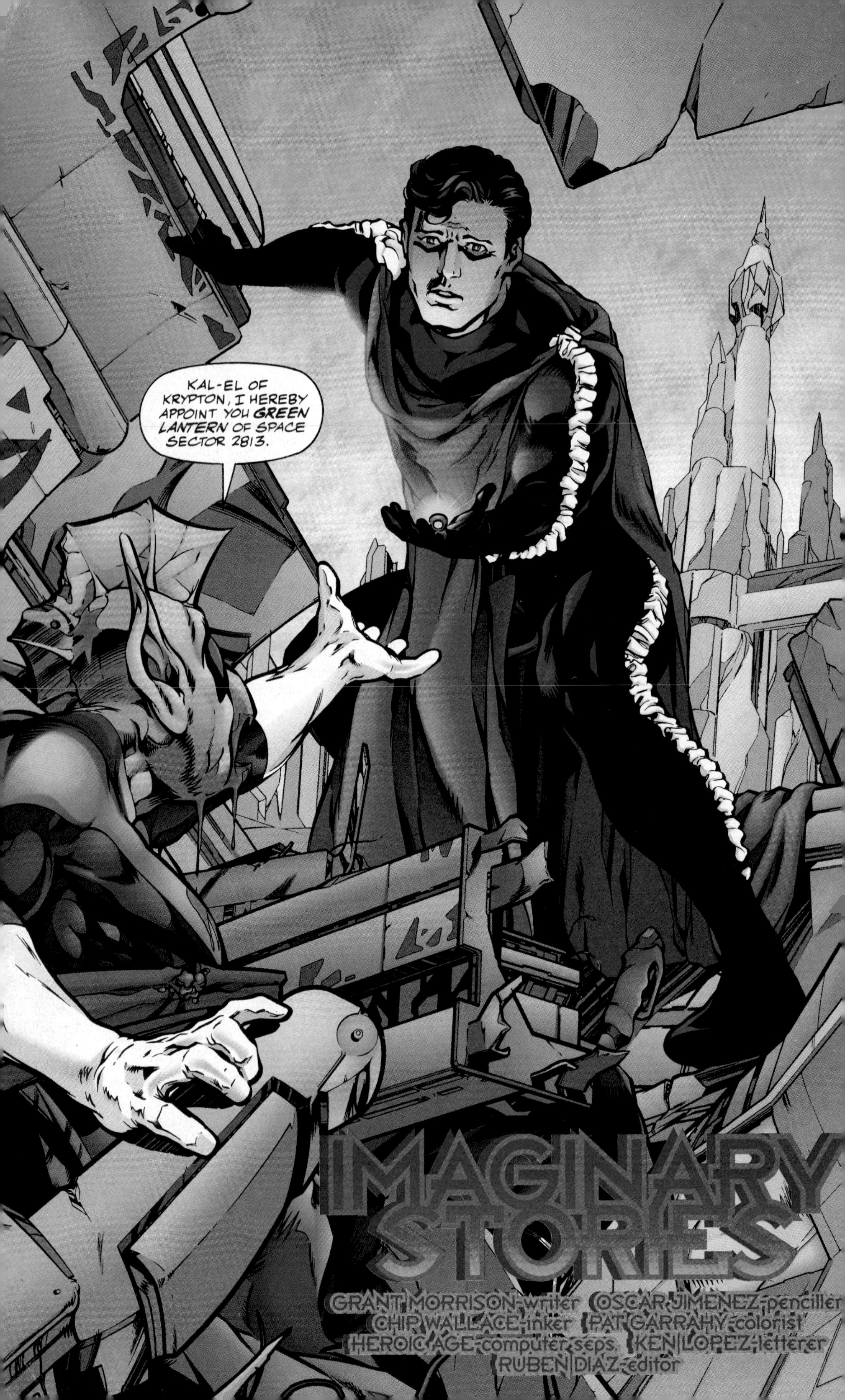
KAL-EL OF KRYPTON, I HEREBY APPOINT YOU GREEN LANTERN OF SPACE SECTOR 2813.
IMAGINARY STORIES
GRANT MORRISON-writer OSCAR JIMENEZ-penciller
CHIP WALLACE-inker PAT GARRAHY-colorist
HEROIC AGE-computer seps. KEN LOPEZ-letterer
RUBEN DIAZ-editor

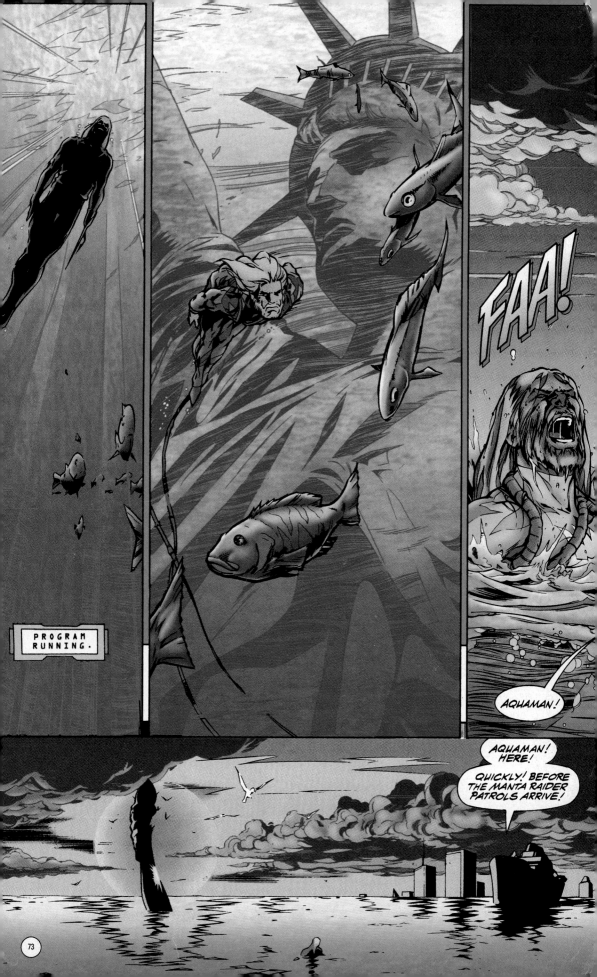

PROGRAM
RUNNING.

FAA!

AQUAMAN!

AQUAMAN!
HERE!

QUICKLY! BEFORE
THE MANTA RAIDER
PATROLS ARRIVE!

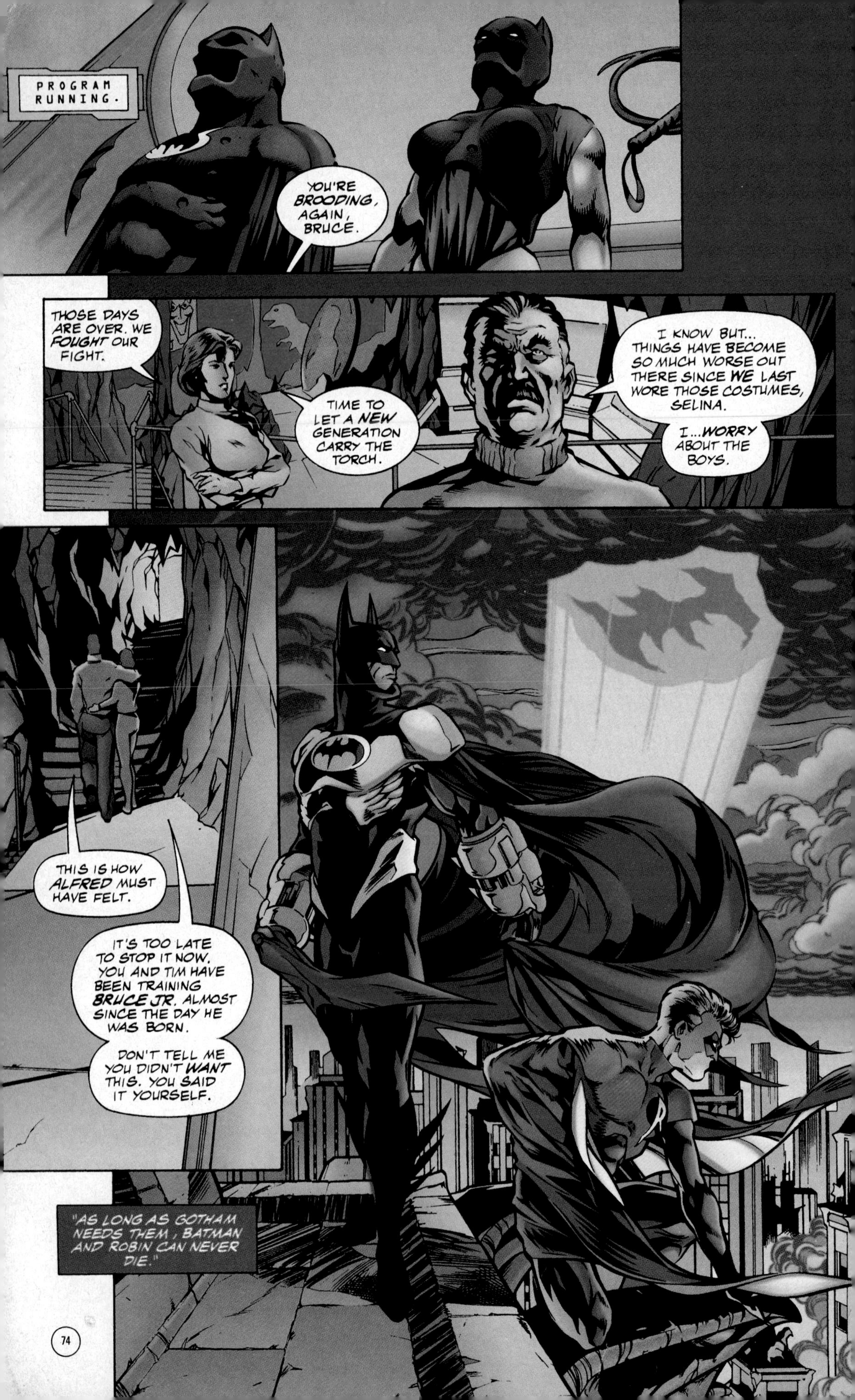
PROGRAM RUNNING.
YOU'RE BROODING, AGAIN, BRUCE.
THOSE DAYS ARE OVER. WE FOUGHT OUR FIGHT.
TIME TO LET A NEW GENERATION CARRY THE TORCH.
I KNOW BUT... THINGS HAVE BECOME SO MUCH WORSE OUT THERE SINCE WE LAST WORE THOSE COSTUMES, SELINA.
I...WORRY ABOUT THE BOYS.
THIS IS HOW ALFRED MUST HAVE FELT.
IT'S TOO LATE TO STOP IT NOW. YOU AND TIM HAVE BEEN TRAINING BRUCE JR. ALMOST SINCE THE DAY HE WAS BORN.
DON'T TELL ME YOU DIDN'T WANT THIS. YOU SAID IT YOURSELF.
"AS LONG AS GOTHAM NEEDS THEM, BATMAN AND ROBIN CAN NEVER DIE."

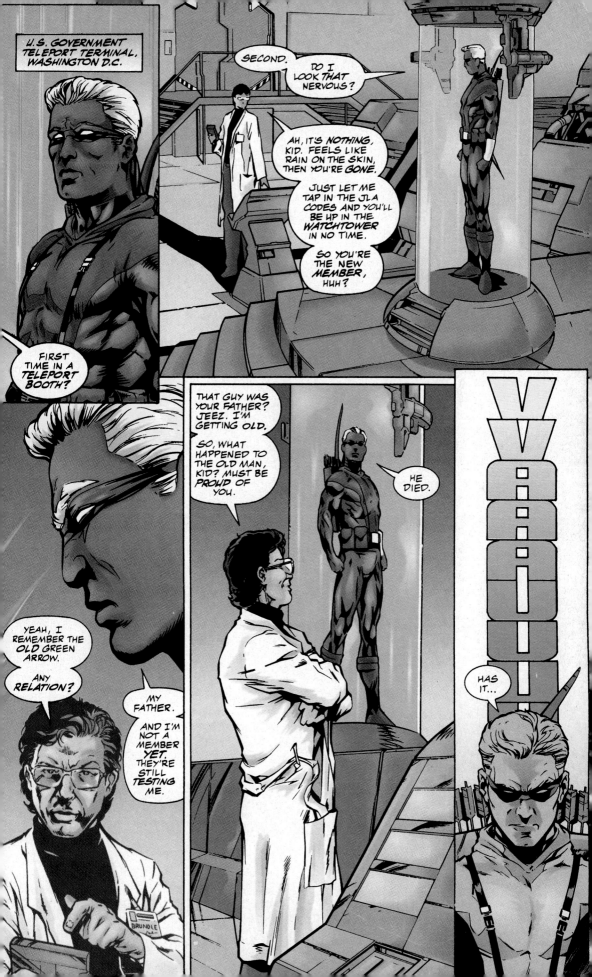

U.S. GOVERNMENT TELEPORT TERMINAL, WASHINGTON D.C.

SECOND.

DO I LOOK *THAT* NERVOUS?

AH, IT'S *NOTHING*, KID. FEELS LIKE RAIN ON THE SKIN, THEN *YOU'RE GONE*.

JUST LET ME TAP IN THE JLA CODES AND YOU'LL BE UP IN THE *WATCHTOWER* IN NO TIME.

SO YOU'RE THE NEW *MEMBER*, HUH?

FIRST TIME IN A *TELEPORT* BOOTH?

THAT GUY WAS YOUR FATHER? JEEZ. I'M GETTING OLD.

SO, WHAT HAPPENED TO THE OLD MAN, KID? MUST BE *PROUD* OF YOU.

HE DIED.

VZAAUUU

YEAH, I REMEMBER THE OLD GREEN ARROW. ANY *RELATION*?

MY FATHER.

AND I'M NOT A MEMBER *YET*. THEY'RE STILL *TESTING* ME.

HAS IT...

BRUNDLE

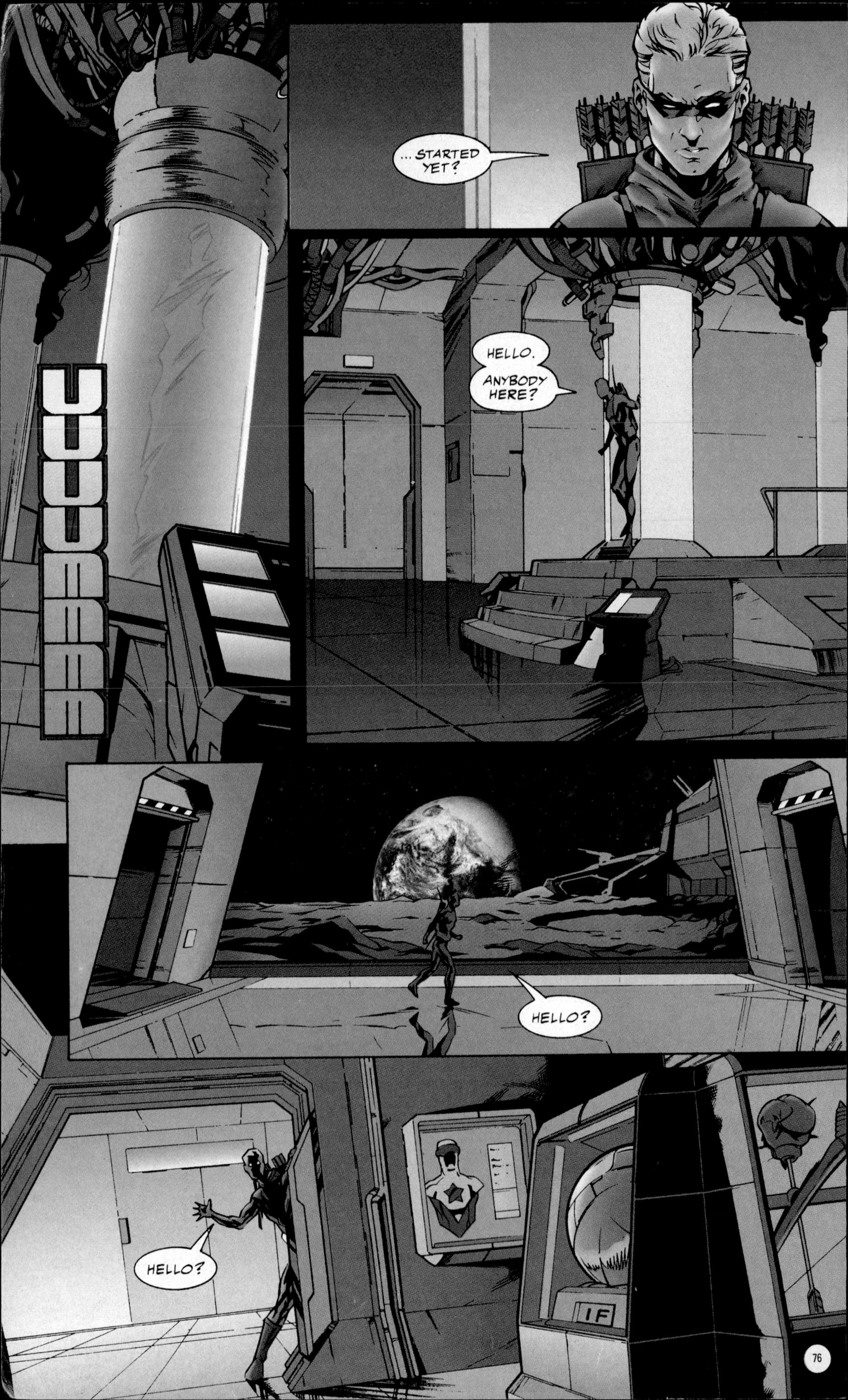

...STARTED YET?
UUUMMMMM
HELLO. ANYBODY HERE?
HELLO?
HELLO?
IF

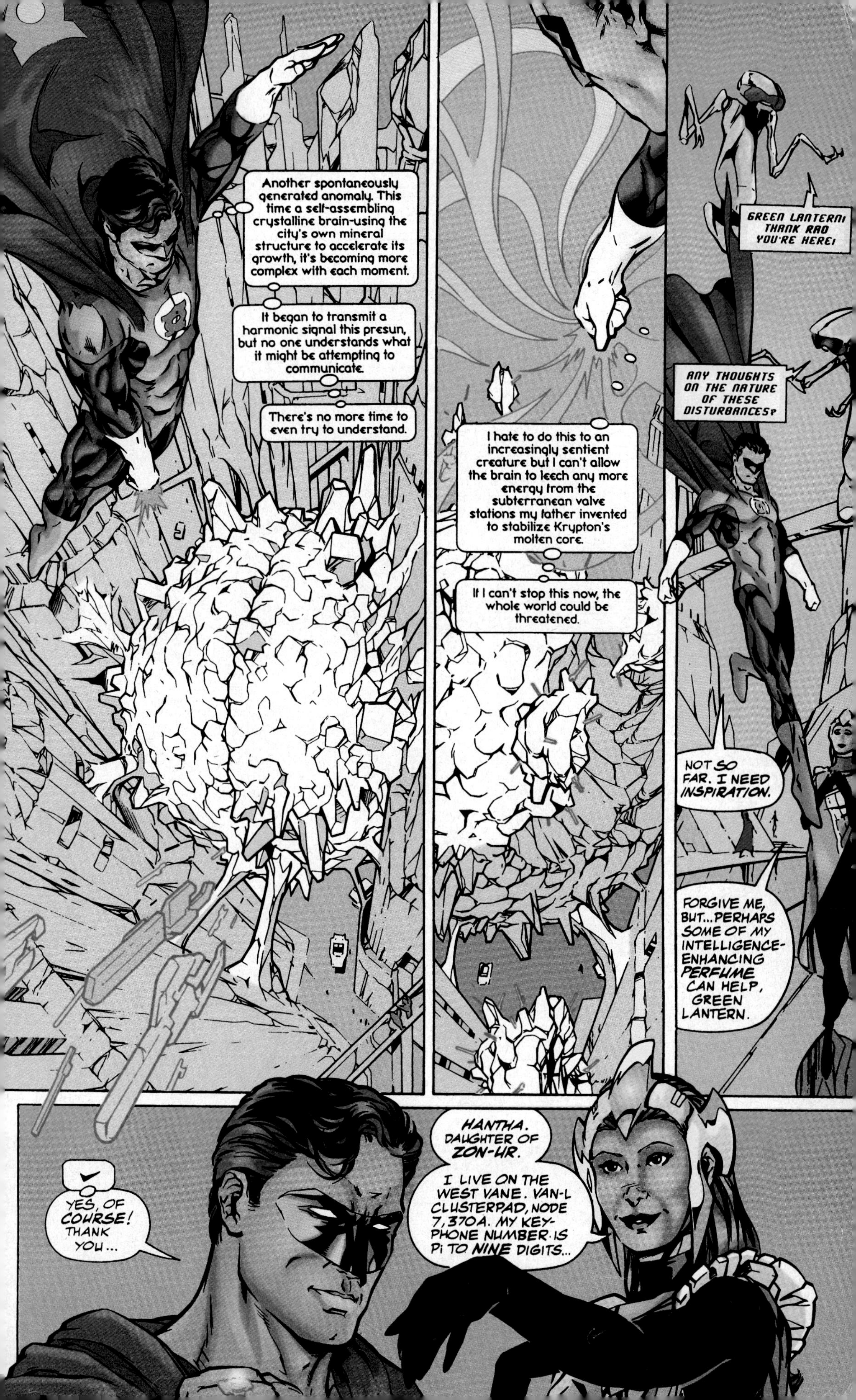

Another spontaneously generated anomaly. This time a self-assembling crystalline brain-using the city's own mineral structure to accelerate its growth, it's becoming more complex with each moment.
It began to transmit a harmonic signal this presun, but no one understands what it might be attempting to communicate.
There's no more time to even try to understand.
I hate to do this to an increasingly sentient creature but I can't allow the brain to leech any more energy from the subterranean valve stations my father invented to stabilize Krypton's molten core.
If I can't stop this now, the whole world could be threatened.
GREEN LANTERN! THANK RAO YOU'RE HERE!
ANY THOUGHTS ON THE NATURE OF THESE DISTURBANCES?
NOT SO FAR. I NEED INSPIRATION.
FORGIVE ME, BUT...PERHAPS SOME OF MY INTELLIGENCE-ENHANCING PERFUME CAN HELP, GREEN LANTERN.
HANTHA. DAUGHTER OF ZON-UR.
I LIVE ON THE WEST VANE. VAN-L CLUSTERPAD, NODE 7,370A. MY KEY-PHONE NUMBER IS PI TO NINE DIGITS...
YES, OF COURSE! THANK YOU...

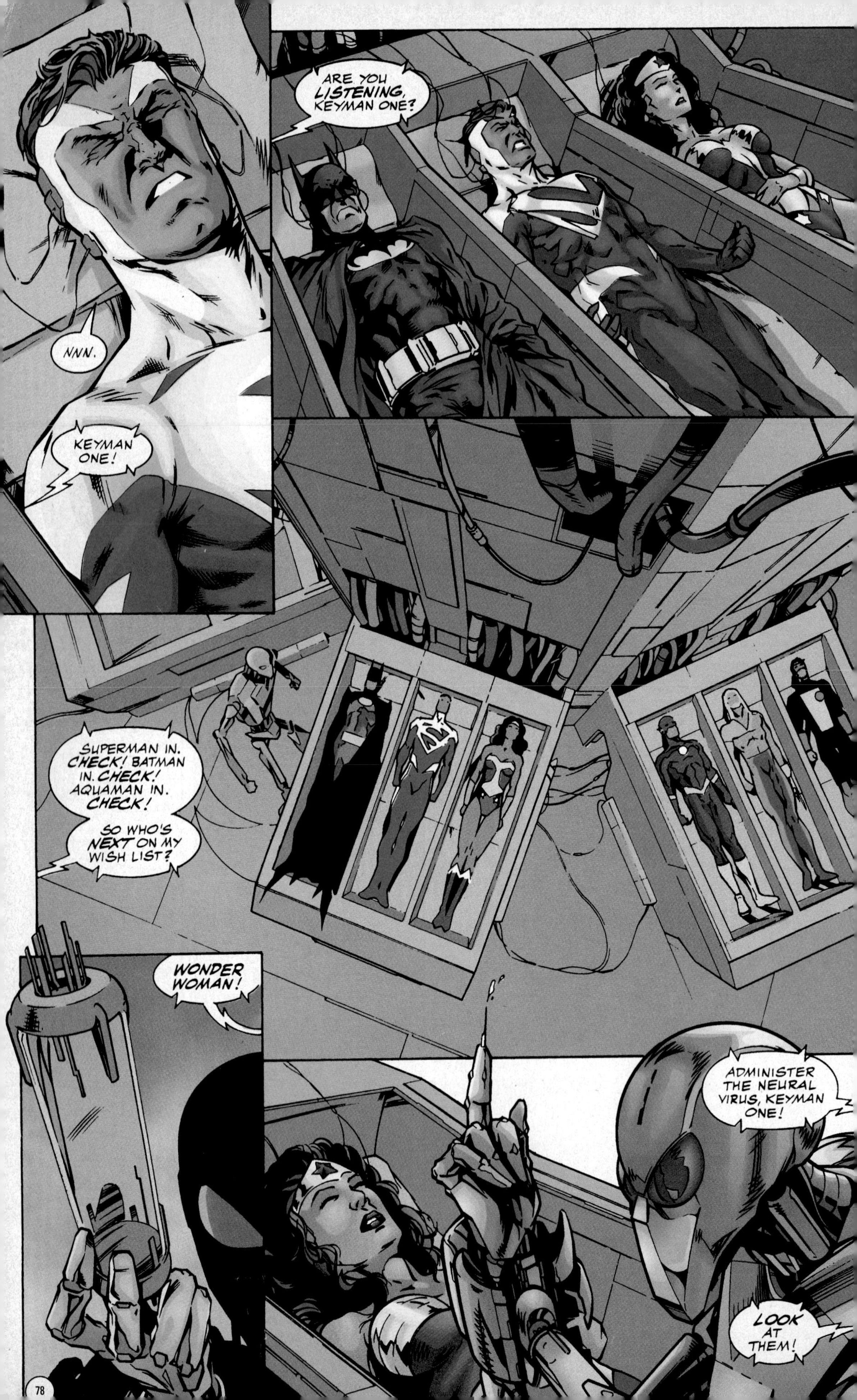
NNN.
KEYMAN ONE!
ARE YOU LISTENING, KEYMAN ONE?
SUPERMAN IN. CHECK! BATMAN IN. CHECK! AQUAMAN IN. CHECK!
SO WHO'S NEXT ON MY WISH LIST?
WONDER WOMAN!
ADMINISTER THE NEURAL VIRUS, KEYMAN ONE!
LOOK AT THEM!

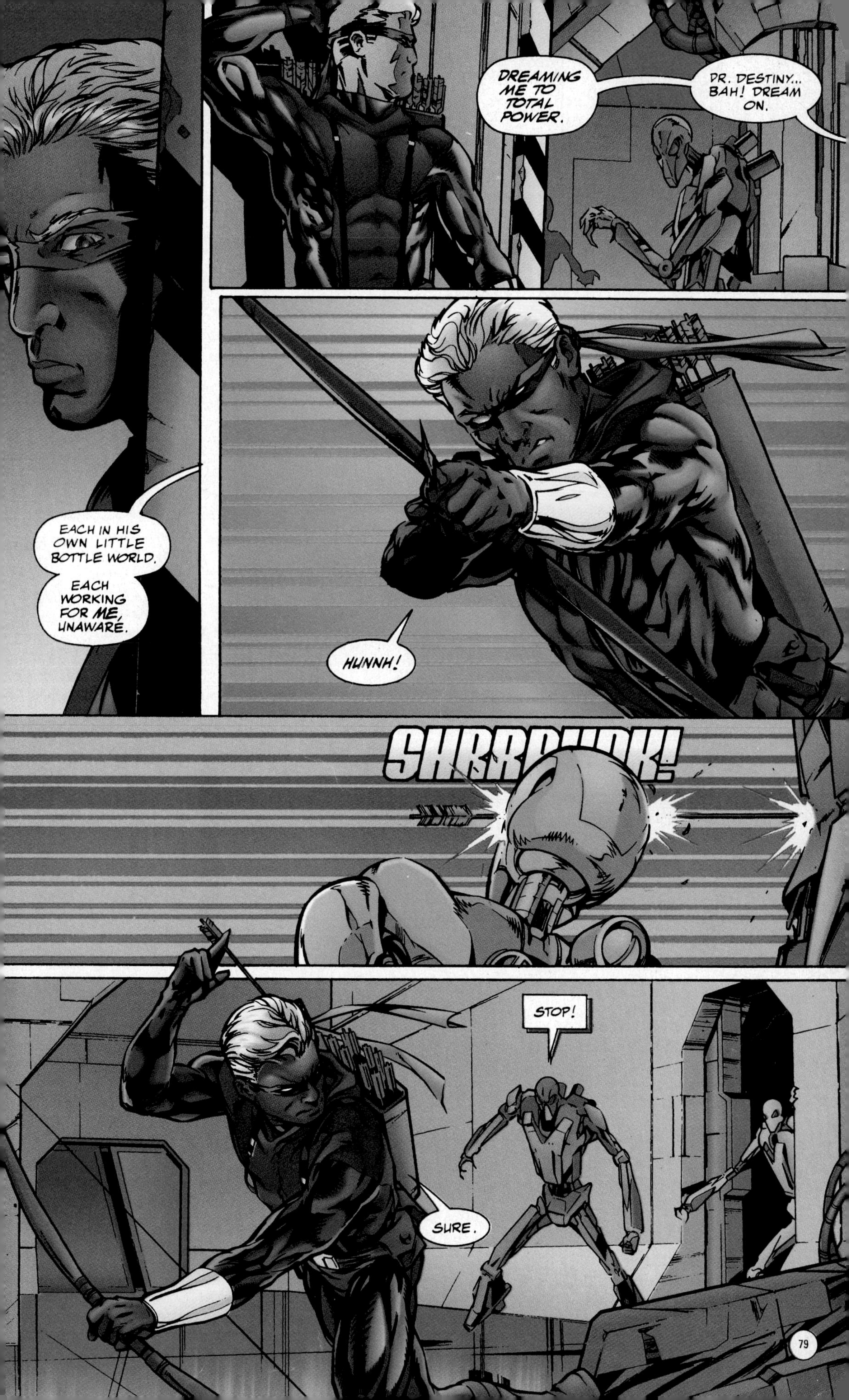

DREAMING ME TO TOTAL POWER.
DR. DESTINY... BAH! DREAM ON.
EACH IN HIS OWN LITTLE BOTTLE WORLD.
EACH WORKING FOR ME, UNAWARE.
HUNNH!
SHRRDUNK!
STOP!
SURE.

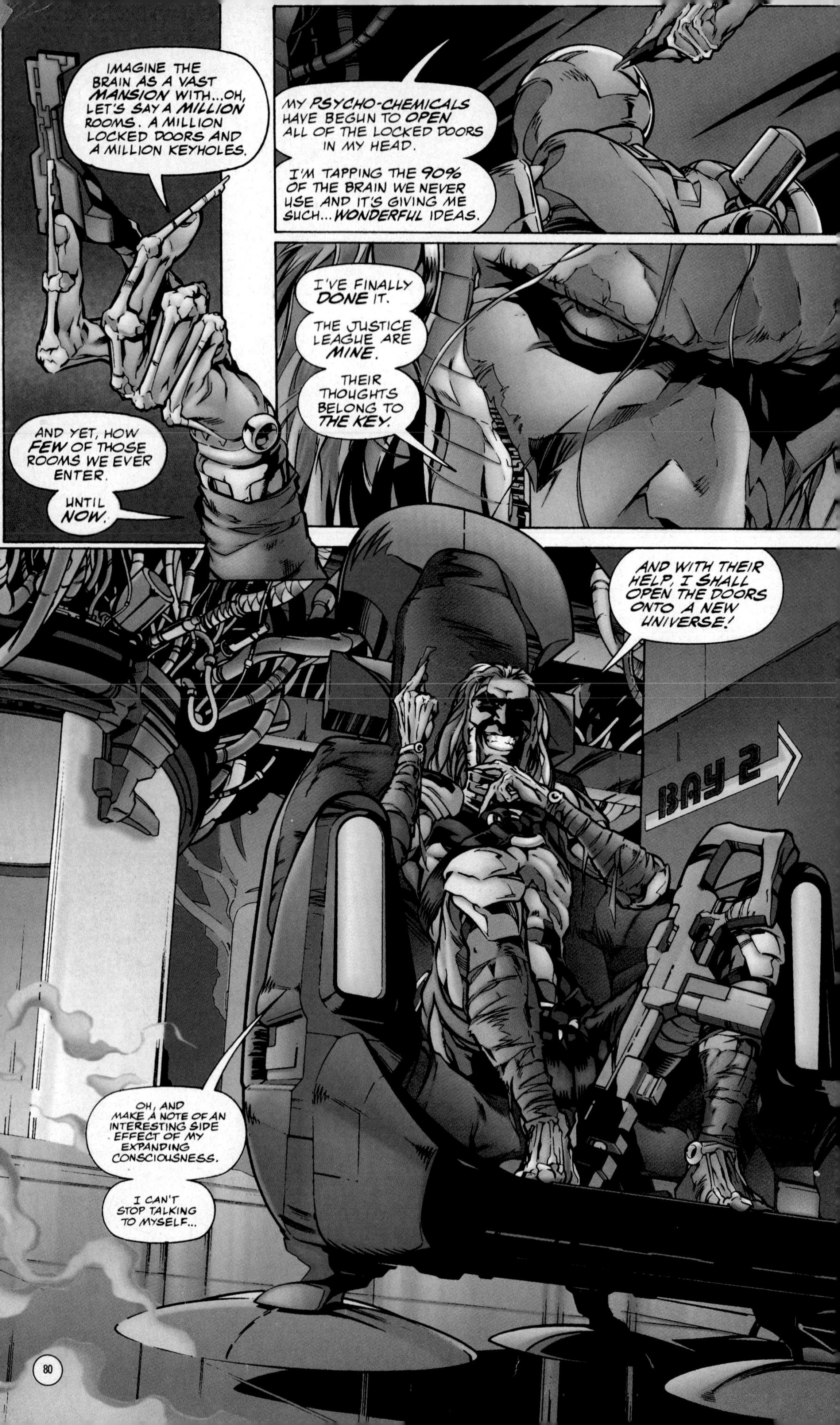
IMAGINE THE BRAIN AS A VAST MANSION WITH...OH, LET'S SAY A MILLION ROOMS. A MILLION LOCKED DOORS AND A MILLION KEYHOLES.
MY PSYCHO-CHEMICALS HAVE BEGUN TO OPEN ALL OF THE LOCKED DOORS IN MY HEAD.
I'M TAPPING THE 90% OF THE BRAIN WE NEVER USE AND IT'S GIVING ME SUCH... WONDERFUL IDEAS.
AND YET, HOW FEW OF THOSE ROOMS WE EVER ENTER.
UNTIL NOW.
I'VE FINALLY DONE IT.
THE JUSTICE LEAGUE ARE MINE.
THEIR THOUGHTS BELONG TO THE KEY.
AND WITH THEIR HELP, I SHALL OPEN THE DOORS ONTO A NEW UNIVERSE!
BAY 2
OH, AND MAKE A NOTE OF AN INTERESTING SIDE EFFECT OF MY EXPANDING CONSCIOUSNESS.
I CAN'T STOP TALKING TO MYSELF...

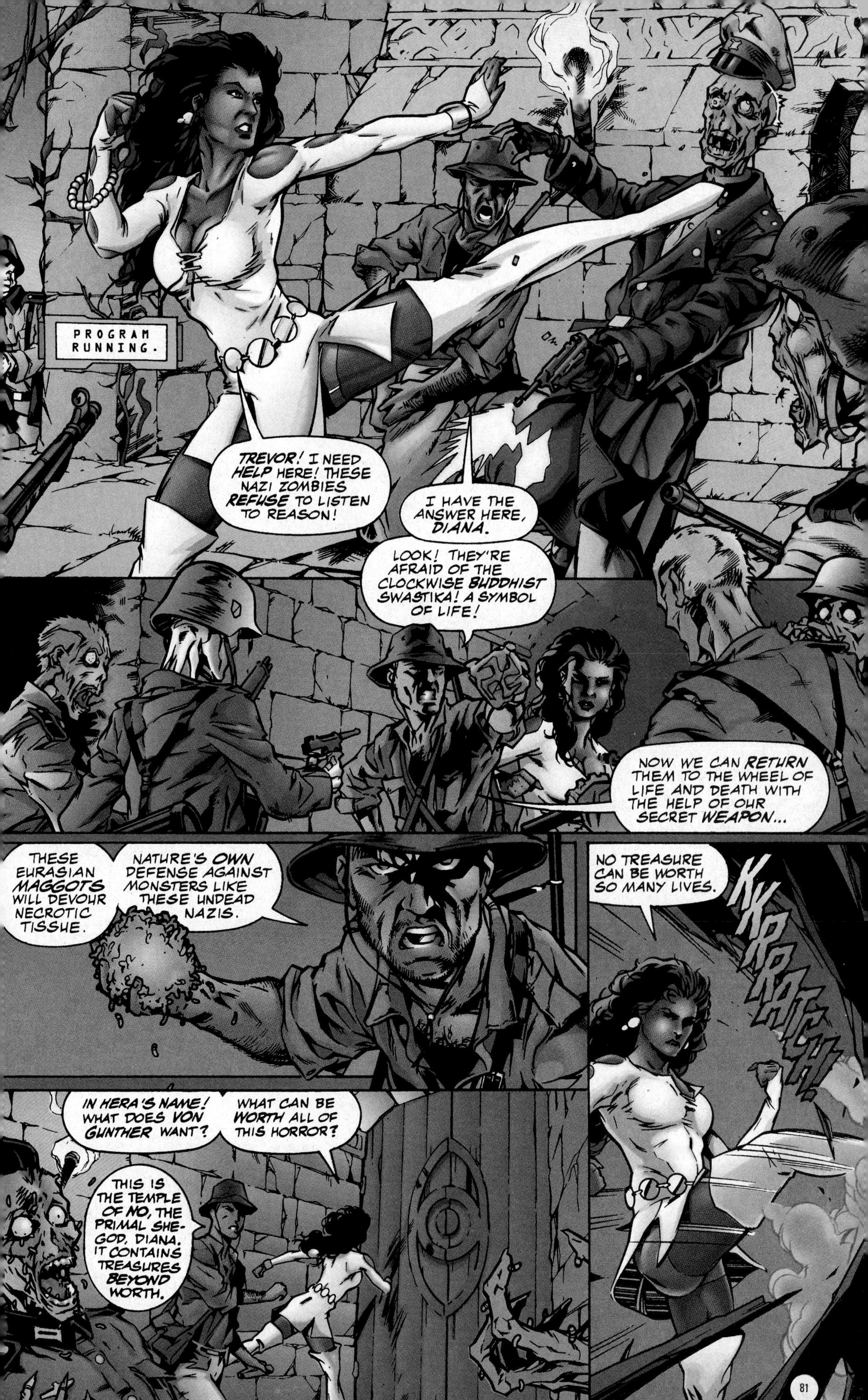

PROGRAM RUNNING.
TREVOR! I NEED HELP HERE! THESE NAZI ZOMBIES REFUSE TO LISTEN TO REASON!
I HAVE THE ANSWER HERE, DIANA.
LOOK! THEY'RE AFRAID OF THE CLOCKWISE BUDDHIST SWASTIKA! A SYMBOL OF LIFE!
NOW WE CAN RETURN THEM TO THE WHEEL OF LIFE AND DEATH WITH THE HELP OF OUR SECRET WEAPON...
THESE EURASIAN MAGGOTS WILL DEVOUR NECROTIC TISSUE.
NATURE'S OWN DEFENSE AGAINST MONSTERS LIKE THESE UNDEAD NAZIS.
NO TREASURE CAN BE WORTH SO MANY LIVES.
KKRATCH
IN HERA'S NAME! WHAT DOES VON GUNTHER WANT?
WHAT CAN BE WORTH ALL OF THIS HORROR?
THIS IS THE TEMPLE OF NO, THE PRIMAL SHE-GOD, DIANA. IT CONTAINS TREASURES BEYOND WORTH.

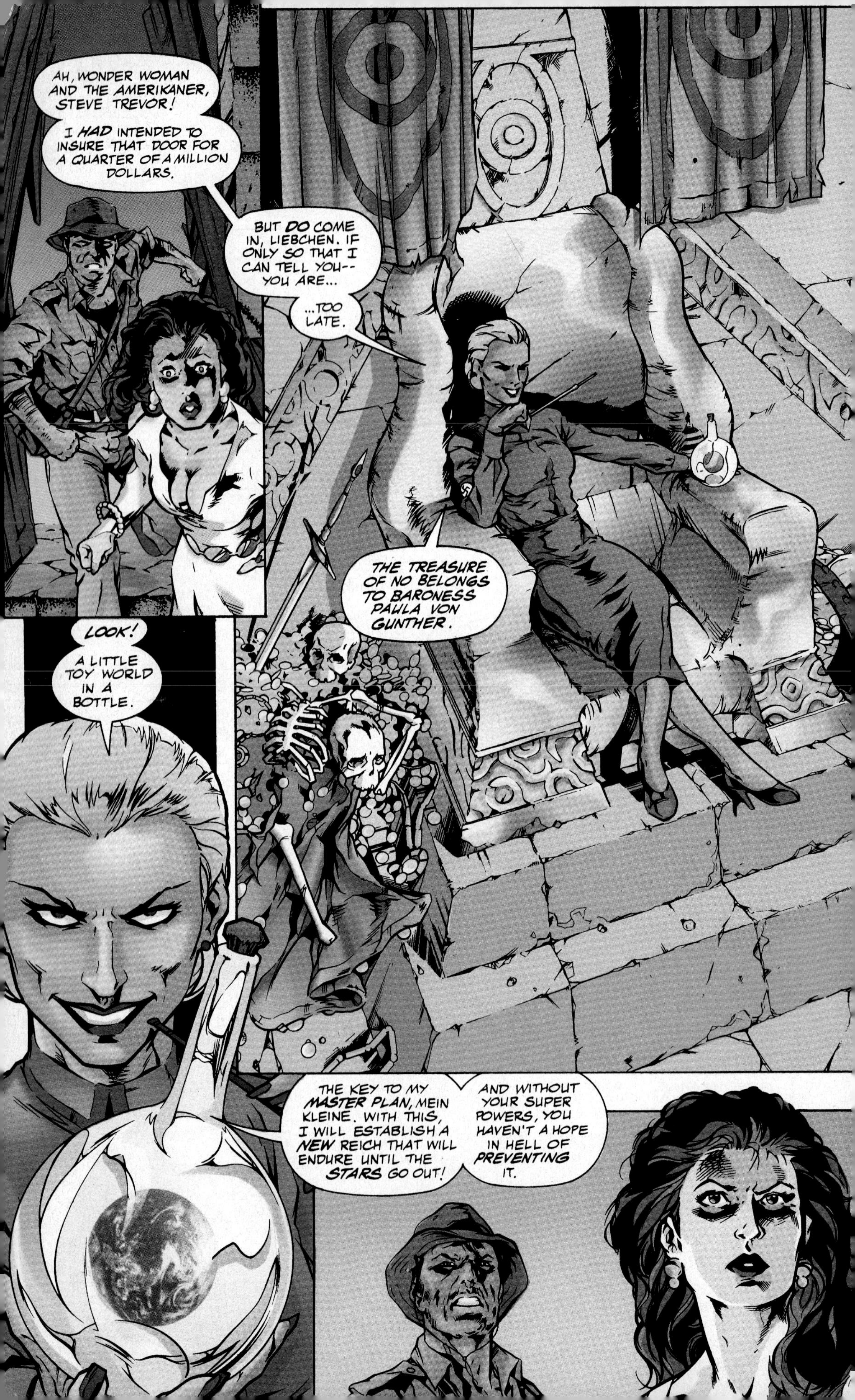
AH, WONDER WOMAN AND THE AMERIKANER, STEVE TREVOR!
I HAD INTENDED TO INSURE THAT DOOR FOR A QUARTER OF A MILLION DOLLARS.
BUT DO COME IN, LIEBCHEN. IF ONLY SO THAT I CAN TELL YOU-- YOU ARE...
...TOO LATE.
THE TREASURE OF NO BELONGS TO BARONESS PAULA VON GUNTHER.
LOOK!
A LITTLE TOY WORLD IN A BOTTLE.
THE KEY TO MY MASTER PLAN, MEIN KLEINE. WITH THIS, I WILL ESTABLISH A NEW REICH THAT WILL ENDURE UNTIL THE STARS GO OUT!
AND WITHOUT YOUR SUPER POWERS, YOU HAVEN'T A HOPE IN HELL OF PREVENTING IT.

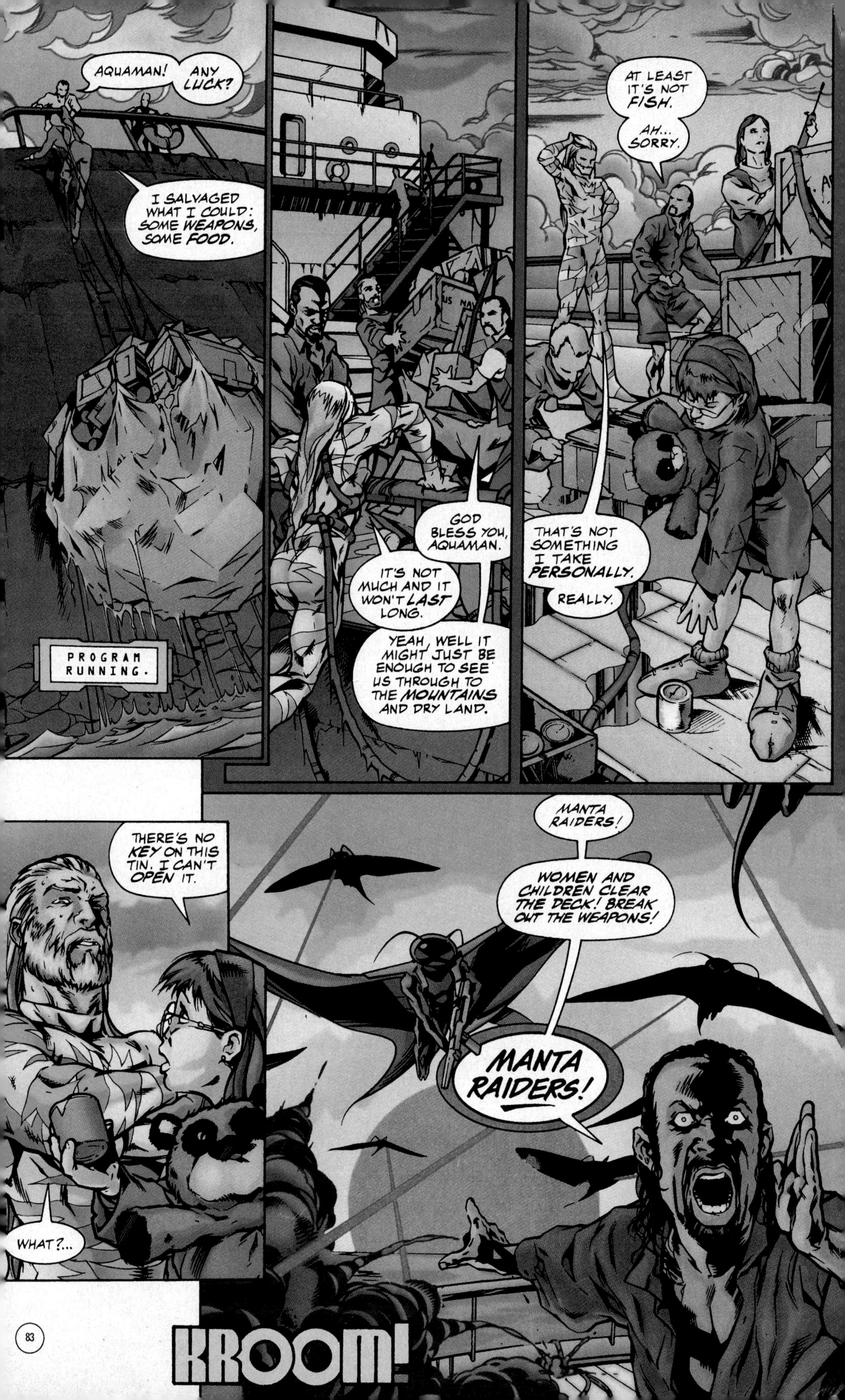
AQUAMAN! ANY LUCK?
I SALVAGED WHAT I COULD: SOME WEAPONS, SOME FOOD.
PROGRAM RUNNING.
GOD BLESS YOU, AQUAMAN.
IT'S NOT MUCH AND IT WON'T LAST LONG.
YEAH, WELL IT MIGHT JUST BE ENOUGH TO SEE US THROUGH TO THE MOUNTAINS AND DRY LAND.
AT LEAST IT'S NOT FISH.
AH... SORRY.
THAT'S NOT SOMETHING I TAKE PERSONALLY.
REALLY.
THERE'S NO KEY ON THIS TIN. I CAN'T OPEN IT.
WHAT?...
MANTA RAIDERS!
WOMEN AND CHILDREN CLEAR THE DECK! BREAK OUT THE WEAPONS!
MANTA RAIDERS!
KROOM!

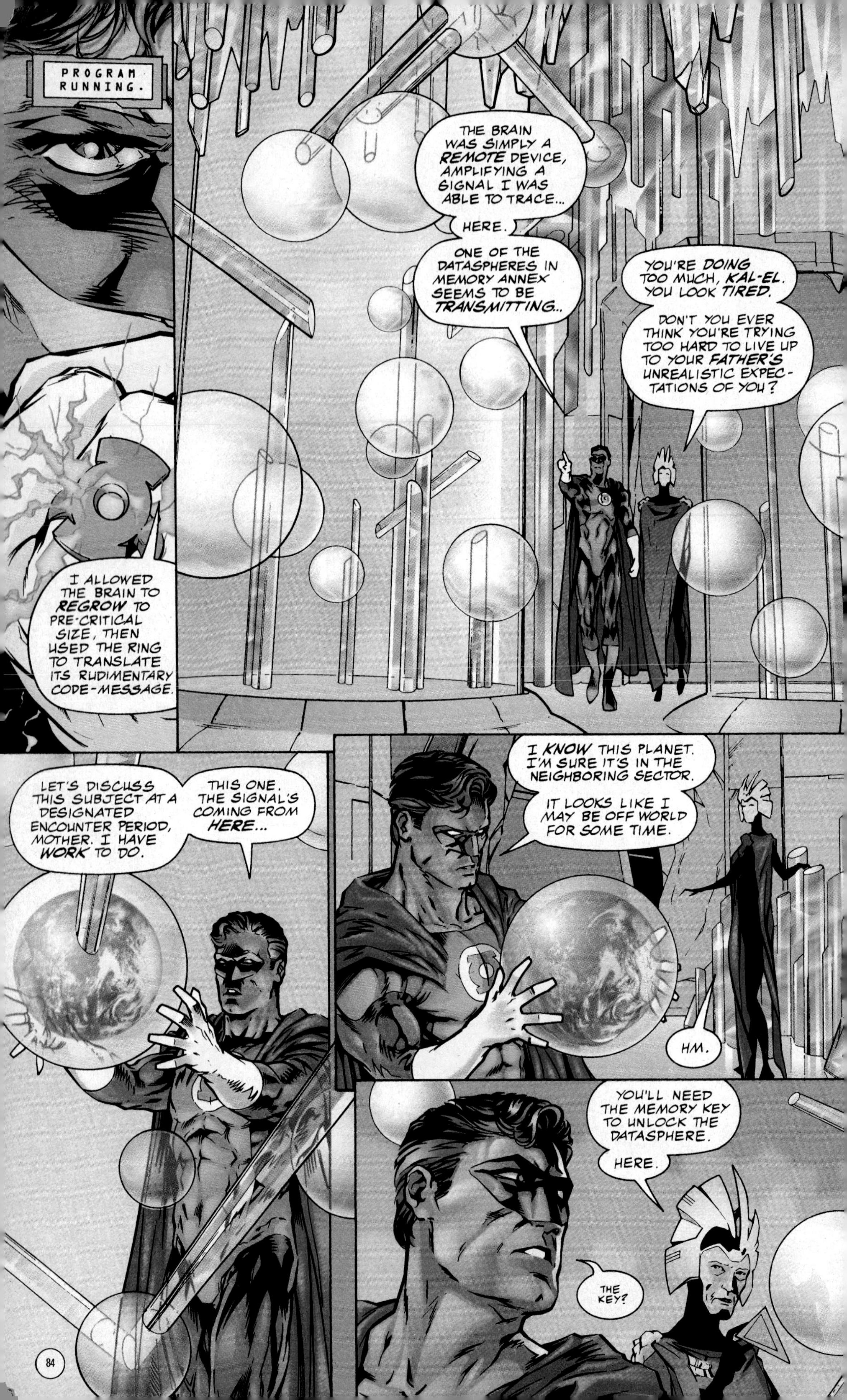

PROGRAM RUNNING.
THE BRAIN WAS SIMPLY A REMOTE DEVICE, AMPLIFYING A SIGNAL I WAS ABLE TO TRACE...
HERE.
ONE OF THE DATASPHERES IN MEMORY ANNEX SEEMS TO BE TRANSMITTING...
YOU'RE DOING TOO MUCH, KAL-EL. YOU LOOK TIRED.
DON'T YOU EVER THINK YOU'RE TRYING TOO HARD TO LIVE UP TO YOUR FATHER'S UNREALISTIC EXPECTATIONS OF YOU?
I ALLOWED THE BRAIN TO REGROW TO PRE-CRITICAL SIZE, THEN USED THE RING TO TRANSLATE ITS RUDIMENTARY CODE-MESSAGE.
LET'S DISCUSS THIS SUBJECT AT A DESIGNATED ENCOUNTER PERIOD, MOTHER. I HAVE WORK TO DO.
THIS ONE. THE SIGNAL'S COMING FROM HERE...
I KNOW THIS PLANET. I'M SURE IT'S IN THE NEIGHBORING SECTOR.
IT LOOKS LIKE I MAY BE OFF WORLD FOR SOME TIME.
HM.
YOU'LL NEED THE MEMORY KEY TO UNLOCK THE DATASPHERE.
HERE.
THE KEY?

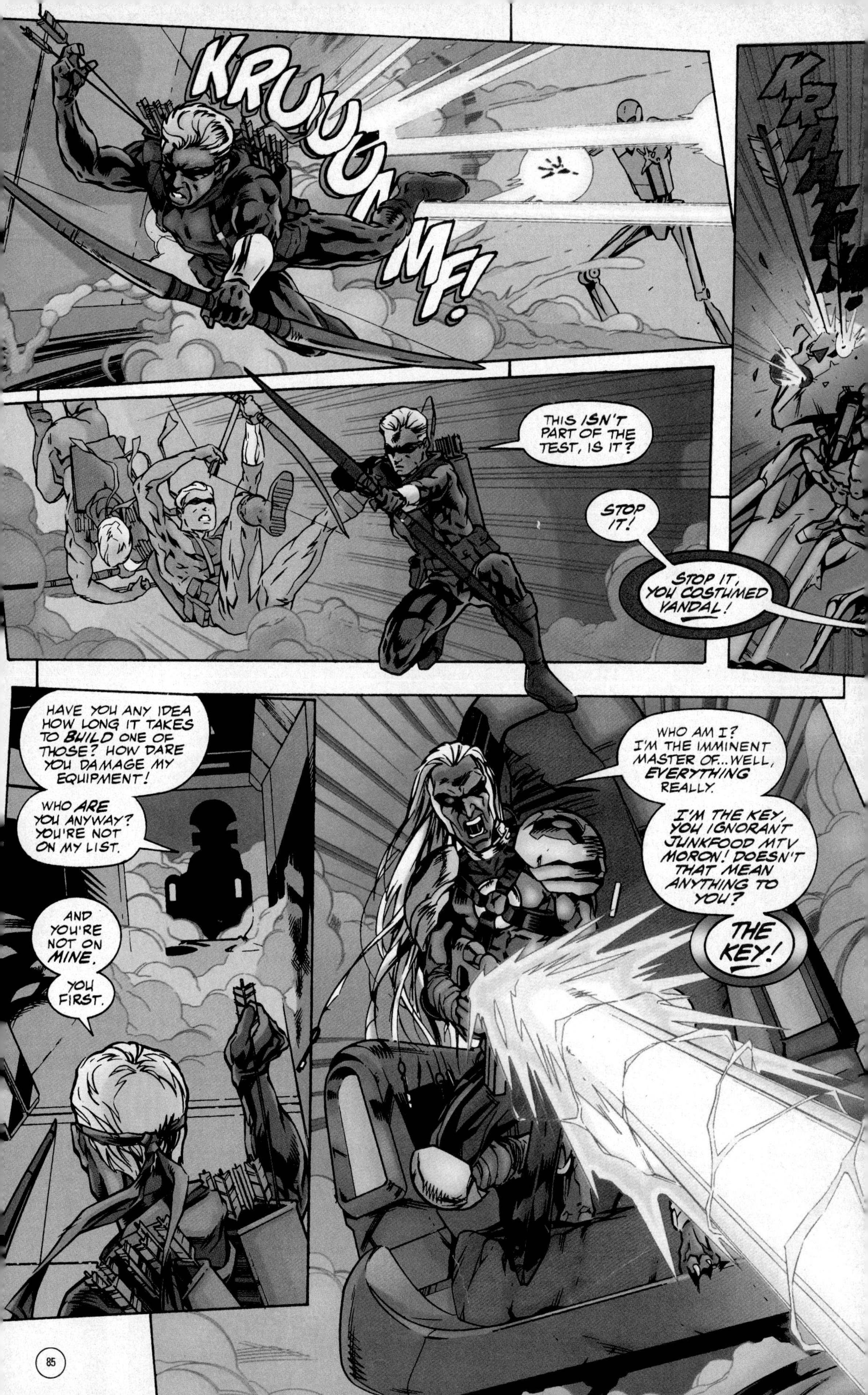
KRUUUUMMF!
KRAAAKK!
THIS ISN'T PART OF THE TEST, IS IT?
STOP IT!
STOP IT, YOU COSTUMED VANDAL!
HAVE YOU ANY IDEA HOW LONG IT TAKES TO BUILD ONE OF THOSE? HOW DARE YOU DAMAGE MY EQUIPMENT!
WHO ARE YOU ANYWAY? YOU'RE NOT ON MY LIST.
AND YOU'RE NOT ON MINE.
YOU FIRST.
WHO AM I? I'M THE IMMINENT MASTER OF...WELL, EVERYTHING REALLY.
I'M THE KEY, YOU IGNORANT JUNKFOOD MTV MORON! DOESN'T THAT MEAN ANYTHING TO YOU?
THE KEY!

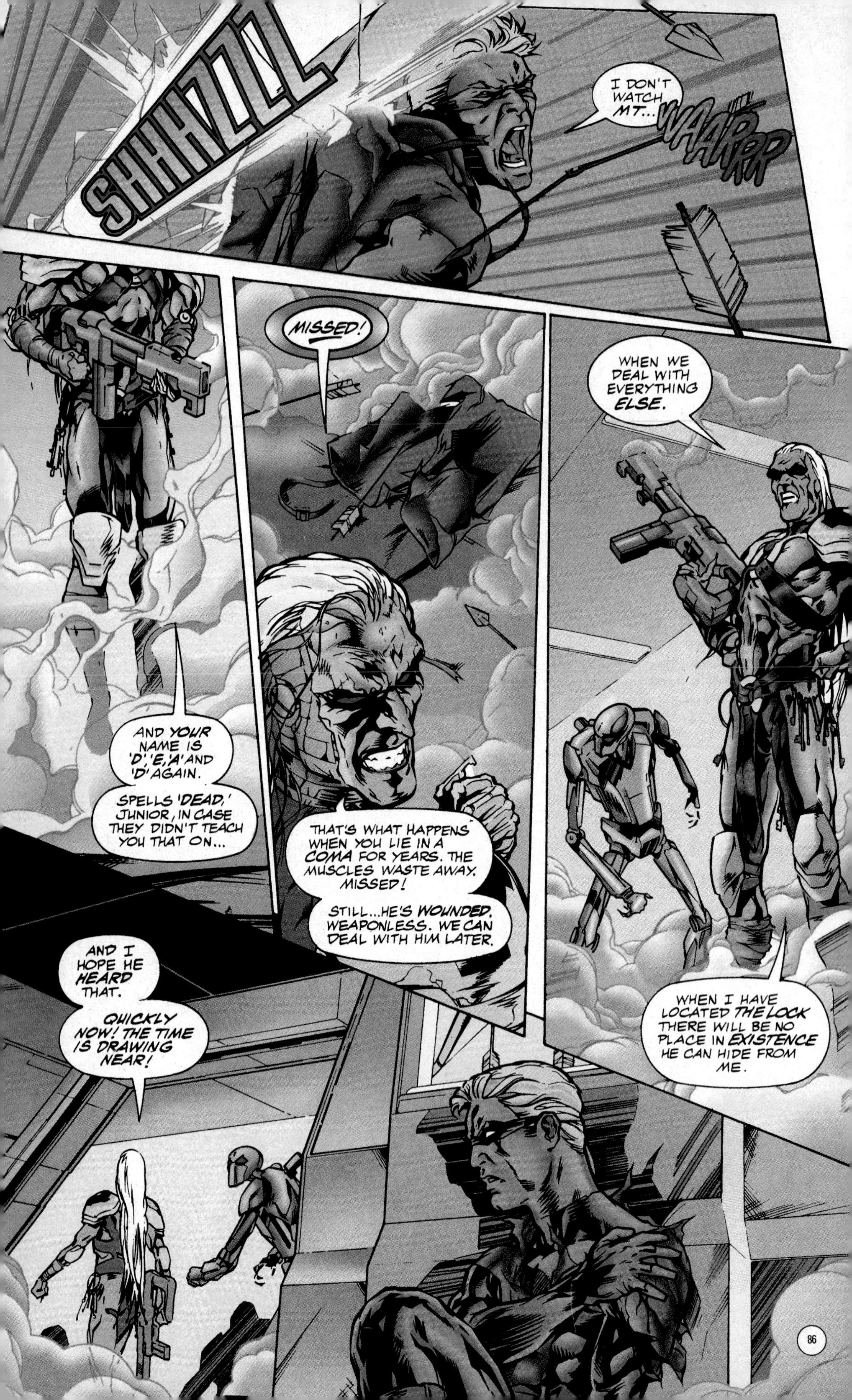
SHHHZZZZ
I DON'T WATCH MT...
WAARRR
MISSED!
AND YOUR NAME IS 'D','E,'A' AND 'D' AGAIN.
SPELLS 'DEAD,' JUNIOR, IN CASE THEY DIDN'T TEACH YOU THAT ON...
THAT'S WHAT HAPPENS WHEN YOU LIE IN A COMA FOR YEARS. THE MUSCLES WASTE AWAY. MISSED!
STILL...HE'S WOUNDED, WEAPONLESS. WE CAN DEAL WITH HIM LATER.
WHEN WE DEAL WITH EVERYTHING ELSE.
AND I HOPE HE HEARD THAT.
QUICKLY NOW! THE TIME IS DRAWING NEAR!
WHEN I HAVE LOCATED THE LOCK THERE WILL BE NO PLACE IN EXISTENCE HE CAN HIDE FROM ME.

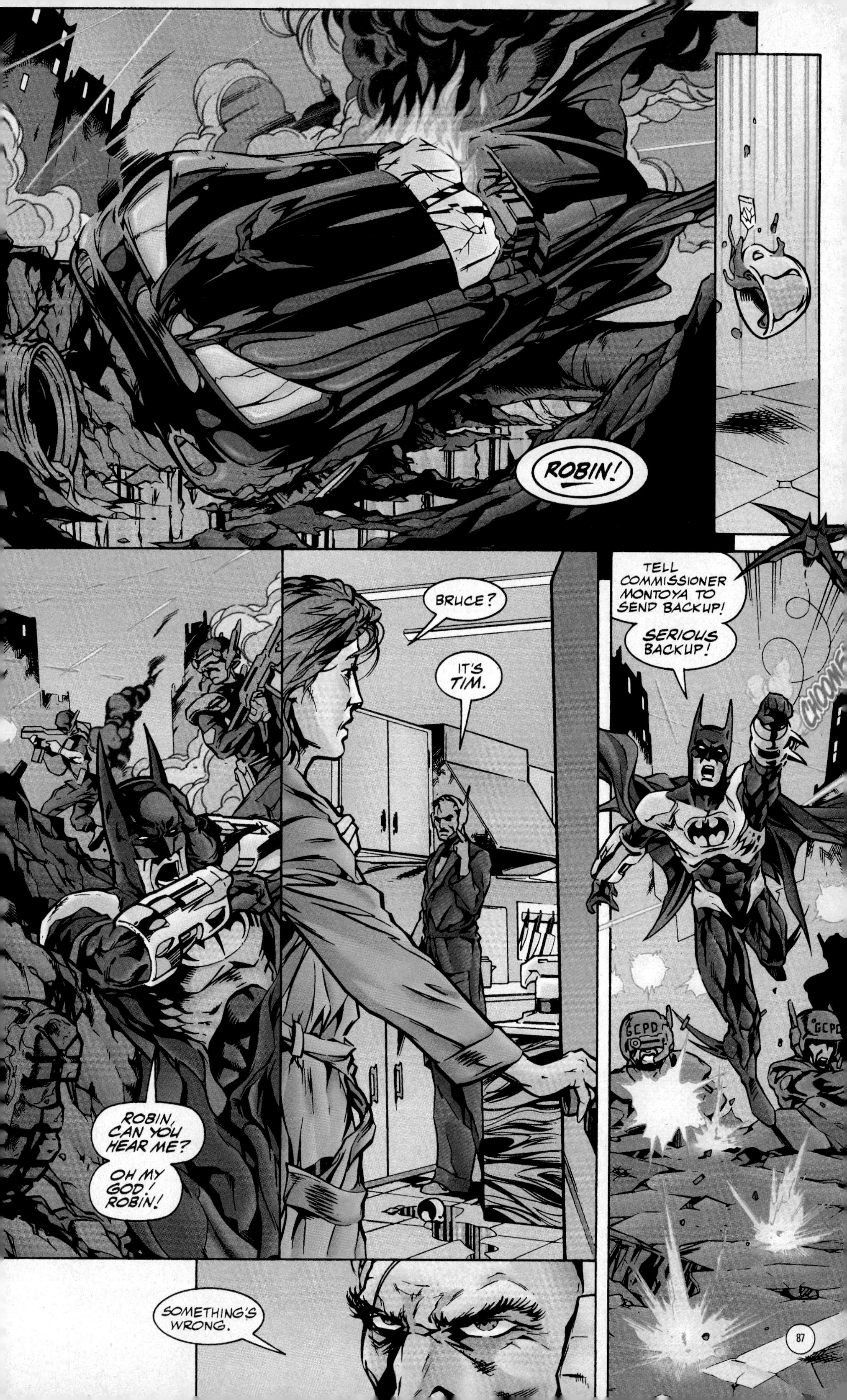
ROBIN!
BRUCE?
IT'S TIM.
TELL COMMISSIONER MONTOYA TO SEND BACKUP!
SERIOUS BACKUP!
ROBIN, CAN YOU HEAR ME?
OH MY GOD! ROBIN!
SOMETHING'S WRONG.

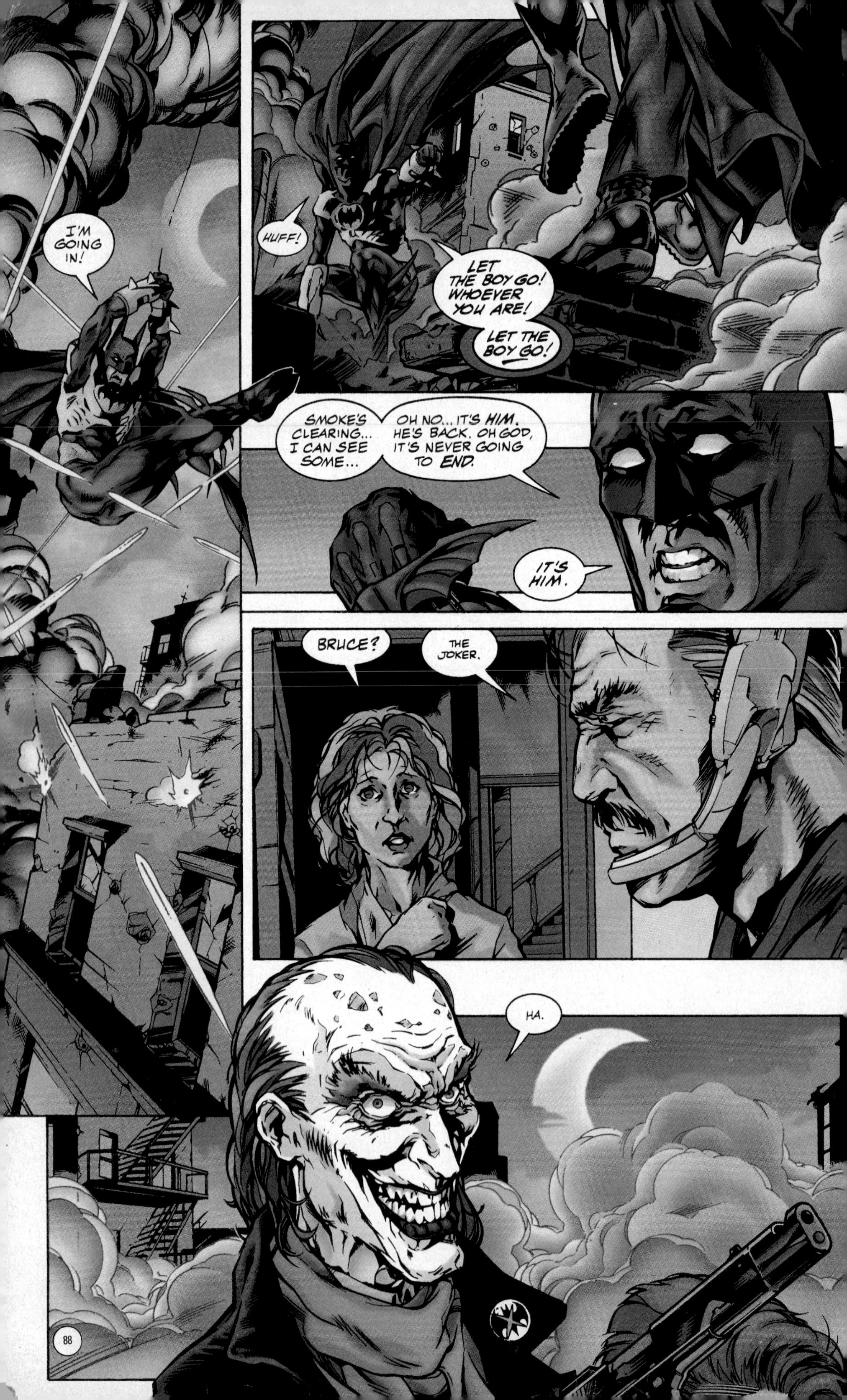
I'M GOING IN!
HUFF!
LET THE BOY GO! WHOEVER YOU ARE!
LET THE BOY GO!
SMOKE'S CLEARING... I CAN SEE SOME...
OH NO... IT'S HIM. HE'S BACK. OH GOD, IT'S NEVER GOING TO END.
IT'S HIM.
BRUCE?
THE JOKER.
HA.

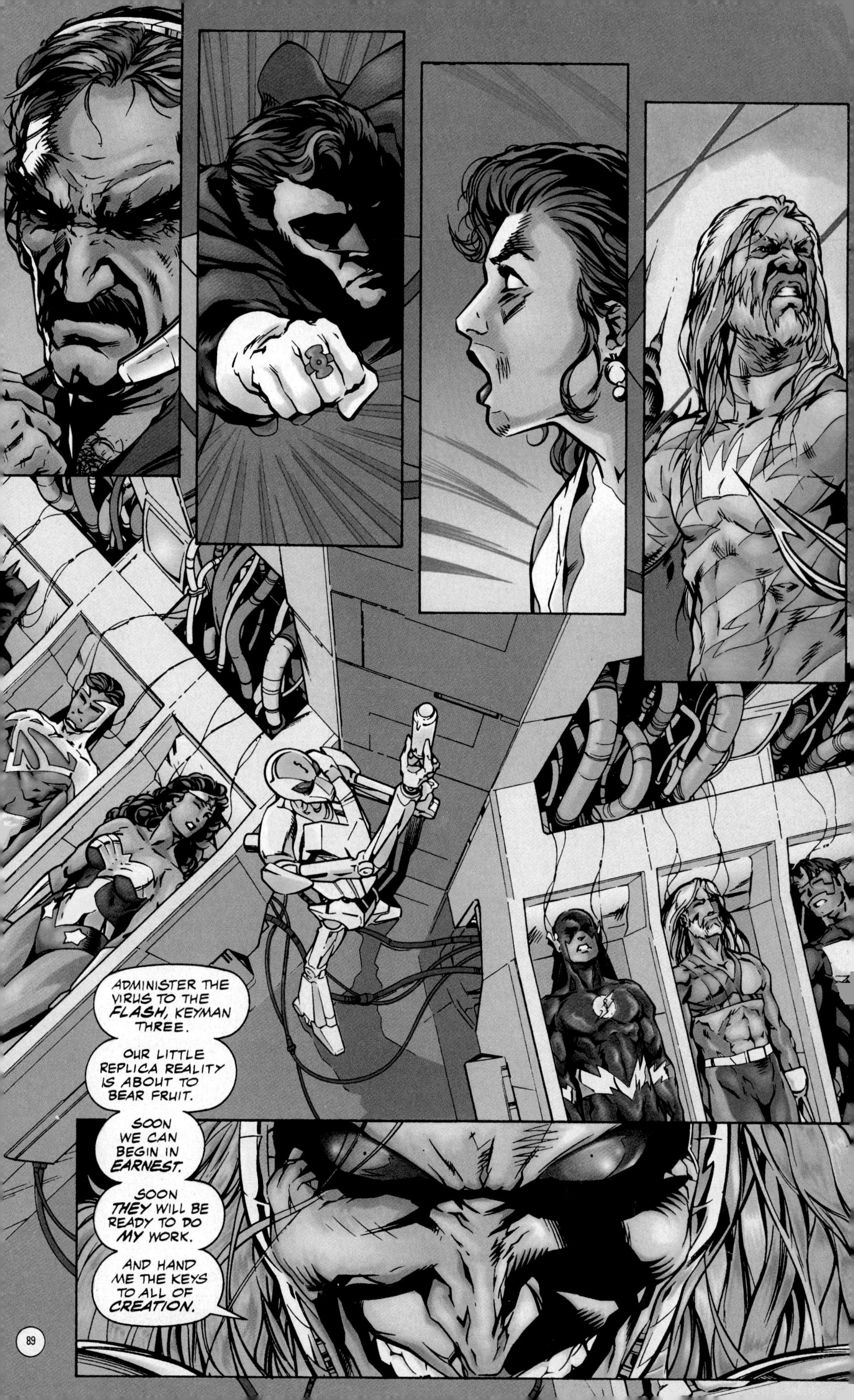
ADMINISTER THE VIRUS TO THE FLASH, KEYMAN THREE.
OUR LITTLE REPLICA REALITY IS ABOUT TO BEAR FRUIT.
SOON WE CAN BEGIN IN EARNEST.
SOON THEY WILL BE READY TO DO MY WORK.
AND HAND ME THE KEYS TO ALL OF CREATION.

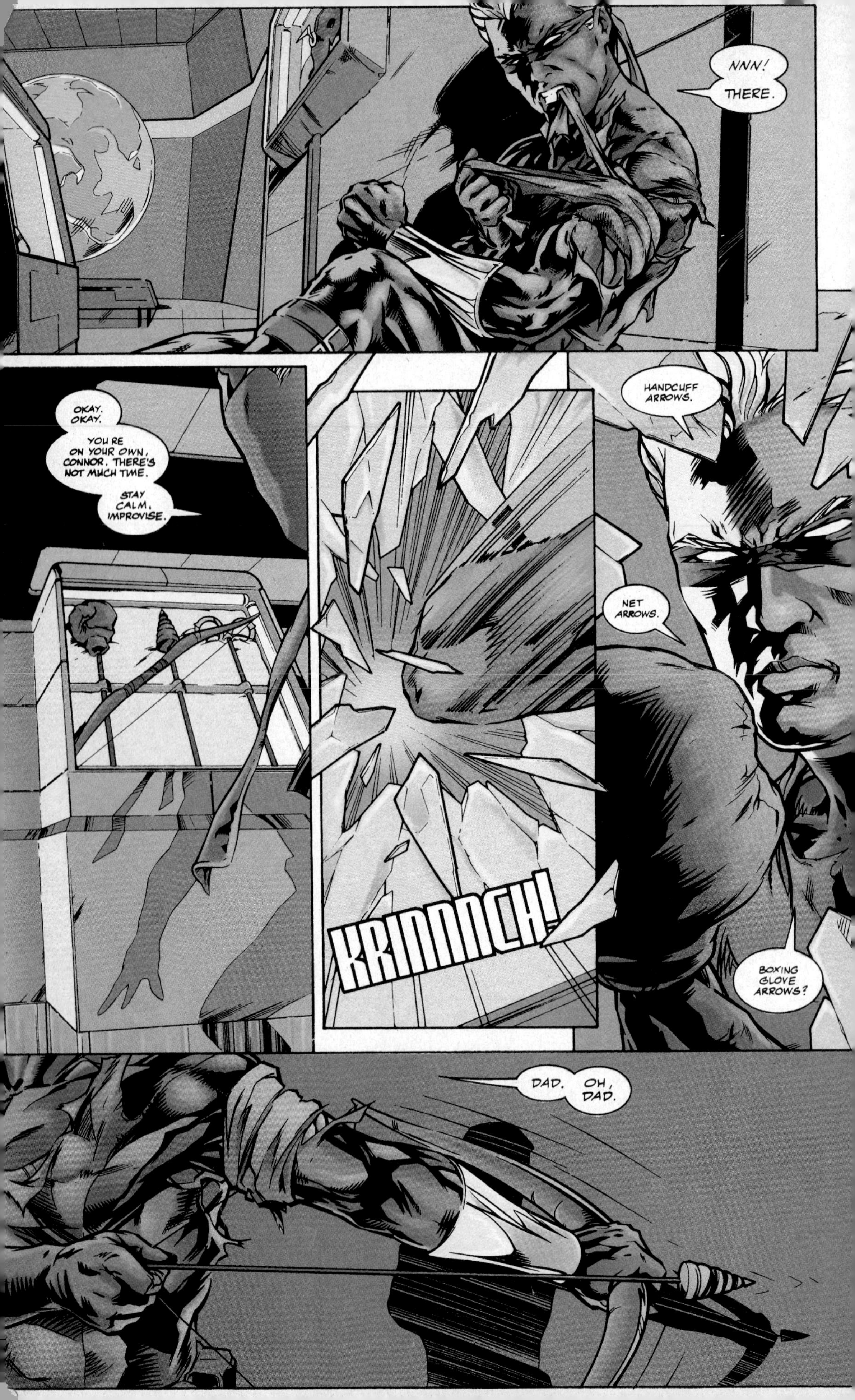
NNN!
THERE.
OKAY. OKAY.
YOU'RE ON YOUR OWN, CONNOR. THERE'S NOT MUCH TIME.
STAY CALM. IMPROVISE.
KRINNNCH!
HANDCUFF ARROWS.
NET ARROWS.
BOXING GLOVE ARROWS?
DAD. OH, DAD.

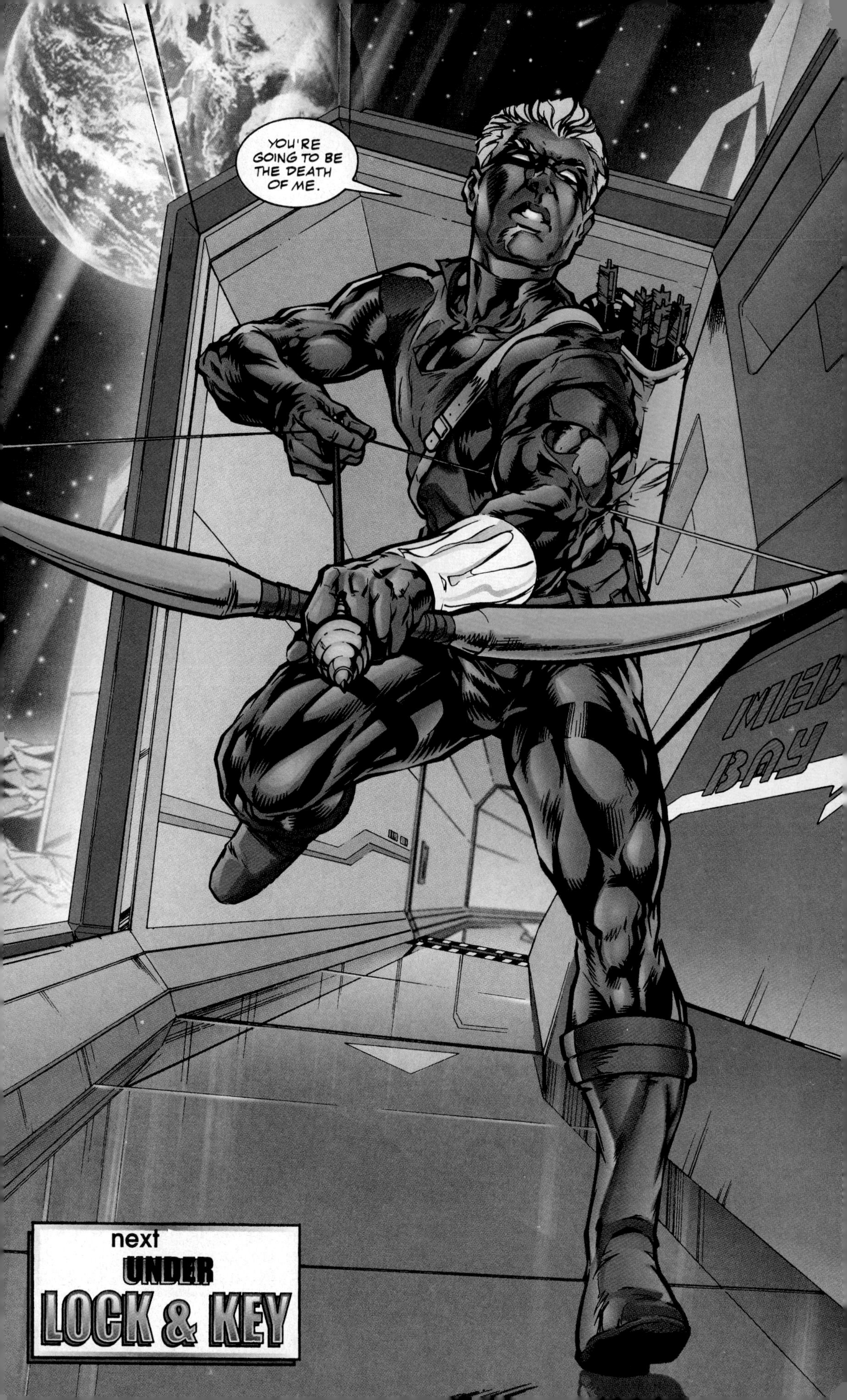
YOU'RE GOING TO BE THE DEATH OF ME.
MED BAY
next
UNDER
LOCK & KEY

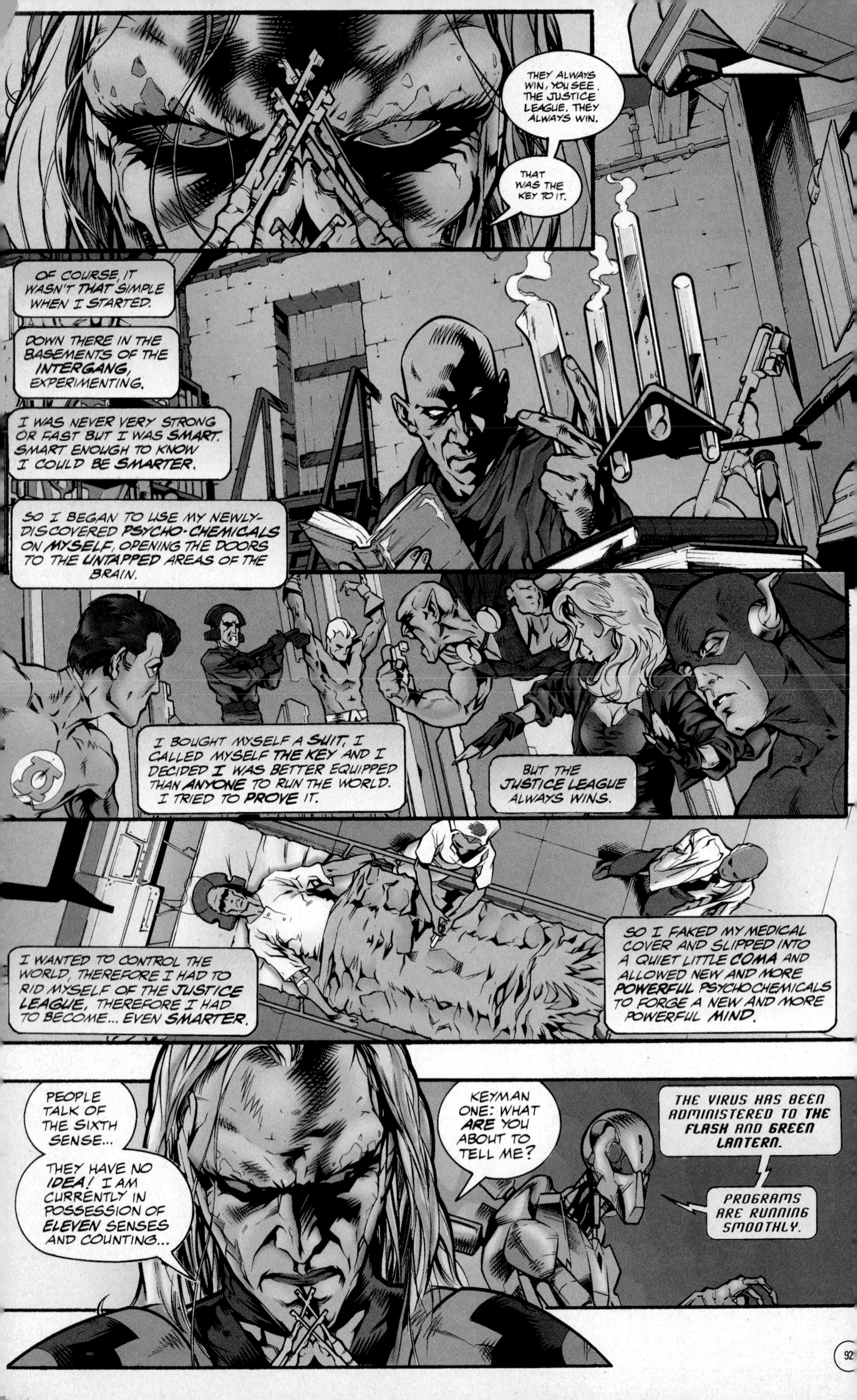
THEY ALWAYS WIN, YOU SEE. THE JUSTICE LEAGUE. THEY ALWAYS WIN.
THAT WAS THE KEY TO IT.
OF COURSE, IT WASN'T THAT SIMPLE WHEN I STARTED.
DOWN THERE IN THE BASEMENTS OF THE INTERGANG, EXPERIMENTING.
I WAS NEVER VERY STRONG OR FAST BUT I WAS SMART. SMART ENOUGH TO KNOW I COULD BE SMARTER.
SO I BEGAN TO USE MY NEWLY-DISCOVERED PSYCHO-CHEMICALS ON MYSELF, OPENING THE DOORS TO THE UNTAPPED AREAS OF THE BRAIN.
I BOUGHT MYSELF A SUIT, I CALLED MYSELF THE KEY AND I DECIDED I WAS BETTER EQUIPPED THAN ANYONE TO RUN THE WORLD. I TRIED TO PROVE IT.
BUT THE JUSTICE LEAGUE ALWAYS WINS.
I WANTED TO CONTROL THE WORLD, THEREFORE I HAD TO RID MYSELF OF THE JUSTICE LEAGUE, THEREFORE I HAD TO BECOME... EVEN SMARTER.
SO I FAKED MY MEDICAL COVER AND SLIPPED INTO A QUIET LITTLE COMA AND ALLOWED NEW AND MORE POWERFUL PSYCHOCHEMICALS TO FORGE A NEW AND MORE POWERFUL MIND.
PEOPLE TALK OF THE SIXTH SENSE...
THEY HAVE NO IDEA! I AM CURRENTLY IN POSSESSION OF ELEVEN SENSES AND COUNTING...
KEYMAN ONE: WHAT ARE YOU ABOUT TO TELL ME?
THE VIRUS HAS BEEN ADMINISTERED TO THE FLASH AND GREEN LANTERN.
PROGRAMS ARE RUNNING SMOOTHLY.

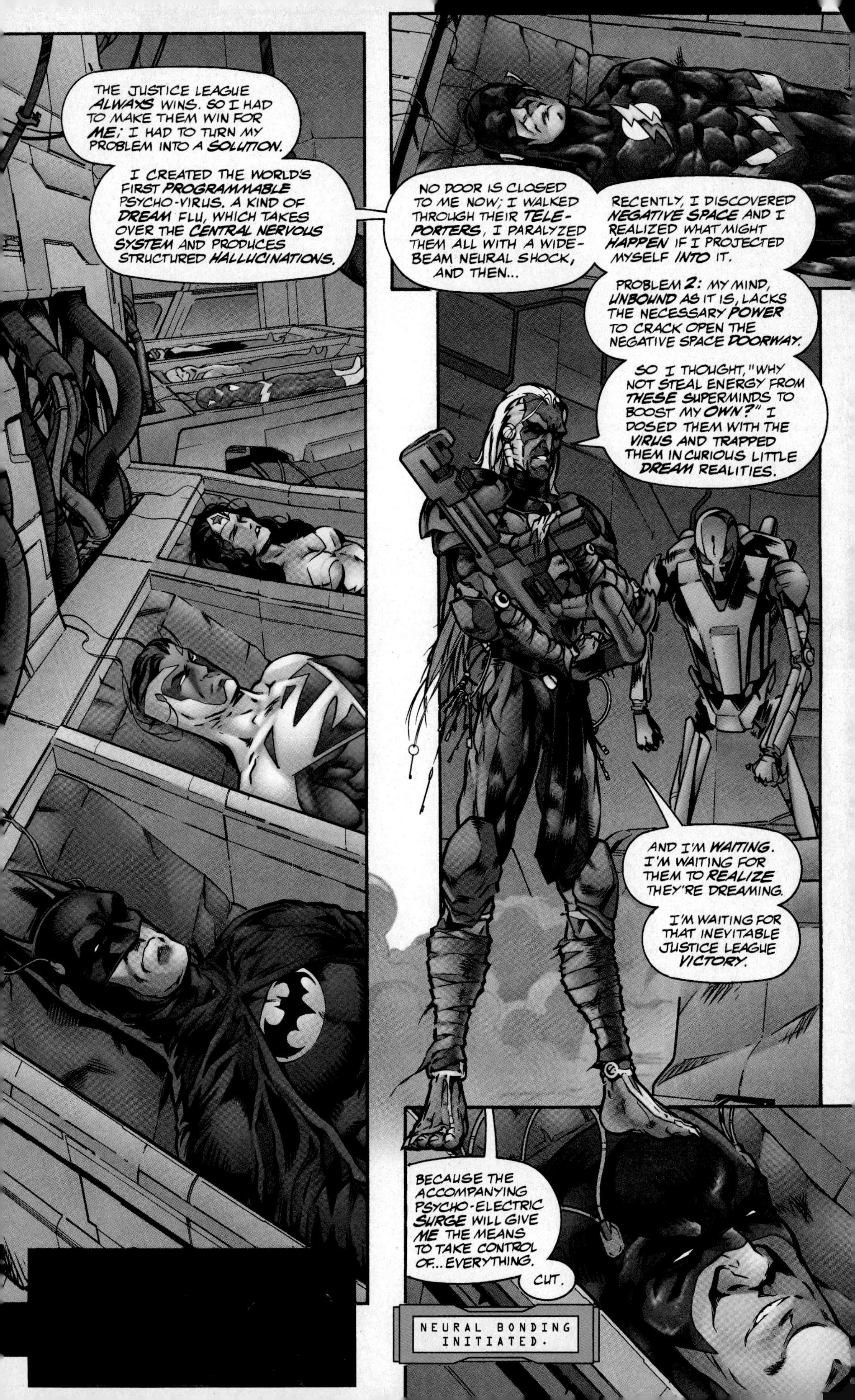

THE JUSTICE LEAGUE ALWAYS WINS. SO I HAD TO MAKE THEM WIN FOR ME; I HAD TO TURN MY PROBLEM INTO A SOLUTION.
I CREATED THE WORLD'S FIRST PROGRAMMABLE PSYCHO-VIRUS. A KIND OF DREAM FLU, WHICH TAKES OVER THE CENTRAL NERVOUS SYSTEM AND PRODUCES STRUCTURED HALLUCINATIONS.
NO DOOR IS CLOSED TO ME NOW; I WALKED THROUGH THEIR TELE-PORTERS, I PARALYZED THEM ALL WITH A WIDE-BEAM NEURAL SHOCK, AND THEN...
RECENTLY, I DISCOVERED NEGATIVE SPACE AND I REALIZED WHAT MIGHT HAPPEN IF I PROJECTED MYSELF INTO IT.
PROBLEM 2: MY MIND, UNBOUND AS IT IS, LACKS THE NECESSARY POWER TO CRACK OPEN THE NEGATIVE SPACE DOORWAY.
SO I THOUGHT, "WHY NOT STEAL ENERGY FROM THESE SUPERMINDS TO BOOST MY OWN?" I DOSED THEM WITH THE VIRUS AND TRAPPED THEM IN CURIOUS LITTLE DREAM REALITIES.
AND I'M WAITING. I'M WAITING FOR THEM TO REALIZE THEY'RE DREAMING.
I'M WAITING FOR THAT INEVITABLE JUSTICE LEAGUE VICTORY.
BECAUSE THE ACCOMPANYING PSYCHO-ELECTRIC SURGE WILL GIVE ME THE MEANS TO TAKE CONTROL OF... EVERYTHING.
CUT.
NEURAL BONDING INITIATED.

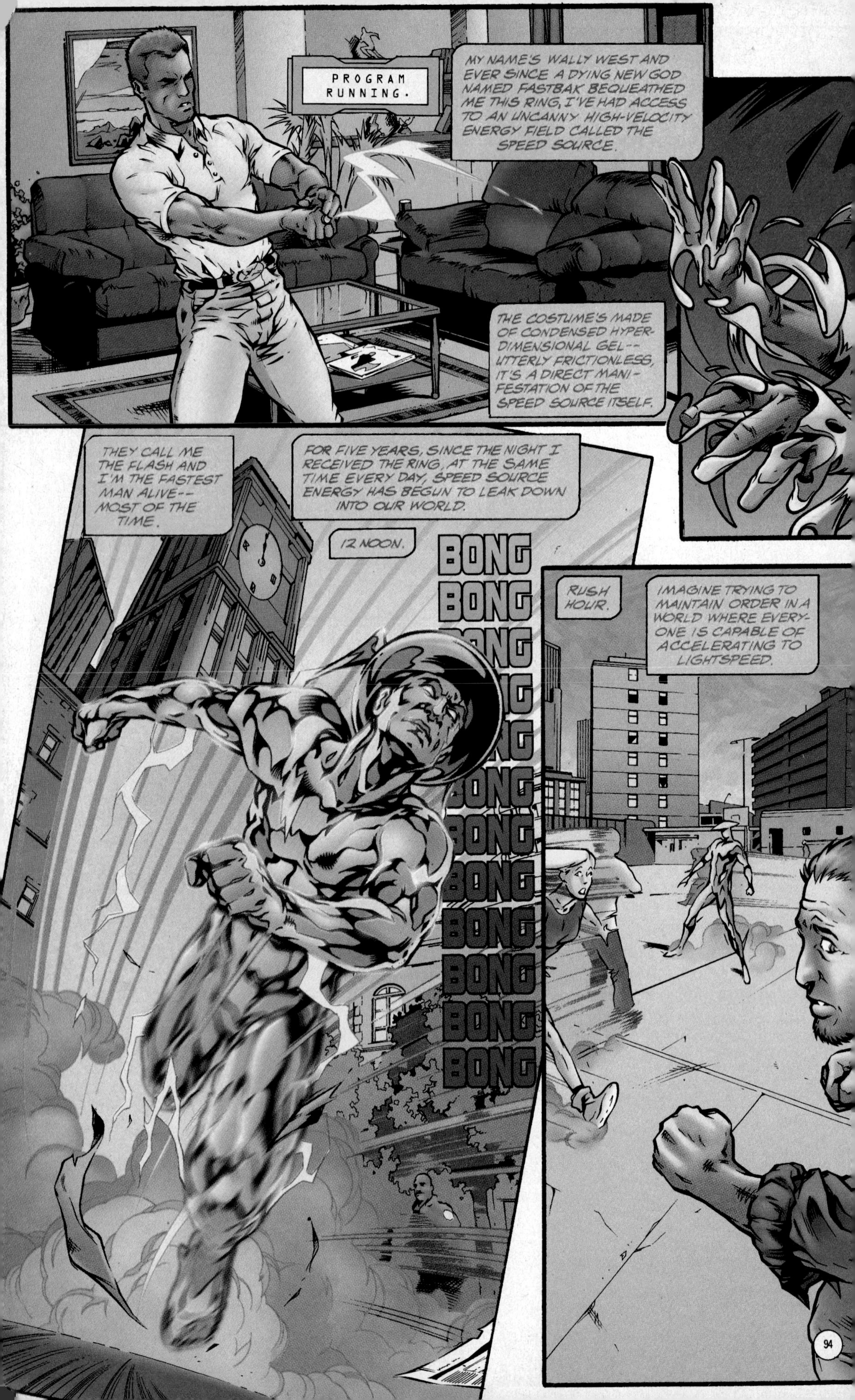
PROGRAM RUNNING.
MY NAME'S WALLY WEST AND EVER SINCE A DYING NEW GOD NAMED FASTBAK BEQUEATHED ME THIS RING, I'VE HAD ACCESS TO AN UNCANNY HIGH-VELOCITY ENERGY FIELD CALLED THE SPEED SOURCE.
THE COSTUME'S MADE OF CONDENSED HYPER-DIMENSIONAL GEL-- UTTERLY FRICTIONLESS, IT'S A DIRECT MANI-FESTATION OF THE SPEED SOURCE ITSELF.
THEY CALL ME THE FLASH AND I'M THE FASTEST MAN ALIVE-- MOST OF THE TIME.
FOR FIVE YEARS, SINCE THE NIGHT I RECEIVED THE RING, AT THE SAME TIME EVERY DAY, SPEED SOURCE ENERGY HAS BEGUN TO LEAK DOWN INTO OUR WORLD.
12 NOON.
BONG
BONG
BONG
BONG
BONG
BONG
BONG
BONG
BONG
BONG
RUSH HOUR.
IMAGINE TRYING TO MAINTAIN ORDER IN A WORLD WHERE EVERY-ONE IS CAPABLE OF ACCELERATING TO LIGHTSPEED.

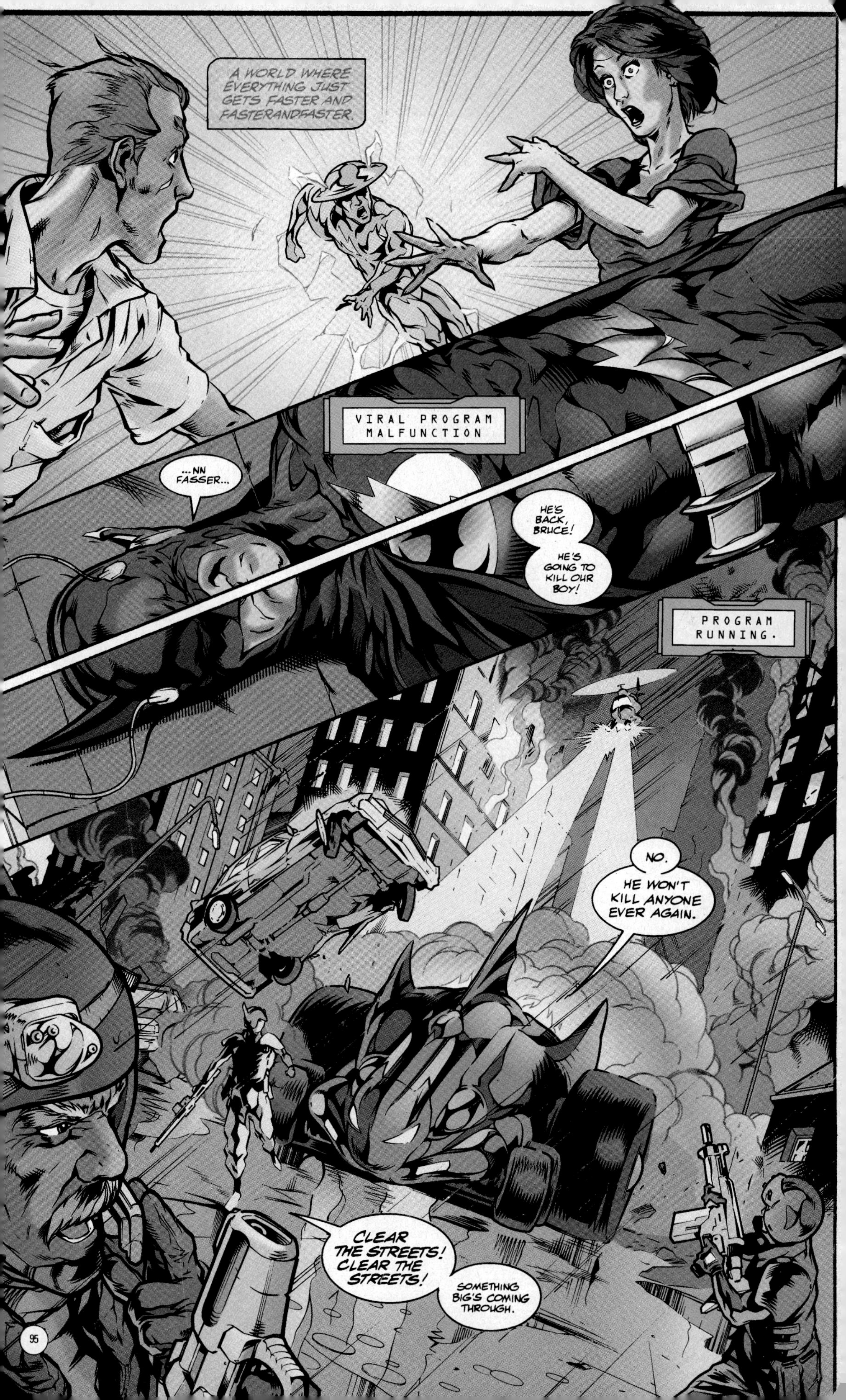
A WORLD WHERE EVERYTHING JUST GETS FASTER AND FASTERANDFASTER.
VIRAL PROGRAM MALFUNCTION
...NN FASSER...
HE'S BACK, BRUCE!
HE'S GOING TO KILL OUR BOY!
PROGRAM RUNNING.
NO.
HE WON'T KILL ANYONE EVER AGAIN.
CLEAR THE STREETS! CLEAR THE STREETS!
SOMETHING BIG'S COMING THROUGH.

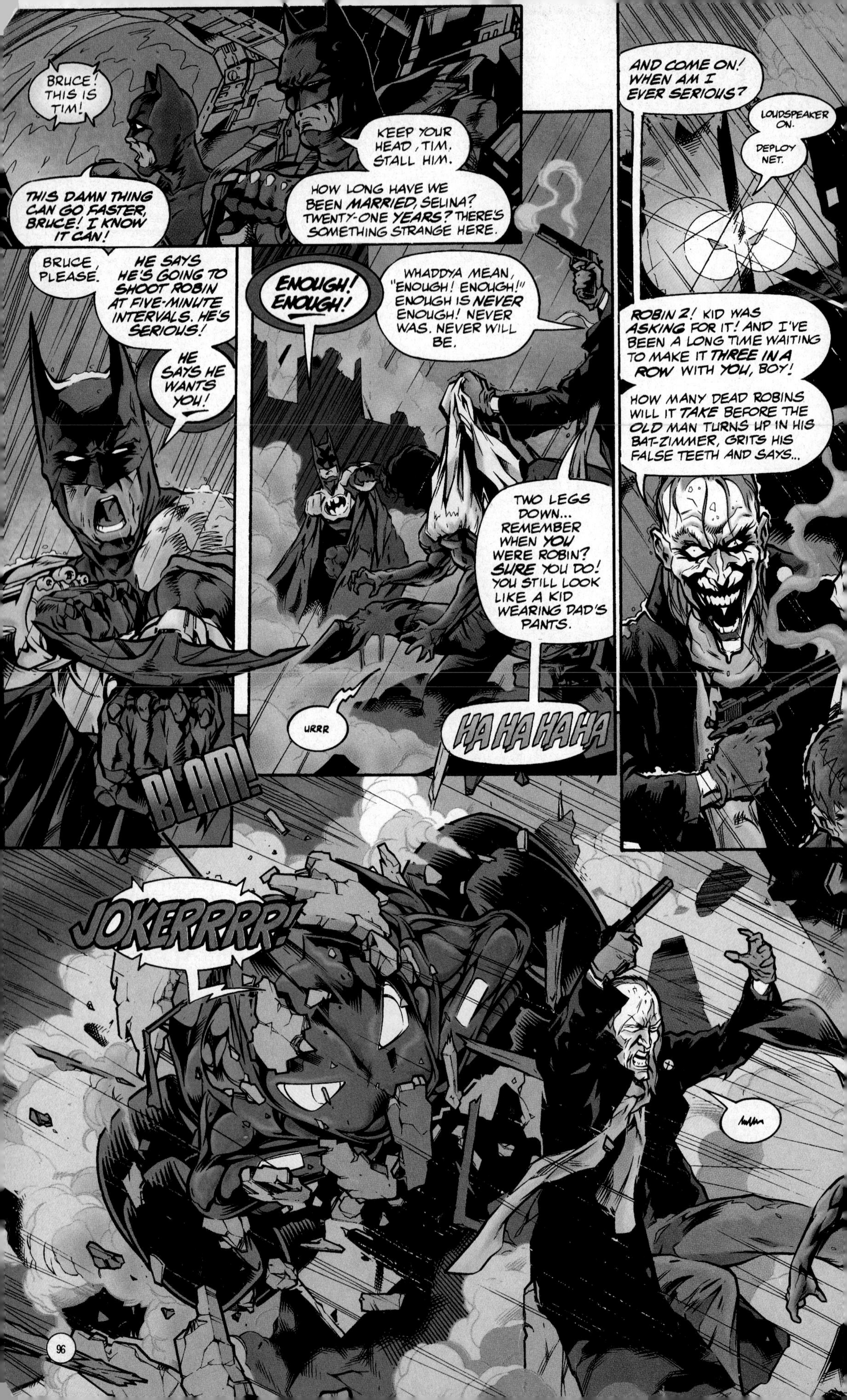

BRUCE! THIS IS TIM!
THIS DAMN THING CAN GO FASTER, BRUCE! I KNOW IT CAN!
KEEP YOUR HEAD, TIM. STALL HIM.
HOW LONG HAVE WE BEEN MARRIED, SELINA? TWENTY-ONE YEARS? THERE'S SOMETHING STRANGE HERE.
AND COME ON! WHEN AM I EVER SERIOUS?
LOUDSPEAKER ON.
DEPLOY NET.
BRUCE PLEASE.
HE SAYS HE'S GOING TO SHOOT ROBIN AT FIVE-MINUTE INTERVALS. HE'S SERIOUS!
HE SAYS HE WANTS YOU!
BLAM!
ENOUGH! ENOUGH!
WHADDYA MEAN, "ENOUGH! ENOUGH!" ENOUGH IS NEVER ENOUGH! NEVER WAS. NEVER WILL BE.
TWO LEGS DOWN... REMEMBER WHEN YOU WERE ROBIN? SURE YOU DO! YOU STILL LOOK LIKE A KID WEARING DAD'S PANTS.
URRR
HA HA HA HA HA
ROBIN 2! KID WAS ASKING FOR IT! AND I'VE BEEN A LONG TIME WAITING TO MAKE IT THREE IN A ROW WITH YOU, BOY!
HOW MANY DEAD ROBINS WILL IT TAKE BEFORE THE OLD MAN TURNS UP IN HIS BAT-ZIMMER, GRITS HIS FALSE TEETH AND SAYS...
JOKERRRR!

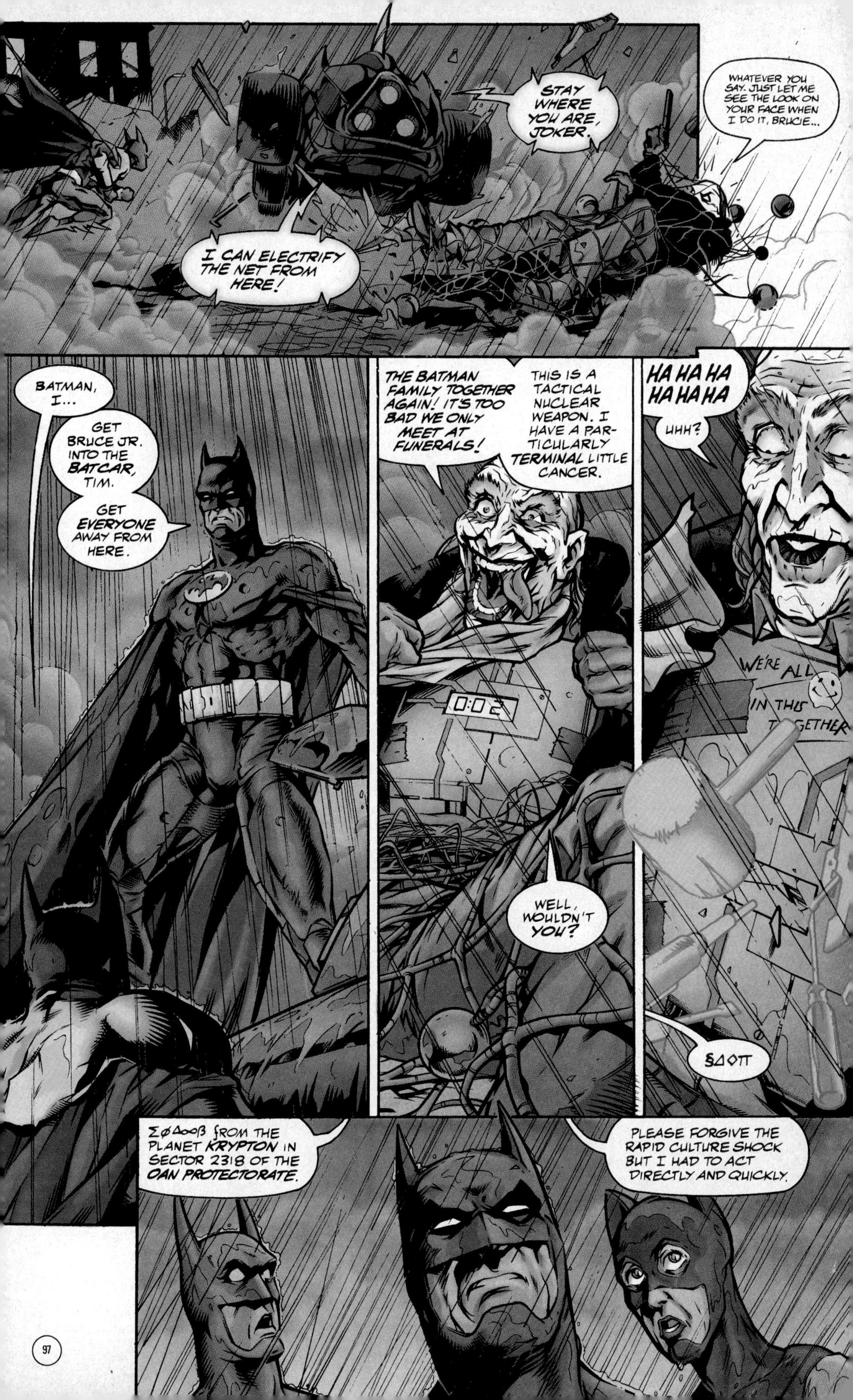

STAY WHERE YOU ARE, JOKER.
I CAN ELECTRIFY THE NET FROM HERE!
WHATEVER YOU SAY. JUST LET ME SEE THE LOOK ON YOUR FACE WHEN I DO IT, BRUCIE...
BATMAN, I...
GET BRUCE JR. INTO THE BATCAR, TIM.
GET EVERYONE AWAY FROM HERE.
THE BATMAN FAMILY TOGETHER AGAIN! IT'S TOO BAD WE ONLY MEET AT FUNERALS!
THIS IS A TACTICAL NUCLEAR WEAPON. I HAVE A PARTICULARLY TERMINAL LITTLE CANCER.
0:02
WELL, WOULDN'T YOU?
HA HA HA HA HA HA
UHH?
WE'RE ALL IN THIS TOGETHER
§ΔΟΠ
ΣØΔοοβ FROM THE PLANET KRYPTON IN SECTOR 2318 OF THE OAN PROTECTORATE.
PLEASE FORGIVE THE RAPID CULTURE SHOCK BUT I HAD TO ACT DIRECTLY AND QUICKLY.

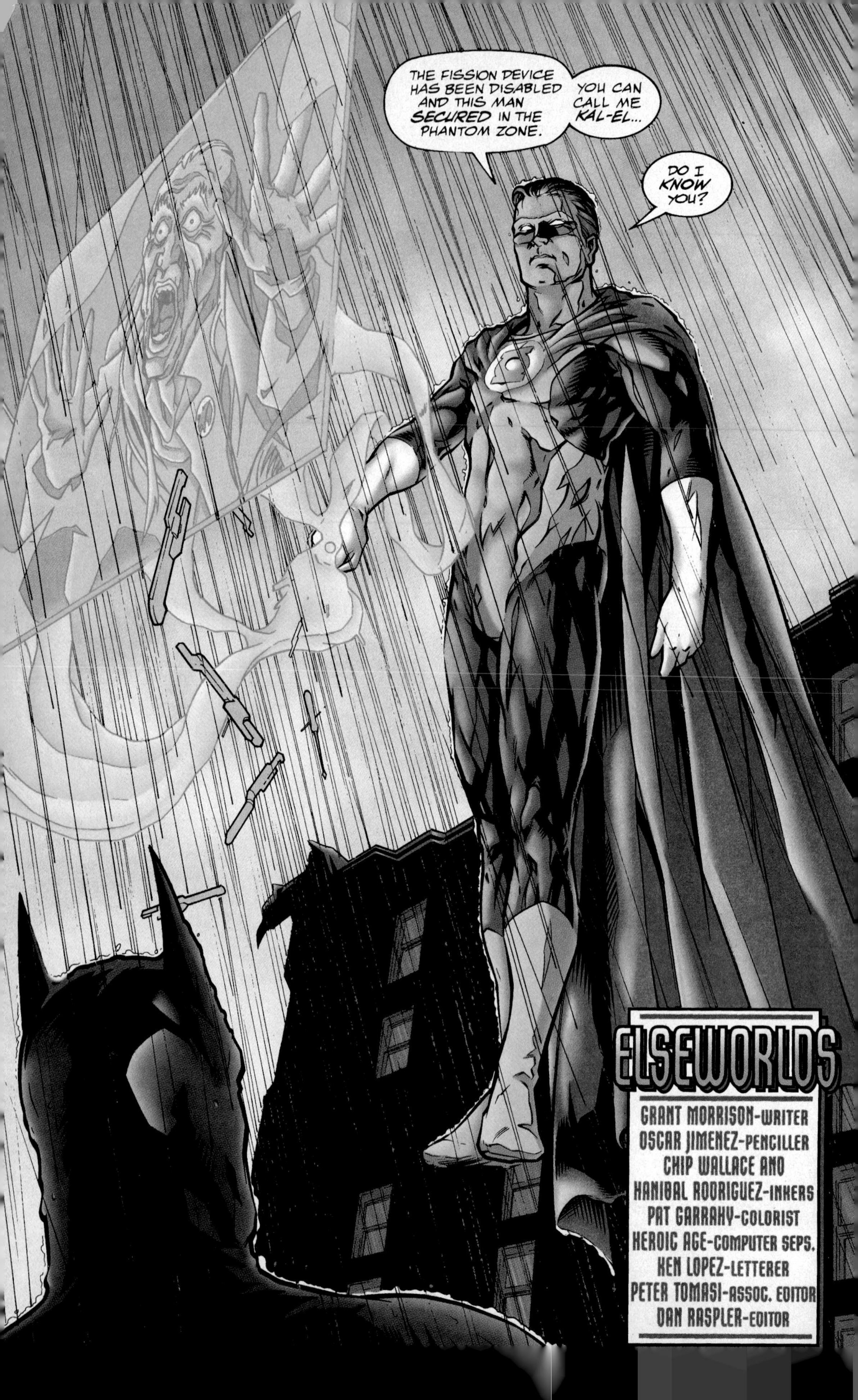
THE FISSION DEVICE HAS BEEN DISABLED AND THIS MAN SECURED IN THE PHANTOM ZONE.
YOU CAN CALL ME KAL-EL...
DO I KNOW YOU?
ELSEWORLDS
GRANT MORRISON-WRITER
OSCAR JIMENEZ-PENCILLER
CHIP WALLACE AND
HANIBAL RODRIGUEZ-INKERS
PAT GARRAHY-COLORIST
HEROIC AGE-COMPUTER SEPS.
KEN LOPEZ-LETTERER
PETER TOMASI-ASSOC. EDITOR
DAN RASPLER-EDITOR

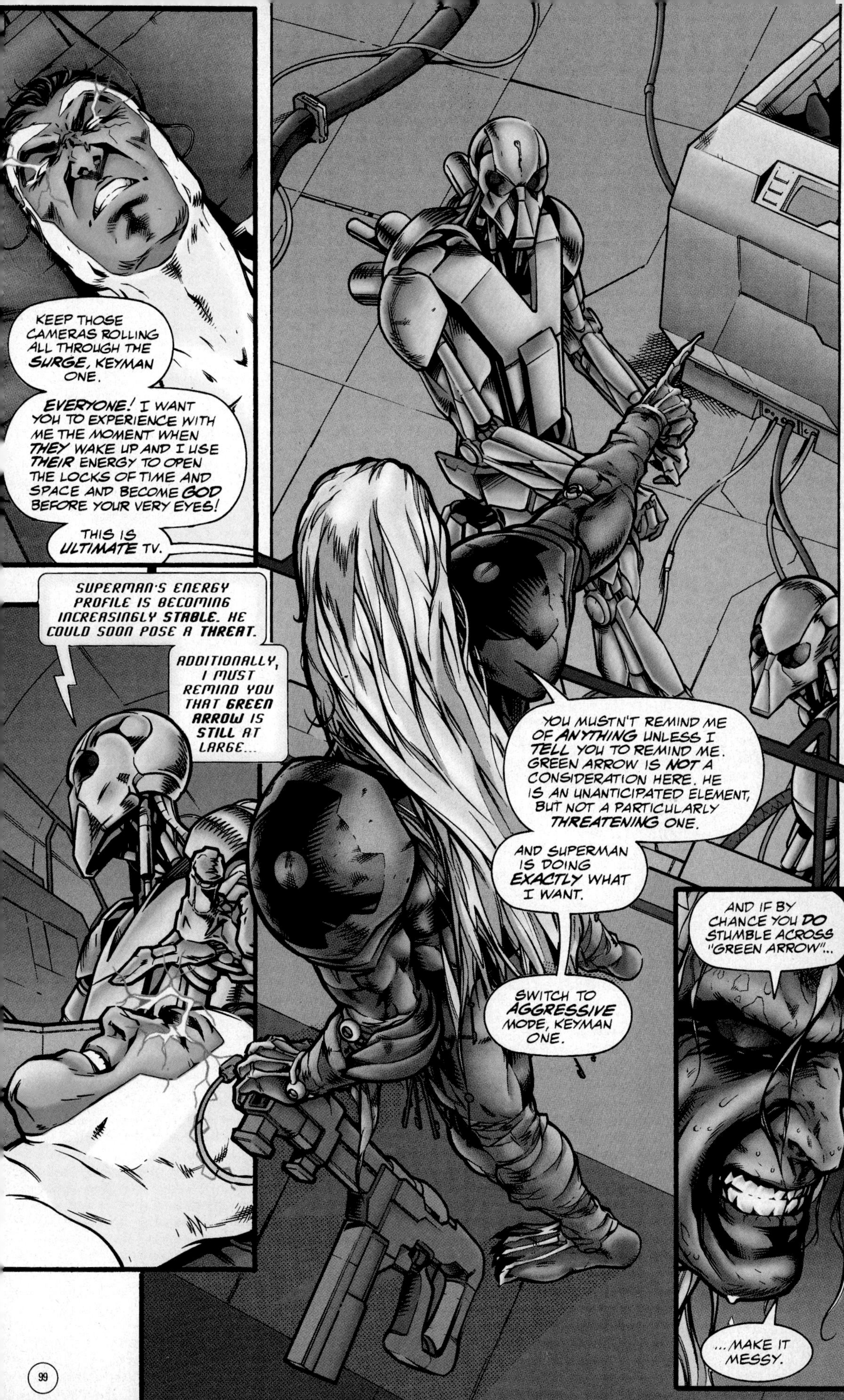

KEEP THOSE CAMERAS ROLLING ALL THROUGH THE SURGE, KEYMAN ONE.
EVERYONE! I WANT YOU TO EXPERIENCE WITH ME THE MOMENT WHEN THEY WAKE UP AND I USE THEIR ENERGY TO OPEN THE LOCKS OF TIME AND SPACE AND BECOME GOD BEFORE YOUR VERY EYES!
THIS IS ULTIMATE TV.
SUPERMAN'S ENERGY PROFILE IS BECOMING INCREASINGLY STABLE. HE COULD SOON POSE A THREAT.
ADDITIONALLY, I MUST REMIND YOU THAT GREEN ARROW IS STILL AT LARGE...
YOU MUSTN'T REMIND ME OF ANYTHING UNLESS I TELL YOU TO REMIND ME. GREEN ARROW IS NOT A CONSIDERATION HERE. HE IS AN UNANTICIPATED ELEMENT, BUT NOT A PARTICULARLY THREATENING ONE.
AND SUPERMAN IS DOING EXACTLY WHAT I WANT.
SWITCH TO AGGRESSIVE MODE, KEYMAN ONE.
AND IF BY CHANCE YOU DO STUMBLE ACROSS "GREEN ARROW"...
...MAKE IT MESSY.

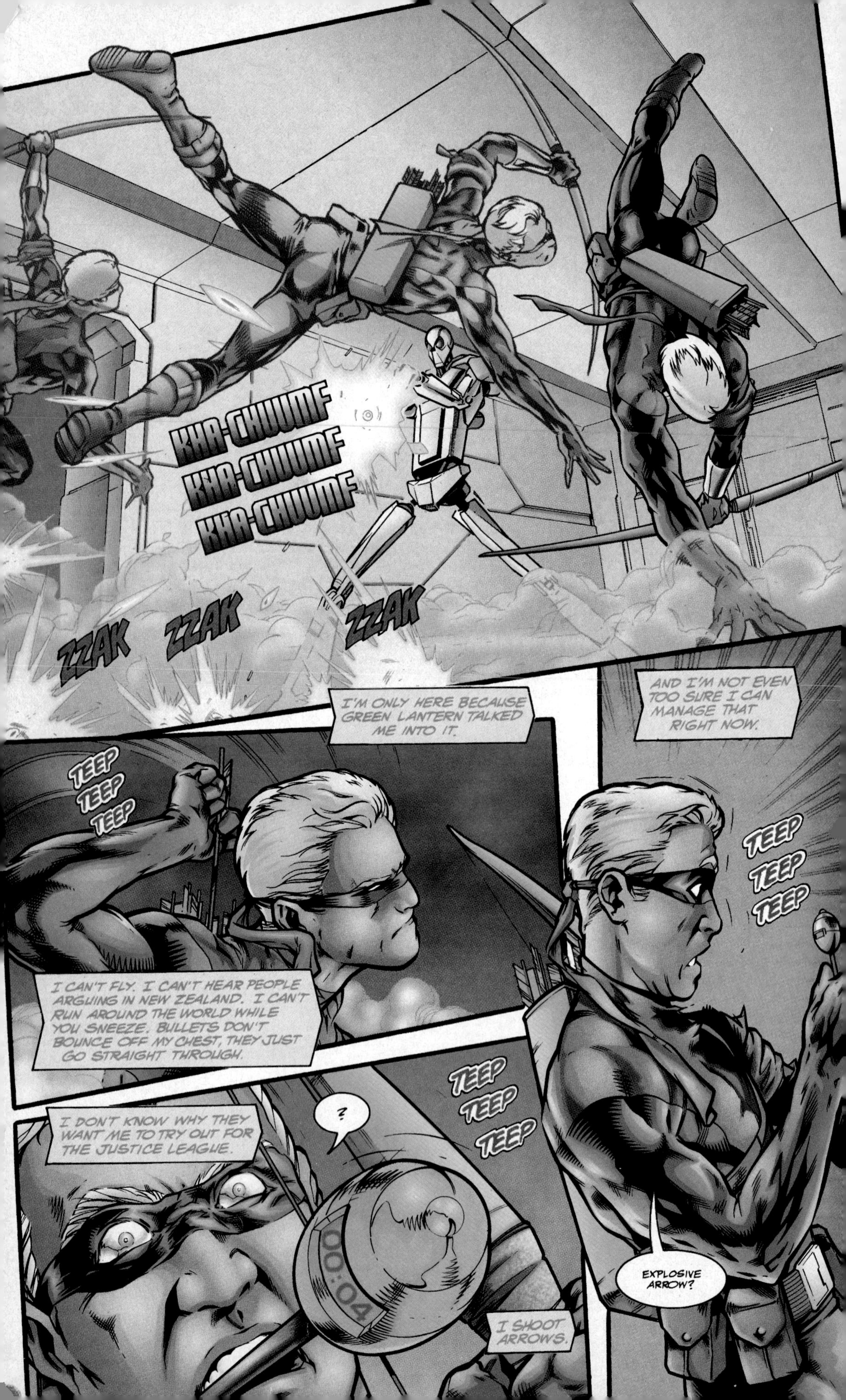
KHA-CHUUMF
KHA-CHUUMF
KHA-CHUUMF
ZZAK
ZZAK
ZZAK
I'M ONLY HERE BECAUSE GREEN LANTERN TALKED ME INTO IT.
AND I'M NOT EVEN TOO SURE I CAN MANAGE THAT RIGHT NOW.
TEEP TEEP TEEP
I CAN'T FLY. I CAN'T HEAR PEOPLE ARGUING IN NEW ZEALAND. I CAN'T RUN AROUND THE WORLD WHILE YOU SNEEZE. BULLETS DON'T BOUNCE OFF MY CHEST, THEY JUST GO STRAIGHT THROUGH.
TEEP TEEP TEEP
TEEP TEEP TEEP
I DON'T KNOW WHY THEY WANT ME TO TRY OUT FOR THE JUSTICE LEAGUE.
?
00:04
I SHOOT ARROWS.
EXPLOSIVE ARROW?

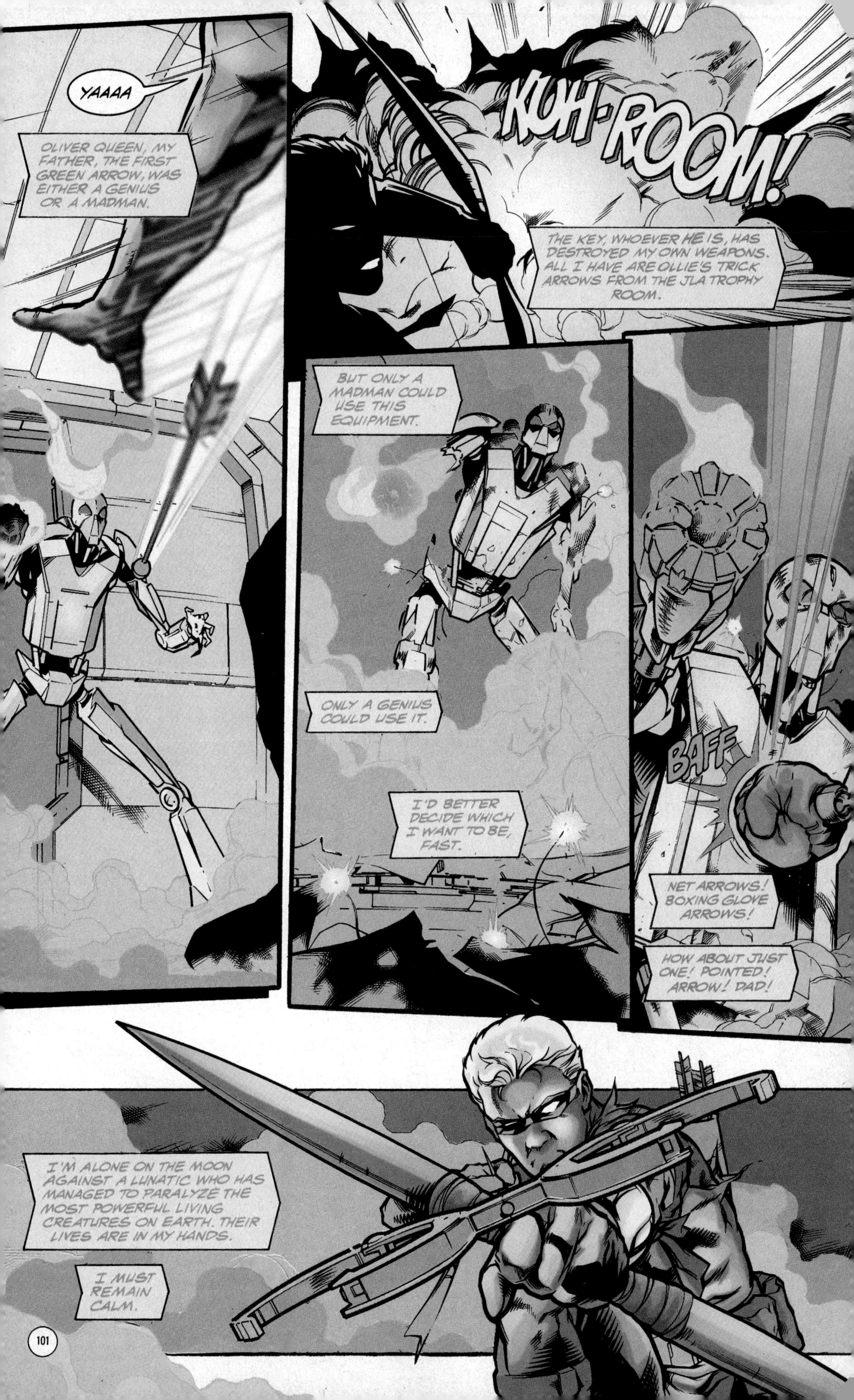
YAAAA
OLIVER QUEEN, MY FATHER, THE FIRST GREEN ARROW, WAS EITHER A GENIUS OR A MADMAN.
KUH-ROOM!
THE KEY, WHOEVER HE IS, HAS DESTROYED MY OWN WEAPONS. ALL I HAVE ARE OLLIE'S TRICK ARROWS FROM THE JLA TROPHY ROOM.
BUT ONLY A MADMAN COULD USE THIS EQUIPMENT.
ONLY A GENIUS COULD USE IT.
I'D BETTER DECIDE WHICH I WANT TO BE, FAST.
BAFF
NET ARROWS! BOXING GLOVE ARROWS!
HOW ABOUT JUST ONE! POINTED! ARROW! DAD!
I'M ALONE ON THE MOON AGAINST A LUNATIC WHO HAS MANAGED TO PARALYZE THE MOST POWERFUL LIVING CREATURES ON EARTH. THEIR LIVES ARE IN MY HANDS.
I MUST REMAIN CALM.

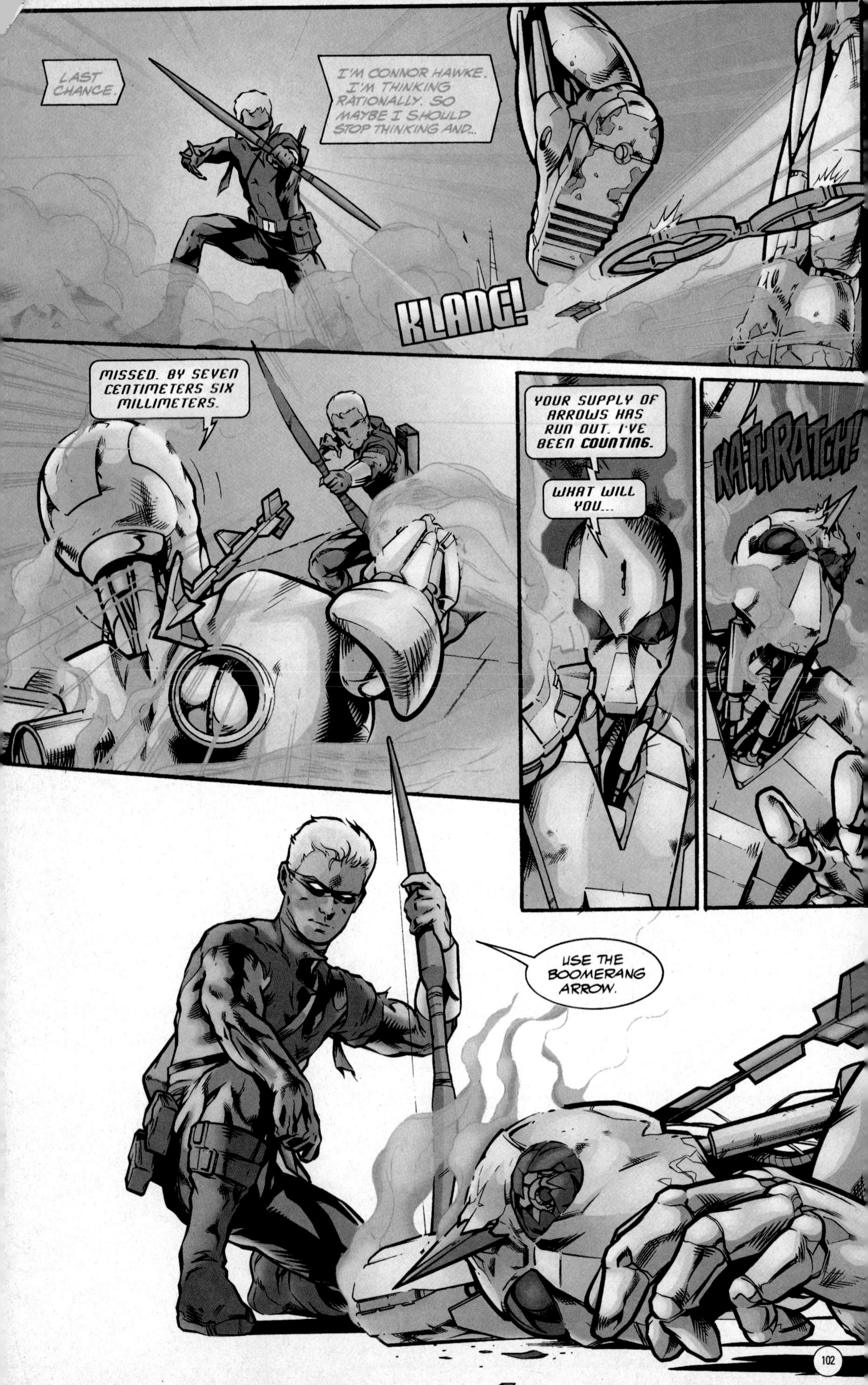
LAST CHANCE.
I'M CONNOR HAWKE. I'M THINKING RATIONALLY. SO MAYBE I SHOULD STOP THINKING AND...
KLANG!
MISSED. BY SEVEN CENTIMETERS SIX MILLIMETERS.
YOUR SUPPLY OF ARROWS HAS RUN OUT. I'VE BEEN COUNTING.
WHAT WILL YOU...
KA-THRATCH!
USE THE BOOMERANG ARROW.

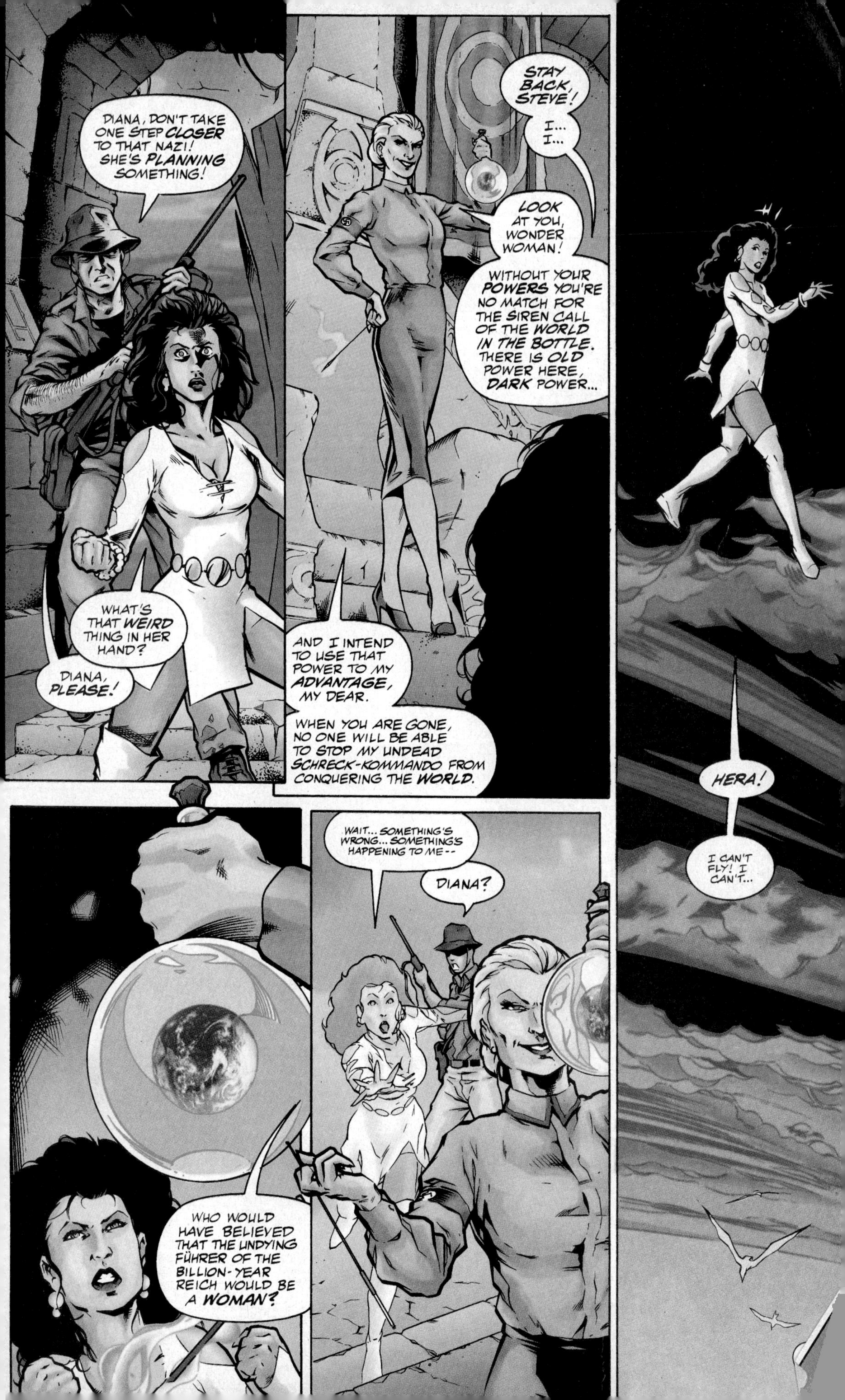
DIANA, DON'T TAKE ONE STEP CLOSER TO THAT NAZI! SHE'S PLANNING SOMETHING!
WHAT'S THAT WEIRD THING IN HER HAND?
DIANA, PLEASE!
STAY BACK, STEVE!
I... I...
LOOK AT YOU, WONDER WOMAN!
WITHOUT YOUR POWERS YOU'RE NO MATCH FOR THE SIREN CALL OF THE WORLD IN THE BOTTLE. THERE IS OLD POWER HERE, DARK POWER...
AND I INTEND TO USE THAT POWER TO MY ADVANTAGE, MY DEAR.
WHEN YOU ARE GONE, NO ONE WILL BE ABLE TO STOP MY UNDEAD SCHRECK-KOMMANDO FROM CONQUERING THE WORLD.
HERA!
I CAN'T FLY! I CAN'T...
WHO WOULD HAVE BELIEVED THAT THE UNDYING FÜHRER OF THE BILLION-YEAR REICH WOULD BE A WOMAN?
WAIT... SOMETHING'S WRONG... SOMETHING'S HAPPENING TO ME--
DIANA?

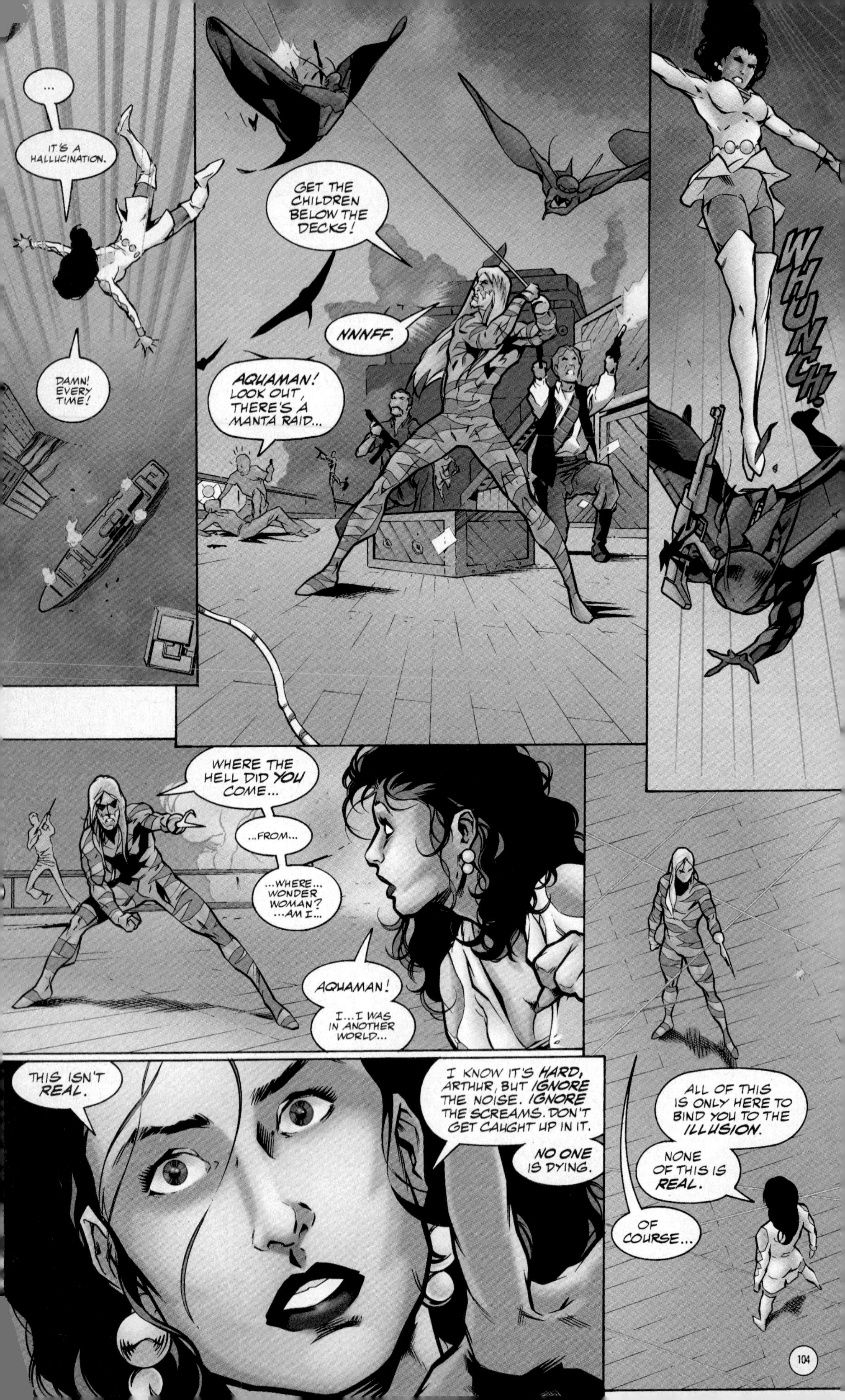
...
IT'S A HALLUCINATION.
DAMN! EVERY TIME!
GET THE CHILDREN BELOW THE DECKS!
NNNFF.
AQUAMAN! LOOK OUT, THERE'S A MANTA RAID...
WHUNCH!
WHERE THE HELL DID YOU COME...
...FROM...
...WHERE... WONDER WOMAN? ...AM I...
AQUAMAN!
I...I WAS IN ANOTHER WORLD...
THIS ISN'T REAL.
I KNOW IT'S HARD, ARTHUR, BUT IGNORE THE NOISE. IGNORE THE SCREAMS. DON'T GET CAUGHT UP IN IT.
NO ONE IS DYING.
ALL OF THIS IS ONLY HERE TO BIND YOU TO THE ILLUSION.
NONE OF THIS IS REAL.
OF COURSE...

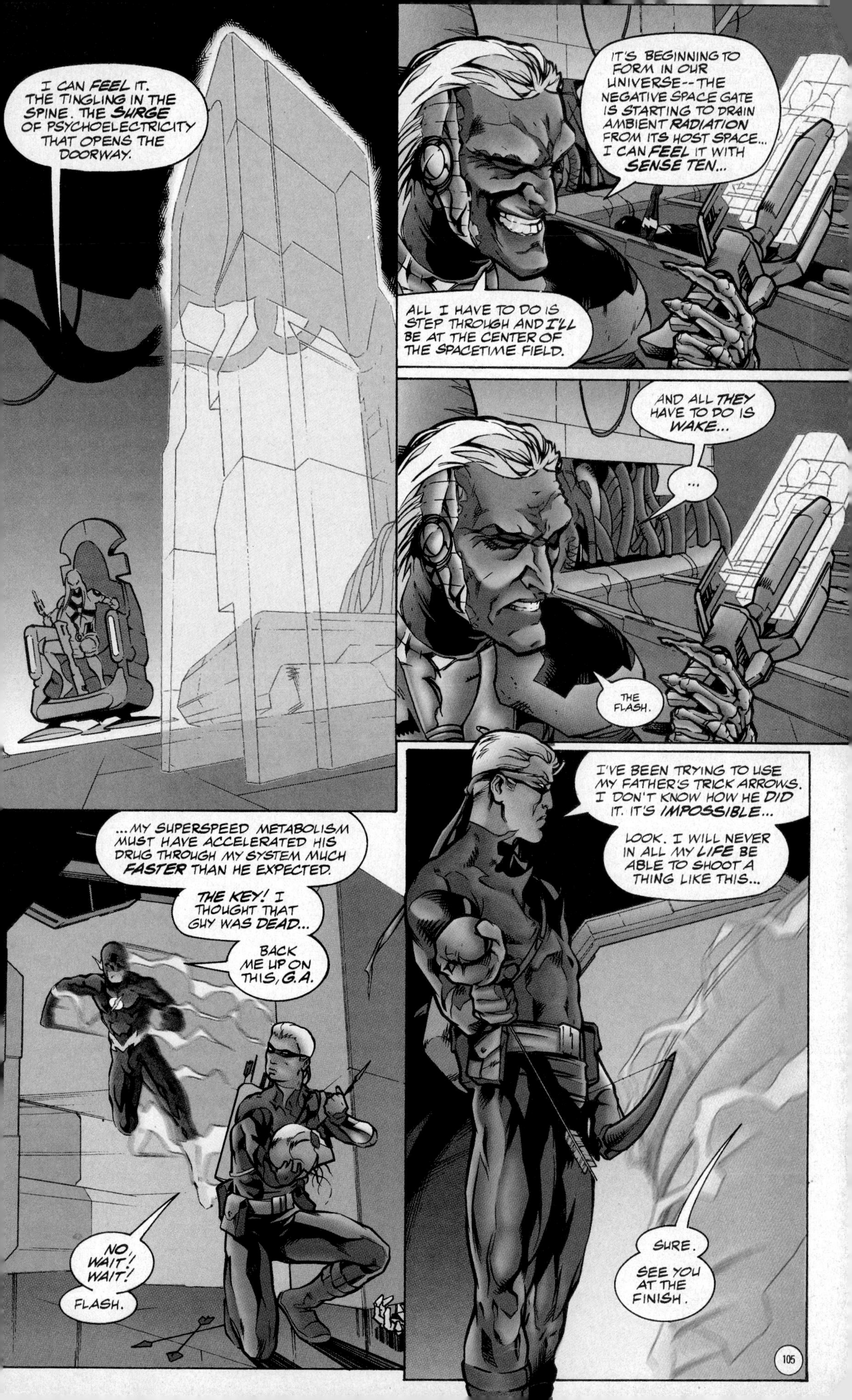

I CAN FEEL IT. THE TINGLING IN THE SPINE. THE SURGE OF PSYCHOELECTRICITY THAT OPENS THE DOORWAY.
IT'S BEGINNING TO FORM IN OUR UNIVERSE--THE NEGATIVE SPACE GATE IS STARTING TO DRAIN AMBIENT RADIATION FROM ITS HOST SPACE... I CAN FEEL IT WITH SENSE TEN...
ALL I HAVE TO DO IS STEP THROUGH AND I'LL BE AT THE CENTER OF THE SPACETIME FIELD.
AND ALL THEY HAVE TO DO IS WAKE...
...
THE FLASH.
...MY SUPERSPEED METABOLISM MUST HAVE ACCELERATED HIS DRUG THROUGH MY SYSTEM MUCH FASTER THAN HE EXPECTED.
THE KEY! I THOUGHT THAT GUY WAS DEAD...
BACK ME UP ON THIS, G.A.
NO, WAIT! WAIT!
FLASH.
I'VE BEEN TRYING TO USE MY FATHER'S TRICK ARROWS. I DON'T KNOW HOW HE DID IT. IT'S IMPOSSIBLE...
LOOK. I WILL NEVER IN ALL MY LIFE BE ABLE TO SHOOT A THING LIKE THIS...
SURE.
SEE YOU AT THE FINISH.

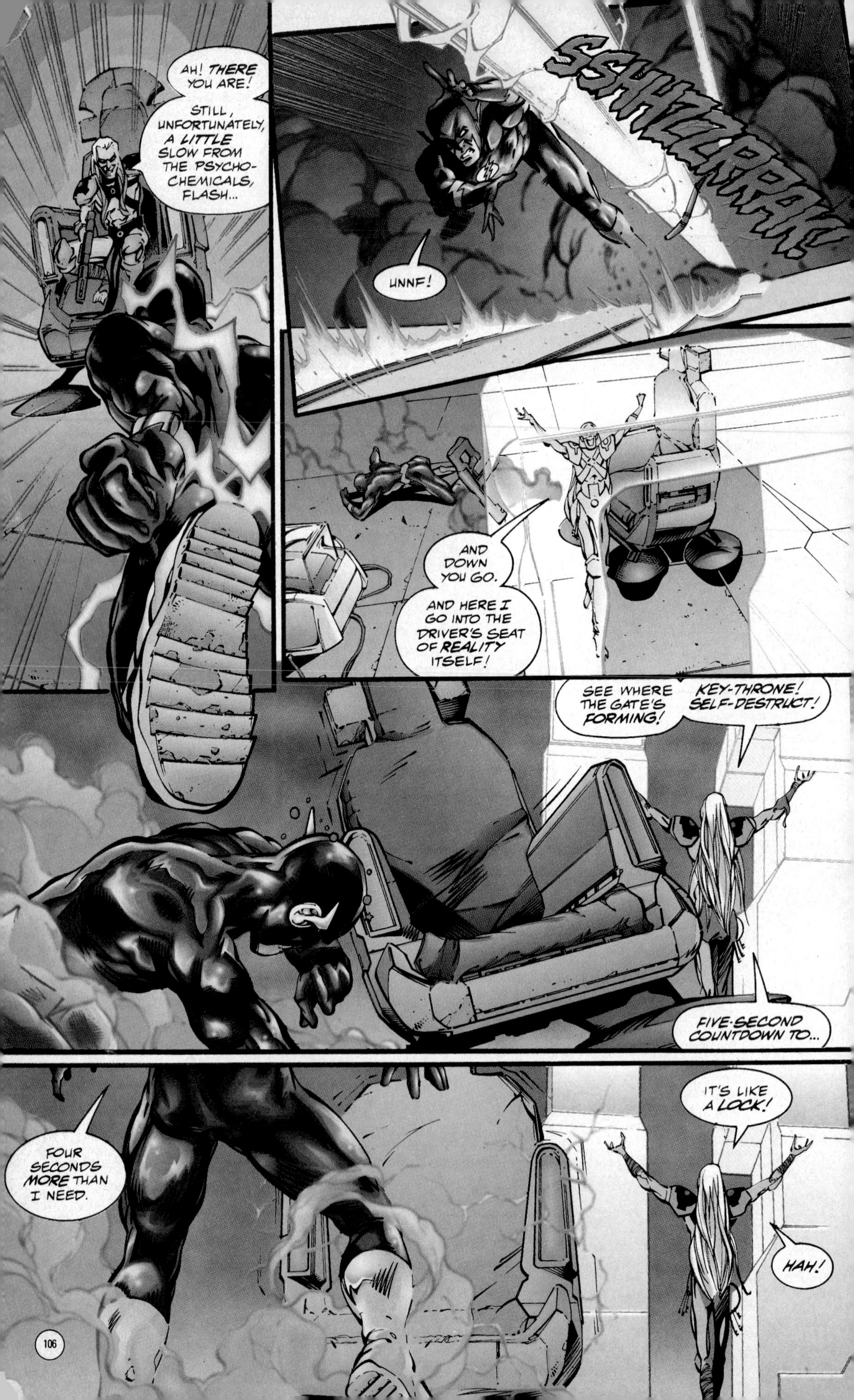
AH! THERE YOU ARE!
STILL, UNFORTUNATELY, A LITTLE SLOW FROM THE PSYCHO-CHEMICALS, FLASH...
SSHHZZRRAK!
UNNF!
AND DOWN YOU GO.
AND HERE I GO INTO THE DRIVER'S SEAT OF REALITY ITSELF!
SEE WHERE THE GATE'S FORMING!
KEY-THRONE! SELF-DESTRUCT!
FIVE-SECOND COUNTDOWN TO...
IT'S LIKE A LOCK!
FOUR SECONDS MORE THAN I NEED.
HAH!

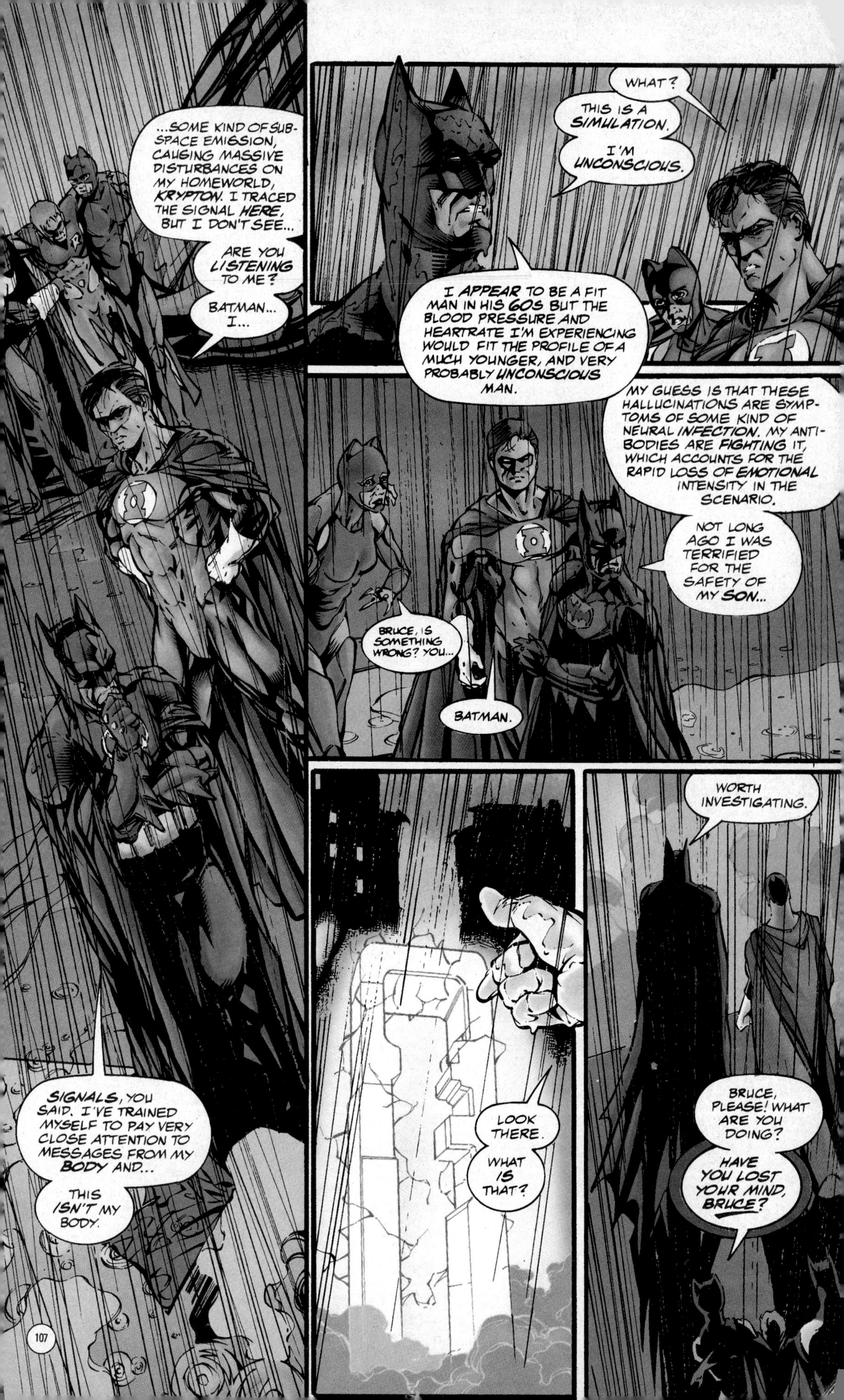
...SOME KIND OF SUB-SPACE EMISSION, CAUSING MASSIVE DISTURBANCES ON MY HOMEWORLD, KRYPTON. I TRACED THE SIGNAL HERE, BUT I DON'T SEE...
ARE YOU LISTENING TO ME?
BATMAN... I...
SIGNALS, YOU SAID. I'VE TRAINED MYSELF TO PAY VERY CLOSE ATTENTION TO MESSAGES FROM MY BODY AND...
THIS ISN'T MY BODY.
WHAT?
THIS IS A SIMULATION.
I'M UNCONSCIOUS.
I APPEAR TO BE A FIT MAN IN HIS 60S BUT THE BLOOD PRESSURE AND HEARTRATE I'M EXPERIENCING WOULD FIT THE PROFILE OF A MUCH YOUNGER, AND VERY PROBABLY UNCONSCIOUS MAN.
MY GUESS IS THAT THESE HALLUCINATIONS ARE SYMPTOMS OF SOME KIND OF NEURAL INFECTION. MY ANTI-BODIES ARE FIGHTING IT, WHICH ACCOUNTS FOR THE RAPID LOSS OF EMOTIONAL INTENSITY IN THE SCENARIO.
NOT LONG AGO I WAS TERRIFIED FOR THE SAFETY OF MY SON...
BRUCE, IS SOMETHING WRONG? YOU...
BATMAN.
LOOK THERE.
WHAT IS THAT?
WORTH INVESTIGATING.
BRUCE, PLEASE! WHAT ARE YOU DOING?
HAVE YOU LOST YOUR MIND, BRUCE?

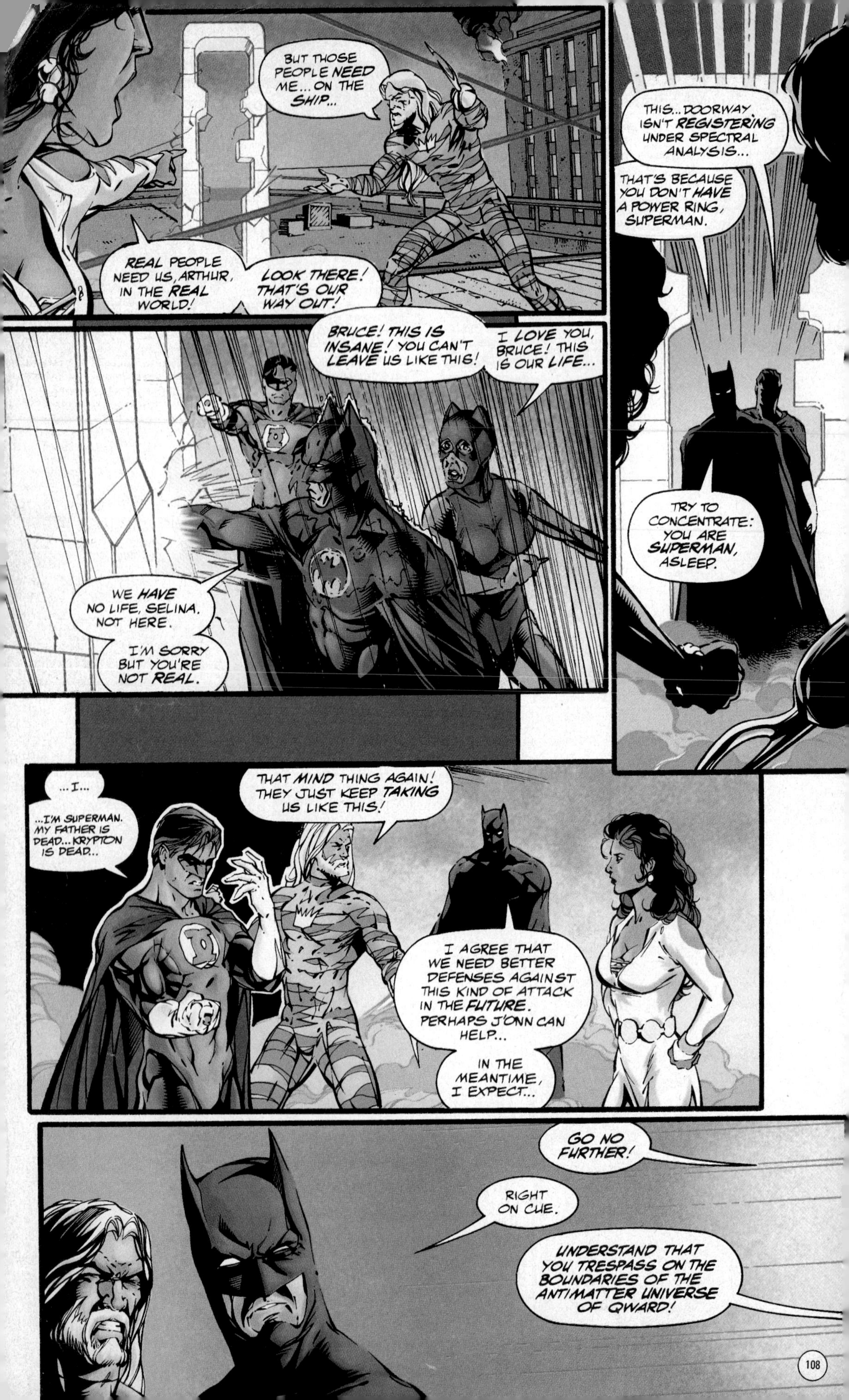
BUT THOSE PEOPLE NEED ME... ON THE SHIP...
REAL PEOPLE NEED US, ARTHUR, IN THE REAL WORLD!
LOOK THERE! THAT'S OUR WAY OUT!
THIS... DOORWAY ISN'T REGISTERING UNDER SPECTRAL ANALYSIS...
THAT'S BECAUSE YOU DON'T HAVE A POWER RING, SUPERMAN.
BRUCE! THIS IS INSANE! YOU CAN'T LEAVE US LIKE THIS!
I LOVE YOU, BRUCE! THIS IS OUR LIFE...
WE HAVE NO LIFE, SELINA. NOT HERE.
I'M SORRY BUT YOU'RE NOT REAL.
TRY TO CONCENTRATE: YOU ARE SUPERMAN, ASLEEP.
...I...
...I'M SUPERMAN. MY FATHER IS DEAD... KRYPTON IS DEAD...
THAT MIND THING AGAIN! THEY JUST KEEP TAKING US LIKE THIS!
I AGREE THAT WE NEED BETTER DEFENSES AGAINST THIS KIND OF ATTACK IN THE FUTURE. PERHAPS J'ONN CAN HELP...
IN THE MEANTIME, I EXPECT...
GO NO FURTHER!
RIGHT ON CUE.
UNDERSTAND THAT YOU TRESPASS ON THE BOUNDARIES OF THE ANTIMATTER UNIVERSE OF QWARD!

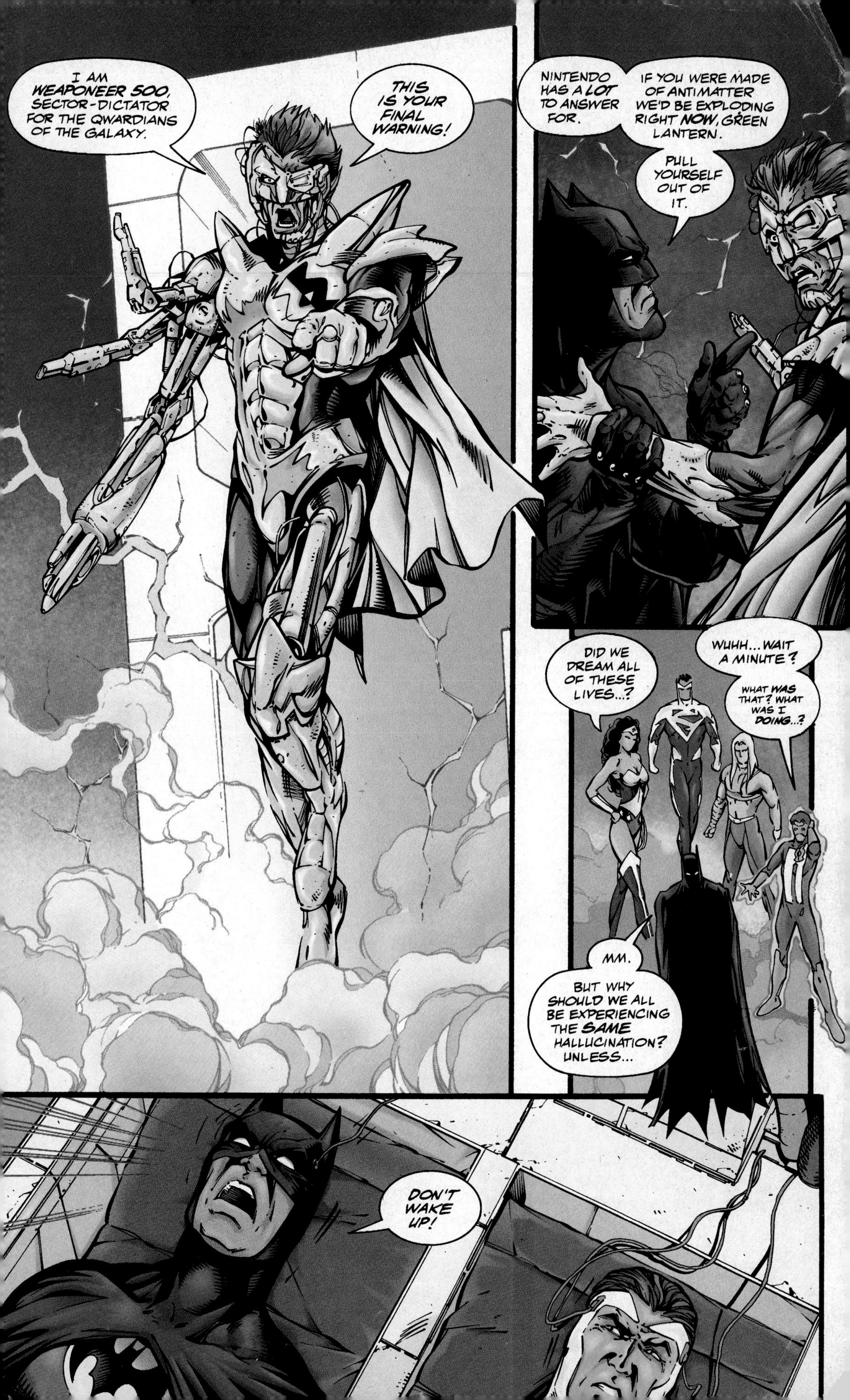
I AM WEAPONEER 500, SECTOR-DICTATOR FOR THE QWARDIANS OF THE GALAXY.
THIS IS YOUR FINAL WARNING!
NINTENDO HAS A LOT TO ANSWER FOR.
IF YOU WERE MADE OF ANTIMATTER WE'D BE EXPLODING RIGHT NOW, GREEN LANTERN.
PULL YOURSELF OUT OF IT.
DID WE DREAM ALL OF THESE LIVES...?
WUHH... WAIT A MINUTE?
WHAT WAS THAT? WHAT WAS I DOING...?
MM.
BUT WHY SHOULD WE ALL BE EXPERIENCING THE SAME HALLUCINATION? UNLESS...
DON'T WAKE UP!
...

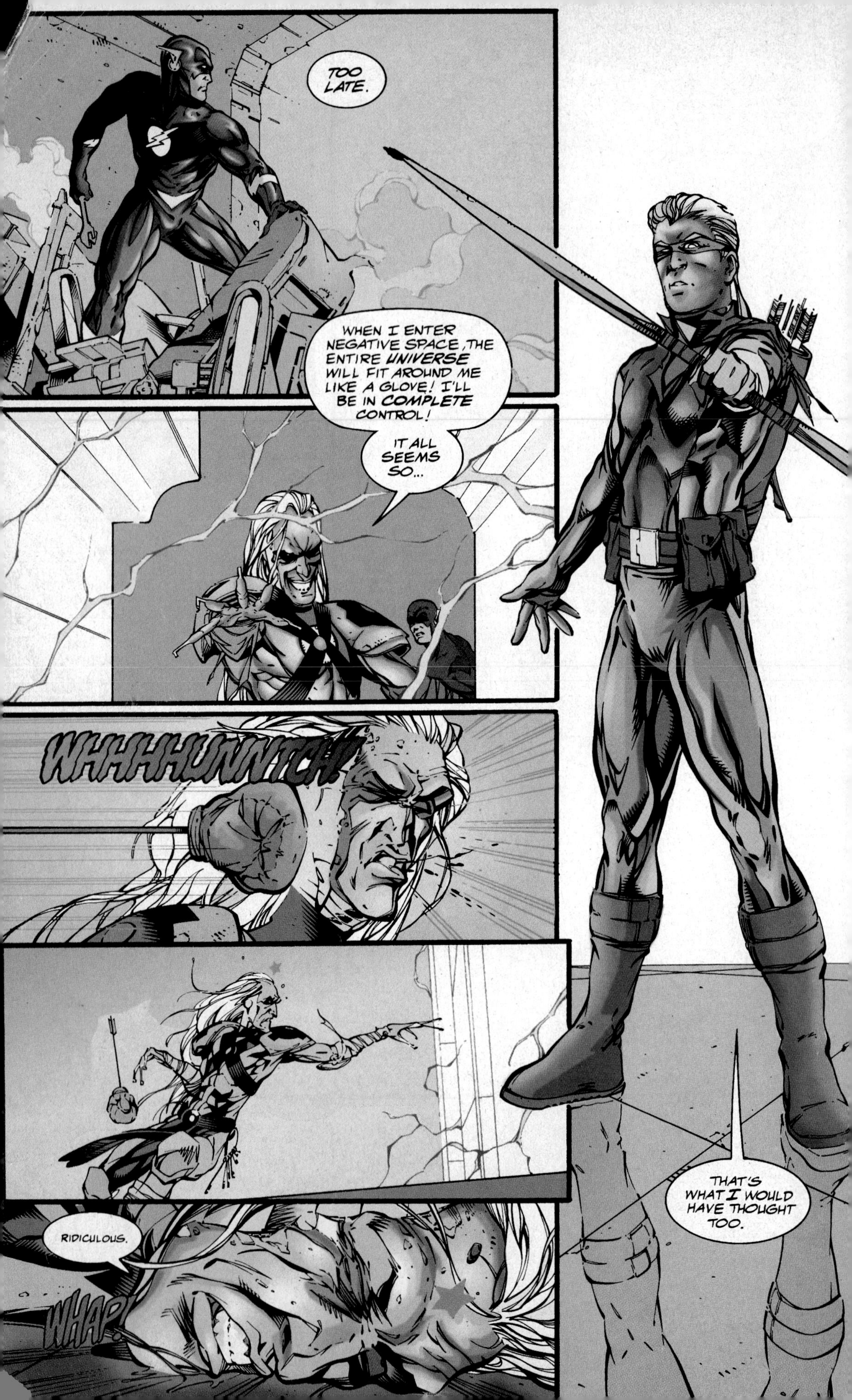
TOO LATE.
WHEN I ENTER NEGATIVE SPACE, THE ENTIRE UNIVERSE WILL FIT AROUND ME LIKE A GLOVE! I'LL BE IN COMPLETE CONTROL!
IT ALL SEEMS SO...
WHHHHUNNTCH!
THAT'S WHAT I WOULD HAVE THOUGHT TOO.
RIDICULOUS.
WHAP!

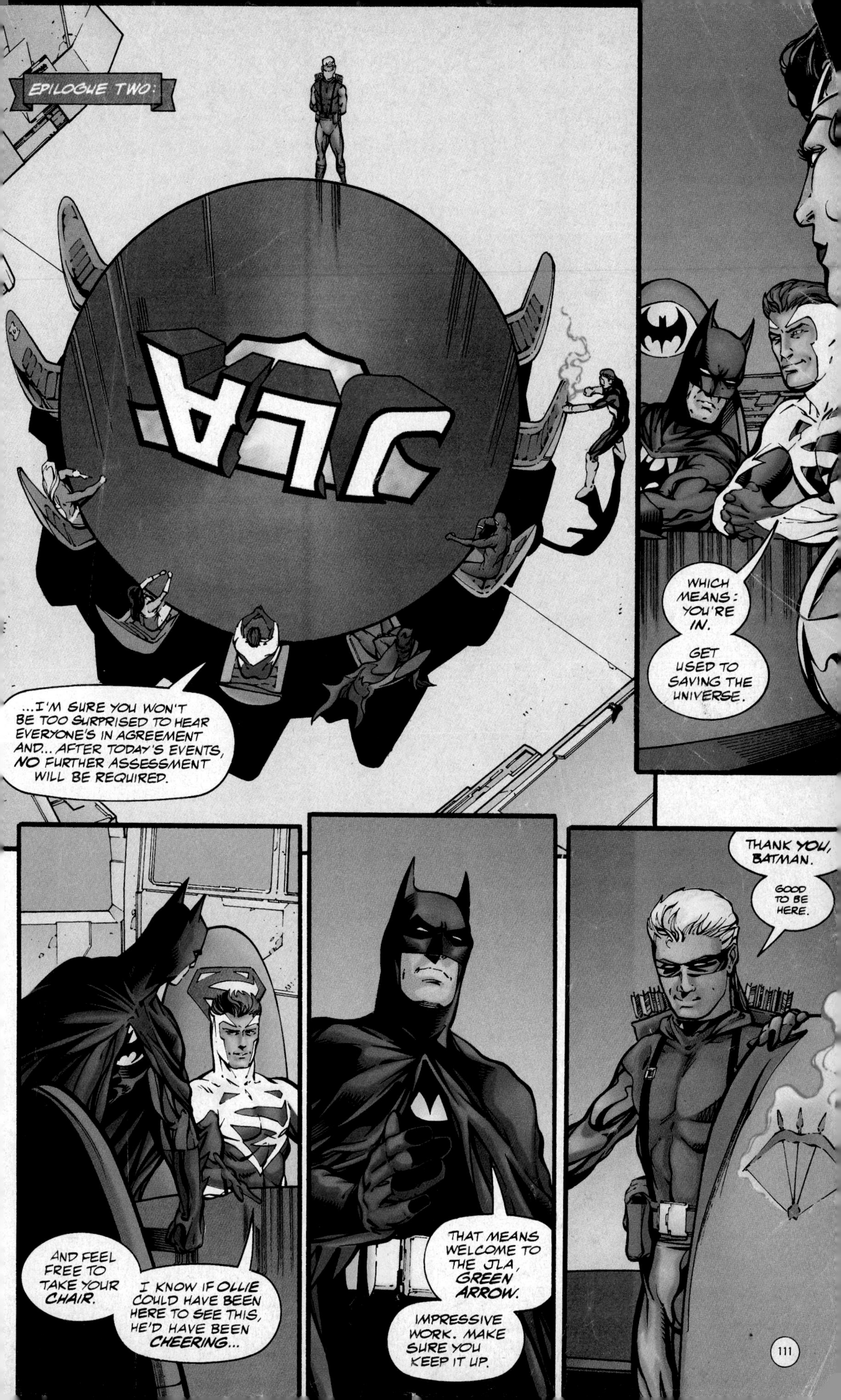

EPILOGUE TWO:
JLA
...I'M SURE YOU WON'T BE TOO SURPRISED TO HEAR EVERYONE'S IN AGREEMENT AND... AFTER TODAY'S EVENTS, NO FURTHER ASSESSMENT WILL BE REQUIRED.
WHICH MEANS: YOU'RE IN.
GET USED TO SAVING THE UNIVERSE.
AND FEEL FREE TO TAKE YOUR CHAIR.
I KNOW IF OLLIE COULD HAVE BEEN HERE TO SEE THIS, HE'D HAVE BEEN CHEERING...
THAT MEANS WELCOME TO THE JLA, GREEN ARROW.
IMPRESSIVE WORK. MAKE SURE YOU KEEP IT UP.
THANK YOU, BATMAN.
GOOD TO BE HERE.

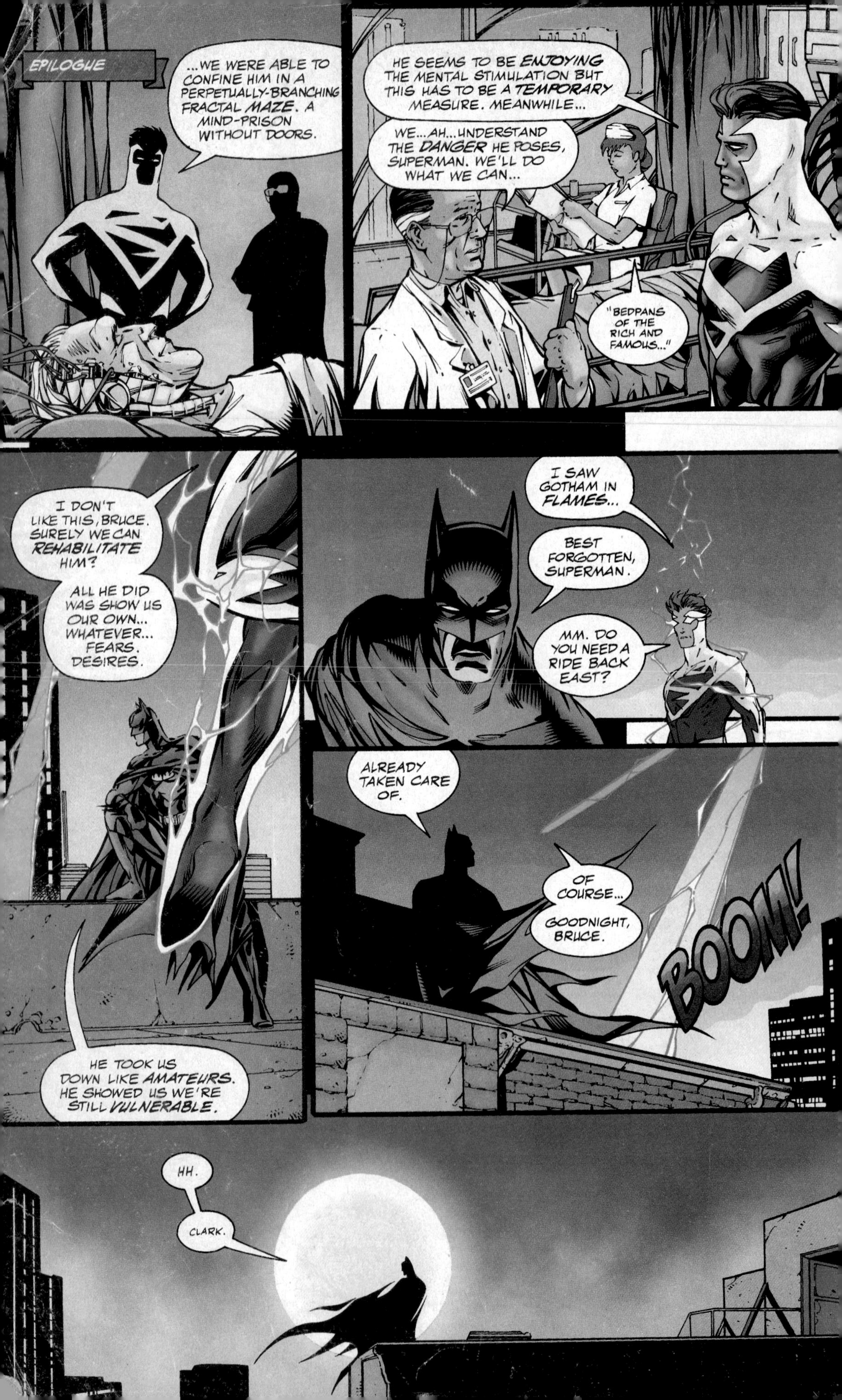
EPILOGUE
...WE WERE ABLE TO CONFINE HIM IN A PERPETUALLY-BRANCHING FRACTAL MAZE. A MIND-PRISON WITHOUT DOORS.
HE SEEMS TO BE ENJOYING THE MENTAL STIMULATION BUT THIS HAS TO BE A TEMPORARY MEASURE. MEANWHILE...
WE...AH...UNDERSTAND THE DANGER HE POSES, SUPERMAN. WE'LL DO WHAT WE CAN...
"BEDPANS OF THE RICH AND FAMOUS..."
I DON'T LIKE THIS, BRUCE. SURELY WE CAN REHABILITATE HIM?
ALL HE DID WAS SHOW US OUR OWN... WHATEVER... FEARS. DESIRES.
HE TOOK US DOWN LIKE AMATEURS. HE SHOWED US WE'RE STILL VULNERABLE.
I SAW GOTHAM IN FLAMES...
BEST FORGOTTEN, SUPERMAN.
MM. DO YOU NEED A RIDE BACK EAST?
ALREADY TAKEN CARE OF.
OF COURSE...
GOODNIGHT, BRUCE.
BOOM!
HH.
CLARK.